Scotland's Shops

Lindsay Lennie

HISTORIC SCOTLAND

2010

Acknowledgements

The research for this publication was funded through a three year Research Fellowship with Technical Conservation Group, Historic Scotland.

Throughout the project there have been numerous people who have assisted in the research and I am grateful for their guidance, support and advice. Many contacted me to suggest where shops of interest could be seen and this was of great assistance in helping me identify places to visit.

I am particularly grateful to the many conservation officers, THI officers, CARS officers and planners as well as City Heritage Trusts throughout Scotland who gave up their time to talk to me about the shops in their areas and the projects they were undertaking.

Thanks also go the staff in the numerous libraries, archives and museums, including RCAHMS, who helped to source drawings, photographs and other images for both the research and this publication.

Notwithstanding the above, particular thanks must go to the following for providing guidance, advice and information over the course of this project:

Dr Deborah Mays, Historic Scotland, Edinburgh
Michael Leybourne, Solway Heritage Trust
Dr Lynn Pearson, Newcastle-upon-Tyne
Tony Herbert, Ironbridge Institute, Jackfield, Ironbridge
Paul Zochowski, East Lothian Council
Mark Douglas, Scottish Borders Council
George Paterson, Bo'ness THI
James Lafferty, Campbeltown
Suzanne and Iain Malcolmson, Nesting, Shetland
Lynda Amos, 138 High Street, Dunbar
Ross Hunter, Graven Images, Glasgow
Fiona MacDonald, Edinburgh World Heritage
Ian Hamilton, Crieff
Sandy Deuchar, Perth
Ian Duncan, Largs
Michael Pearce, Historic Scotland, Edinburgh
Susan Payne and Paul Adair, Perth Museum and Art Gallery
St Andrews Preservation Trust, St Andrews
Professor Phil Banfill, Heriot-Watt University, Edinburgh

I would also like to thank Mark Watson of Historic Scotland, Edinburgh and Liz Davidson of Glasgow Merchant City Townscape Heritage Initiative for commenting on the drafts of this publication and to Ian Riddell for the drawings. Special thanks got to Paul Beaton of Historic Scotland for his guidance, advice and support throughout the period of the Fellowship.

Finally, I am extremely grateful to the shop owners of Scotland who took time out of their busy day to talk to me about the history of their premises and allowed photographs to be taken.

Lindsay Lennie

Figure 1: 1052 Shettleston Road, Glasgow, 1935 © Glasgow City Archives and Special Collections, Mitchell Library (facing page)

Foreword

Figure 2: Cottage Craft Centre, Falkland (facing page)

It is often the buildings that are an integral part of our lives that we take for granted. As we go about our daily lives, we may not notice the subtlety of their architectural detailing or the steady changes taking place, sometimes until much of their original character has been lost. It is probably fair to say we often take our shops for granted, the economic and social building blocks of our town centres yet ever-changing as styles change and retailers come and go. New retailers seek a change of look, new paint or a different design, making their mark on the High Street. This pattern of change is not new; shop owners have been renewing, changing and replacing shopfronts for over 200 hundred years in their attempts to keep up with the latest fashions in retail architecture.

Despite this, retail buildings are often regarded in great affection by people who remember a business now lost or a shopfront now replaced. People are at the heart of buildings of course and many of us remember individuals associated with certain shops. They are woven into the social fabric of our towns and communities and their architecture and conservation is therefore of great importance in retaining town centres that are individual, appealing and meaningful.

This book examines in detail, for the first time, the architectural history of shops in Scotland. The research was part of a three year Research Fellowship funded by Historic Scotland's Technical Conservation Group and involved a survey of shops across Scotland, from Lerwick to Stranraer. Some of the most interesting examples are listed in a gazetteer included in this book, highlighting the many good shopfronts and interiors which survive across Scotland, dispelling the belief that our town centres are becoming homogenous – they are not, yet.

These examples form a timeline of architectural development, of technological advancements, of craft skills and most of all, the needs and aspirations of retailers. From small Georgian bow windows to elaborate Victorian cast iron to minimalist 1930s Vitrolite, these shops map over two centuries of architectural change together with the evolution of shops as an effective marketing device for goods.

This book provides a detailed investigation of shop development, shop types and their architectural elements. It offers examples of good practice in conservation and makes a strong case for the conservation of shops of all periods given the significant contribution which they make to the character of our townscapes.

Retailers of all types face considerable challenges in the twenty-first century. Despite this, and as you can see from this book, many owners and the communities they serve are proud of their shops and the history associated with them. This is the case for both long-established family businesses and for new owners who have inherited a shop with original tiling, shelving or a cast iron frontage. Many recognise the significance of these shops and want to ensure their survival for future generations to appreciate. It is therefore vital that those with appropriate skills work closely with retailers of all types to ensure that this can be achieved. There is much to be celebrated in our retail architecture and this book highlights the tremendous variety of architecture and materials which can be found in towns across Scotland.

Historic Scotland is proud to celebrate an important part of our built environment, a part which can help to give us a sense of place and who we are.

I hope you enjoy this book.

Ruth Parsons
Chief Executive
Historic Scotland

- J. L. GILL. -

Whiskies

Cheeses

NUTS ABOUT BIRDS
the home delivery service
for all wildbird enthusiasts

PRESS
LATCH

WILD BIRD
FOOD

BUCKTONS
QUALITY
ROBIN &
SONGBIRD
FOOD

Contents

Introduction and Overview   **9**

Section 1: Understanding Scotland's Retail Architecture

Chronological Architectural History   **13**

Early Trading: Markets and Fairs   13
Luckenbooths and Piazzas: Scotland's Early
  Fixed Shops   17
Arches, Bows and Pilasters: The Development of
  Formal Shops from Late Eighteenth to Mid
  Nineteenth Century   23
Glass and Iron: Shops from Mid Nineteenth Century   35
Scottish Department Stores   45
Nineteenth Century Market Reform   49
Edwardian Shops   53
Inter-war Shopfronts 1920-1939   59
Post-war to Present Day   71
Summary   75

Retail Buildings: Structures and Types   **77**

Type 1: Domestic style   78
Type 2: Purpose-built tenements with shops   80
Type 3: Kiosks and small temporary shops   82
Type 4: Projecting Shopfronts   84
Type 5: Bungalow Shops: Purpose-built rows   86
Type 6: Purpose-built Commercial Premises and   88
  Showrooms
Type 7: Shopping Arcades   90
Type 8: Scottish Chain Stores   93
Type 9: Scottish Co-operative Society Buildings   96

**Technical Background: Shop Elements
and Materials**   **101**

Shop Windows and Doors   104
Signs, Lettering and Advertising Methods   106
Blinds and Awnings   110
Ventilation   113
Shop Security   116
External Finishes and Cladding   119
Glazing and Glass Products   122
Shop Interiors   125

Section 2: Conserving Scotland's Shops

**Survey of Extant Historic Shops
in Scotland**   **131**

The contribution made by historic retail buildings   131
Survey of extant historic shopfronts and
  regional identity   131
Overview of survey findings   132
Survey Case Studies 1–7   135

The Conservation of Shops   **149**
Legislative framework   149
Conservation philosophy   149
Grant-aided schemes   150
Investigating traditional shopfronts   150
Case studies in the conservation of historic shops   153
Conservation Case Studies 1-6   154

**The Legacy of Historic Retail
Buildings in Scotland**   **167**

Section 3: Gazetteer, Glossary and References

Gazetteer of Historic Shops   172
Shops: Glossary of Terms   184
References and Sources   192

*Figure 3: J.L. Gill, West
High Street, Crieff
(facing page)*

Introduction and Overview

The town's first job is to define space, starting with the ground and finally coming to terms with the sky after accommodating people and their activities on the way…It must first be intelligible, but it must also be partly mysterious, even if only a short interval of time separates you from the answer to the mystery. McWilliam[1]

The history of Scottish shops is linked with its burgh controls, its trading position and changes in retail practices as well as technology and materials. It is a complex picture of aesthetics, economics and satisfying the practical needs of retailers. Other factors like architectural fashions and the introduction of new materials have resulted in a continually changing pattern. This makes this topic both interesting to study but also challenging because of the ever-changing face of retailing and its architecture.

Shops are an integral part of our everyday lives, even in the face of Internet shopping, home catalogues and the domination of large supermarkets in all sectors. However, retailers face many challenges in meeting their customers needs and in keeping their business viable. Shops reflect the needs of retailers to be seen and to stand out, proclaiming the importance of their shop above all others. Unfortunately, this need has sometimes been misplaced, driven by a desire to modernise a shop but, modern materials are not always sympathetic to the parent building and to the wider townscape. The wholesale removal of traditional shopfronts and interiors means a loss of links with the past, those links which form social and cultural bonds with the towns where people live and work.

This book investigates the history of shops in Scotland, how shops have changed over several hundred years of retailing and considers extant examples which are worthy of further investigation and in some cases, conservation. It examines regional and local characteristics which provide towns with a sense of local identity and pride in their townscapes and retail environment, something which has been all too often lost through the march of unsympathetic modern shopfronts.

This text is in two sections. The first section examines how retail architecture developed through a chronological history of shops from medieval times until the post-war period. This is followed with a more detailed examination of certain building types that are familiar in our townscapes and examines their history, style, materials and significance. Further details of shop architecture are provided in the section on shop elements. Although the practice of retailing is not examined in detail, inevitably this is inextricably linked with the architectural history of shops.

This detailed history was derived from both an examination of standing buildings and from archival records. Although the physical evidence for early Scottish retail buildings is lacking, archive records help to piece together their fascinating history and development. Scotland has a rich source of information including burgh records comprising Town Council Minutes and Dean of Guild Court records. Contemporary accounts by visitors to towns in the eighteenth and nineteenth centuries such as Topham, Defoe, Boswell and Pennant offer an interesting insight and are complemented by early newspapers and drawings.

Although these help to build up a picture of Scotland's early shops, it must be recognised that there may be a bias towards the larger towns and cities where fixed shops probably existed first and where burgh records are possibly more complete. It may also be speculated that, in the same way that London led retail development within England, it is likely that that Glasgow and Edinburgh had a similar role within Scotland.

The second section focuses on the conservation of retail buildings by considering extant examples from across Scotland and how they demonstrate local and regional diversity as well as wider national influences. It also outlines the statutory protection mechanisms in place, listing and conservation areas. This is supported by examples of good conservation practice in caring for historic shops.

With rapid changes in retailing over the last two or three decades, a consideration of the importance of historic shopfronts, their place in our townscapes and their future contribution, aesthetically and economically in our High Streets has never been more important. Their conservation is dependent on understanding what is there and how it is significant so that historic shopfronts can continue to contribute to the town, its people and its activities.

Figure 4: Tiled butchers shop, Sanquhar, Dumfries (facing page)

Figure 5: Attractive window display, Dunkeld, Perthshire

Fig: 5

Section 1: Understanding Scotland's Retail Architecture

Chronological Architectural History

EARLY TRADING: MARKETS AND FAIRS

"Animals seldom failed to stick their horns into the first unguarded inhabitants that came their way, resulting in trembling scenes for parents, guardians, and relations… and a rich harvest for surgeon, undertaker and grave digger." On the late eighteenth century street markets in Dundee[2]

Medieval shopping and trade was carried out in the markets and fairs of Scotland's burghs. The right to hold these markets was a precious privilege, especially for Royal burghs who could also trade overseas. Specially designated market places were usually identified by the mercat cross, a sign of the right to hold a market although in smaller towns markets may simply have been held in a wider section of the High Street. Duties were paid by the non-burghers as they passed through the town port bringing with them their myriad of wares to sell. Market trading was the life-blood of Scottish burghs, central to their economic success and to their survival.

Fairs were much larger events with only a few held every year, some of which were associated with religious festivals. These attracted considerable numbers of people from a wide geographical area and lasted several days giving burghers the opportunity to buy more exotic and unusual goods.

The stalls varied depending on the trader and the types of goods they sold. Some were simple wooden chests on which the goods were displayed. Others may have been larger timber structures with a canopy to offer some protection from inclement weather. Peddlers would also have hawked their goods from baskets as they worked their way through the crowds.

Through the medieval period to the seventeenth and early eighteenth century, the street market was the main source for daily food and provisions. Increasing population and urban expansion meant that markets were crowded

Figure 6: Pitlessie Fair, 1804, by Sir David Wilkie © National Gallery of Scotland (previous page)

Figure 7: The Lawnmarket, Edinburgh, 1829 © Courtesy of RCAHMS. Copied from 'Modern Athens'. Licensor www.rcahms.gov.uk (facing page)

Figure 8: The Fish Cross, Ayr, 1814 © South Ayrshire Libraries Local History Collection, Ayr Carnegie Library. Licensor www.scran.ac.uk

Fig: 8

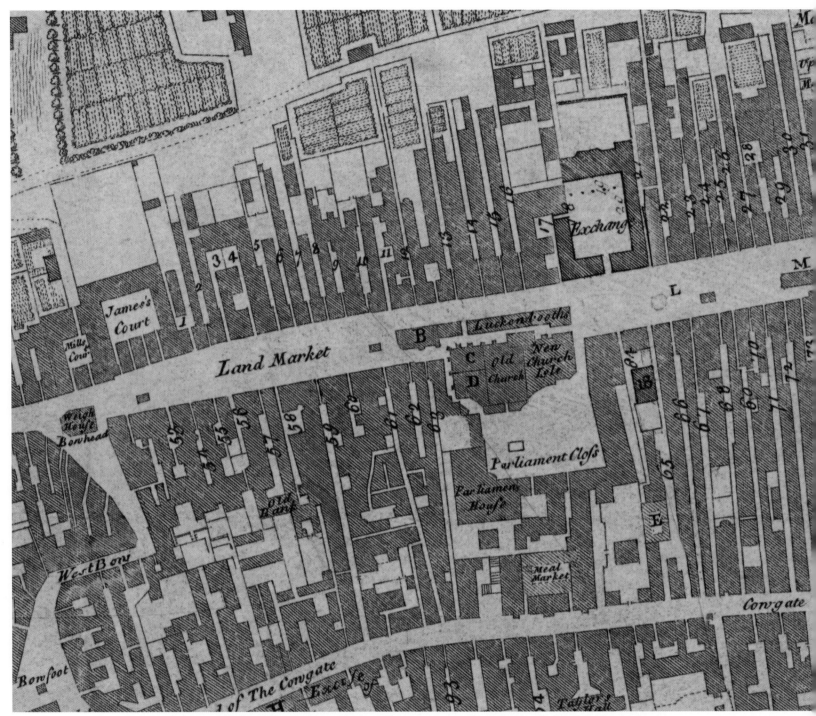

Fig: 9

places, lacking sanitation and sometimes with animals running dangerously loose amongst the crowds. Attempts were made to control the location of markets and fixed positions were sought in order to separate out different uses to try to minimise the disturbance of weekly markets. Topham writing in 1774 comments on the nuisance caused by the holding of these markets in the centre of Edinburgh:

"They suffer a weekly market to be held, in which stalls are erected nearly the whole length of it, and make a confusion almost impossible to be conceived. All sorts of iron and copper ware are exposed to sale; here likewise the herb market is held."[3]

He goes on to describe how the herb women throw the bad vegetables into the street which is a great

14

and drapery goods. William Edgar's map of Edinburgh dated 1765 clearly shows these well-defined market places. (Figure 9) The fact that these markets were "*wall'd in*" means that this must have offered some element of security, protection and control within what was otherwise a chaotic scene. The walls must also have provided a degree of protection from the inclement weather.

Specialised markets therefore became established and Edinburgh's Old Town, for example, had fifteen markets, each in a separate location. Part of this need to localise trades reflected the undesirable nature of some of the selling and it is noticeable how the more noxious trades of slaughtering and meat sale were pushed towards the outskirts of towns. Butchers shambles and fish markets were particularly unpleasant with offal, blood and manufacture of tallow creating offensive smells and a nuisance in the town. In Glasgow the shambles[5] (slaughter-houses) and flesh market were moved nearer to the river and a '*very spacious beef market*' erected in King Street '*the stalls of which are under roofed pillars having in the centre a large paved area open above*'. The market expanded so much that the fish, potato, butter and cheese markets formerly located next to the fleshmarket were moved to behind the weigh-house to allow the whole of the King Street markets to be devoted for a fleshmarket.[6]

The *Perthshire Courier* in 1829 graphically describes the sale of meat at this time in the city of Perth. It also hints at the struggles which went on within the burgh over trading rights:

> "*On Fridays the butchers from the country, who were then a numerous body, sat on horseback on the street with their meat lying over the animal, from which it was sold, as they were denied the use of a stand or stall. So jealous have the free brothers of the Guild in all ages been!*"[7]

The continuing spread of towns and the resultant encroachment on markets remained a problem for town magistrates. The growth of towns and populations caused pressure on the markets, not least because they were being systematically engulfed by the building of houses meaning that they had to be regularly moved to new locations.[8]

inconvenience to passers-by. Writing some 50 years earlier, Defoe describes the markets as not being held in the open street except the herb and fruit markets located in the High Street in the mornings. He says there are *"several distinct Market Places wall'd in, and reserv'd for the particular Things they are appointed for, and very well regulated by the Magistrates, and well supplied also"*.[4] He lists the meal, flesh, poultry and butter markets. Other open markets included the grass and horse markets as well as the weekly land market for linen

Although these markets were central to public life, they also presented a nuisance problem to those in charge of order within the burgh and this was a process of reform that took many decades of the nineteenth century to bring to fruition. Initially small booths and merchants houses existed alongside the markets but we will see that over time they diminished in Scotland and became increasingly marginalised as shops gained supremacy.

LUCKENBOOTHS AND PIAZZAS: SCOTLAND'S EARLY FIXED SHOPS

"Elgin has what in England are called piazzas that run in many places on each side of the street. It must have been a much better place formerly. Probably it had piazzas all along the town as I have seen in Bologna." Boswell on Elgin writing in 1773[9]

While weekly market stalls met the needs of some traders, inevitably there grew a desire for more permanent accommodation and this was met by the establishment of small timber booths, sloping roofs or pentices and buildings with arched ground floors known as piazzas. These were Scotland's earliest fixed shops, located in burghs from at least the fifteenth century, although they bear little resemblance to what we know as a shop today.[10] They were susceptible to the vagaries of the burgh authorities who sought to control encroachments, fire risk and trade and the structures that developed reflected not only retailer needs but also the desire of town councils for order in the society they governed, a situation that was also a potential source of conflict.

Scottish Medieval Shops

The selling of goods in medieval burghs would have been one of three forms.[11] The first was the open sale of primary produce, typically from a market stall; secondly, the sale of manufactured goods from an artisan's shop or at a market stall; thirdly, the sale of imported goods by a merchant who sometimes acted as a wholesaler. None of these would have been recognisable as the types of shops which we see today. The market stalls were simple wooden chests or moveable booths which, over time, became more permanent. Timber fixtures also developed at the front of merchant's houses and neighbouring merchants then followed that example.[12]

Burgh records utilise various terms that were applied to places where selling of goods took place. These suggest that there was perhaps some variation in types of early shops but a lack of detailed evidence makes it difficult to clearly differentiate between them. It may be that the terminology prevailed in certain localities and therefore does not necessarily signify a different type of building and the terms were probably interchangeable:

- Buith or booth: a small timber booth
- Chop, choppe or shop: a shop
- Crame, creame or krame: a very small booth or shop
- Luckenbooth or Luckenbuith: a locked booth or small lock-up shop
- Pent or Pentice: a sloping lean-to roof or porch
- Laigh houses: the ground or lower floors of buildings
- Piazza, piaza or peatches: arcaded ground floors with walkway in front and shops behind

Booths, Luckenbooths and Krames

Medieval markets were typically located in and around the parish church and this central site became the first location for more permanent shops. Edinburgh burgh records refer to 'little chops' which were situated around St Giles in the High Street partly as a way to raise revenue for the church. (Figure 11) These structures were a continual source of trouble for the burgh authorities who tried to exert control over their occupation and to limit their encroachment onto the streets as part of their ongoing attempts to control street nuisances. However, there was always a trade-off between generating income and encouraging trade without permitting excessive nuisances.

Figure 10: High Street, Glasgow, 1840s, showing the piazza with the shops located within the arched openings © Glasgow University Library, Special Collections Department (facing page)

Fig: 11

Figure 11: South side of St Giles, High Street, Edinburgh, 1829 showing shops and booths adjacent to the church. © Royal Commission on the Ancient and Historical Monuments of Scotland. Licensor www.scran.ac.uk

The Edinburgh Luckenbooths, originally known as Buith Raw or Booth Row when erected in the fifteenth century, were located in the ground floor of a five storey tenement in front of St Giles in the High Street. William Edgar's *Plan of the City and Castle of Edinburgh*' (1765) indicates their location and how they narrowed the High Street. (Figure 9) The term 'locked buiths' is used in the Edinburgh burgh records of October 1656 and the term 'Luckenbooths' was well established by the eighteenth century.[13]

Between the tall tenement and the church were small stalls known as 'Krames' or 'Crames'. These tiny wooden buildings were occupied by goldsmiths, watchmakers and jewellers, perhaps seeking the safety and security of booths where they could display their valuable wares. These small structures are described in a burgh account for June 1662 as being sixteen feet in breadth but their depth is not stipulated other than they must not extend out more than a certain distance.[14]

Figure 12:
Luckenbooths, High Street, Edinburgh showing the Krames situated against the wall of St Giles Church © Courtesy of RCAHMS. Licensor www.rcahms.gov.uk

Fig: 12

The burgh authorities controlled the type of tenants, making sure there were no unpleasant trades like tanners or butchers adjacent to a place of worship. Deed of Council restrictions dictated who could occupy these booths as in an entry of 14 April 1643 stating that they shall *"...onlie be sett to goldsmythias to bookbinders to mounter makers and workers of mathematical instruments and to none others"*.[15] Despite endless debates about the defacing of the beauty of St Giles by the juxtaposition of a myriad of shops around its outer walls this did not seem to prevent construction and letting of shops continuing.

An even greater concern for the authorities was the risk of fire in booths and laigh houses, especially as some traders worked with combustible materials. Attempts were made to improve the construction of booths as a burgh account entry for June 1682 shows.[16] Here a goldsmith

was offered a new 19 year lease and as an incentive for him to rebuild his shop in Parliament Close in stone and covered with lead, could pay the old rent with the same clauses in the lease. Thus, the cost of the new building was offset by the lowered rent and the council achieved a more permanent and safer building.

Although the word 'Luckenbooths' was used for a specific tenement in Edinburgh, the term was also used in Dundee suggesting a wider use of this name. A sixteenth century map of Dundee indicates their location in the High Street adjacent to the Meal Market.[17] MacLaren describes them as "*anciently styled, being erected in front of the houses on each side of the street, and thus rendering the passage-way between them very narrow. The entire length of the Overgate presents a continuous line of lucken-booths, very inconvenient as a business thoroughfare, now that wheeled vehicles are almost innumerable*".[18]

It seems that the burgh authorities eventually tired of such encroachments. In Edinburgh the Luckenbooths were removed in 1817 as the High Street was widened and Dundee followed suit later. The move to more permanent buildings was already underway and small timber booths were probably insufficient for many retailers needs.

Pentices

A pent roof or pentice is a small sloping roof at the front of a building. These offered shelter and a degree of permanence for a trader and gradually theses roofs became enclosed, forming booth-like structures on the front of the building. The *Perthshire Courier* describes 'channels' which seem similar to pentices stating:

> *"On the front wall wooden balconies were raised and roofed in with the house, and the ground floor of the balcony was left open in front, which served the purpose of a shop, and was called a channel; on a stand, placed along this channel, the wares of the merchant or craftsman occupying the house were displayed."* [19]

The term 'channel' is also explained as a corruption of the word 'chancel', meaning the lattice work used in churches and which these chancels were similar to. The article describes how the 'channels' described earlier, were demolished and replaced, however, even the new shops appear to have been very basic:

> *"After the channels were pulled down or came to be enclosed, the shops continued to be low, dark and damp places, possessing, with other comforts and conveniences, an earthen floor and a single window, about 3 feet by 18 or 24 inches, and in many cases enclosed within a wooden grating."*

Fig: 13

It is likely that these structures were cheap and easy to erect and would therefore have been common in burghs across Scotland. A painting of Kelso in 1787 shows similar structures on the front of buildings fronting the Market Square. (Figure 13) However, these were also encroachments and caused a narrowing of the street to the undoubted displeasure of the burgh authorities.

Piazzas and Arcades

Shopkeepers understood the benefits of shelter and security for their goods and their customers. Piazzas or peatches were tenements, several storeys high which had impressive arcaded ground floors, the shops being located to the rear of this arched area. Erected in numerous Scottish burghs including Dunfermline, Elgin, Edinburgh, Linlithgow and Glasgow, they were probably inspired by continental architecture. Although Scotland's urban architecture was heavily influenced by France and Holland, the piazzas were definitely Italian in inspiration.

Initially these existed below the timber galleries permitted in Edinburgh from 1508 but during the seventeenth century, burgh bye-laws encouraged construction in stone.[20] Certainly, an entry in the Edinburgh Burgh records for 5 May 1675 notes that the fronts of buildings are to be in stone arches or pillars rather than timber. However, it states that no *"litell pentice or chop"* which is situated below the stairs or at the entrance is to be reinstated, despite the loss of this to the heritor, as these are an encroachment onto the street and must be demolished.[21]

Fig: 14

The main benefits of these piazzas was that they formed an area protected from the weather offering greater security and comfort than an open market stall. Howard[22] suggests that they were indicative of *"classical dignity"* and not designed for shelter. They have also been described as a '*Jacobean shopping mall*'.[23] Certainly Defoe writing of Glasgow in the 1720s was impressed by their style describing them as *"all of stone and generally equal in uniform in Height, as well as in Front; the lower story generally stands on vast square Dorick columns, not round pillars, and Arches between give passage into the shops"*.[24]

MacGibbon and Ross describe examples in Elgin suggesting that *"the arcaded street floor indicates what was a very usual form of construction in this and other Scottish towns"*.[25] (Figure 14) They observe that they have largely disappeared in Elgin except for a remnant leading to a back court, this as a result of the blocking up of the arches. Certainly it seems that they were not universally popular. Dr Johnson and his companion Boswell touring Scotland in 1773 noted the buildings in Elgin stating that there is *"sometimes a walk for a considerable length under a cloister, or portico, which is now indeed frequently broken, because the new houses have another form, but seems to have been uniformly continued in the old city."* Boswell, comparing them to Bologna, Italy, reports that although he liked them for their protection in wet weather, Dr Johnson did not care for them. He felt that they made the shops below too dark and this was not sufficiently compensated for by the protection from occasional bad weather.[26]

Perhaps the greatest insight into these buildings is in the Glasgow burgh records, a city where these buildings were once numerous. Although building in this style was encouraged and even enforced from the early eighteenth century, they do not appear to have been viewed as desirable by all shopkeepers. In February 1758, two petitioners to the Council wanted to rebuild in the Trongate, the entry stating that they are *"praying the councils concurrence for his rebuilding thereof without being unnecessarily burdened with a piazza"*. The petitioners were however unsuccessful in their bid as Council subsequently insisted that the buildings were erected with a piazza.[27]

Figure 15: 42 High Street, Elgin
© T Hay Collection, Moray Council Archives

Fig: 15

However, by the end of the eighteenth century the Council were being forced to abandon their ideal of a continental style parade of arcaded buildings. Burgh records in 1793 offer a fascinating insight into the change of fashion with increasing pressure from shop owners to be allowed to extend to the front of the piazza.[28] The Council also appear to recognise that the unpopularity of these premises makes for a lower rent for such shops and sees an opportunity to increase the rents by allowing the tenants to extend to the front, both enlarging the shop area and making it more desirable.

Ongoing discussions are reported in the burgh records and the matter seems to have finally been resolved in 1799 when the shop proprietors agreed to pay an increased rent for extending into the piazzas.[29] The final death knell was sounded when the piazzas were included in the 1800 Glasgow Police Act which believed them to be *'Receptacles for Thieves, Pickpockets and idle and disorderly persons'*. Brutally condemning the elegant arcaded buildings, the Act states that shop owners are to be encouraged to bring the shops to the front of the building to include the area of the piazzas and that the doors and windows should be altered to allow in light and access by cutting the pillars.[30] Following this Act the piazzas were gradually blocked up.

Elgin seems to have followed Glasgow's example of eradicating the shops below the piazzas. A photograph of Sutherland & Son, 42 High Street depicts the blocked up frontages, the outline of the arches just visible, although the central arch leading to the back court remains open as described by MacGibbon and Ross.[31] (Figure 15)

Although the Glasgow authorities were particularly enthusiastic about constructing these piazzas, none survive in the city. Elgin has retained more of these buildings than any other Scottish burgh with three late seventeenth century examples which have been restored and the arches reinstated, although without the open piazza. (Figure 16) Gladstone's Land, High Street, Edinburgh is the only one to remain in the capital and this has been conserved by the National Trust for Scotland. These few surviving examples of this building type are a link with a former style of retail and domestic Scottish building which effectively fell out of favour and many were ultimately swept away in the nineteenth century street improvements.[32]

Scotland sadly has a poor standing record of medieval shop buildings. However, historical records paint a picture of a thriving retail community, not just in Edinburgh and Glasgow but in other Scottish burghs. Although the early examples were simple timber booths, the aspirations of both shopkeepers and burgh authorities meant that grander buildings like the piazzas were erected. Over time

their unsuitability for purpose became evident, particularly at a time when new types of shop were becoming more commonplace. Like shop buildings throughout history, the fickle nature of retailing meant that shopkeepers had moved on and were seeking more elaborate premises for their business.

Figure 16: Braco's Banking House, Elgin, restored piazza

Fig: 16

ARCHES, BOWS AND PILASTERS:
THE DEVELOPMENT OF FORMAL SHOPS FROM LATE EIGHTEENTH TO MID NINETEENTH CENTURY

"The social fashions of the world were beginning to invade Glasgow, and the inhabitants were full of interest when a shoemaker, a silversmith and a haberdasher opened their shops in the Trongate in 1750, and ladies, instead of waiting for the carrier from Edinburgh to bring special articles, could now put on their pattens and go across to the new shop." Henry Grey Graham[33]

The end of the eighteenth century marks a change in Scotland's retail buildings as the more formal, fixed shops which we recognise as retail premises began to emerge. This shift was in response to greater wealth offering increased retailing opportunities, a focus on classical architecture together with improved availability of suitable materials. These elements combined to allow the gradual development of fixed shops with a formal shop front. More sophisticated design and construction methods together with the wider availability of glass, dressed stone and timber allowed 'polite' retail architecture to develop.

Contemporary records and accounts provide an insight into shops of the eighteenth century. The rapid changes taking place in retailing are evident in letters written by William Creech to Sir John Sinclair, where he notes that in 1763 the profession of haberdasher did not exist but by 1783 it was one of the most common; perfumers were not known in 1763 but by 1783 they "*had splendid shops in every principal street*"; and in that twenty year period hairdresser numbers had tripled.[34] As shops became more numerous and of a greater variety, particularly in what might be termed luxury goods, so improvements in shop design and quality naturally followed. This move to more distinguished retail premises occurred in Scotland from the 1780s onwards.

Other contemporary accounts also detail the improvements underway; an extract from the burgh records of Glasgow in August 1793 reports that "*The improvements lately made in constructing shops with large bow windows and elegant and spacious entries have drawn haberdashers and deallers in fashionable and valuable goods to shops in parts of the town where these improvements can be made*".[35] Dorothy Wordsworth in her tour of Scotland in 1803 confirms this, describing the large Glasgow shops as being similar to those in London.[36] Topham visiting Edinburgh in 1774–75 describes the shops in the High Street where tradesmen were located on ground floors and cellars and *"who style themselves merchants, as in France"*.[37] Even in more remote areas the increase in shop numbers was noticeable. The Statistical Account for Kirkwall, Orkney, notes the increase in shop numbers stating that shopkeepers have "*multiplied almost tenfold of late*".[38]

The introduction of fiscal measures at the end of the eighteenth century also confirms that shop numbers were increasing. A Shop Tax was introduced in 1785 as one of a number of measures to increase taxation and recoup the costs of war with France.[39] The Act states that from 5 July 1785 duty is to be paid on all houses or buildings used as a shop or for trading or selling of retail goods. All shops with a rental value above £5 were liable although wholesale and storage warehouses were exempted unless connected to a shop. Bakers shops were also excluded.[40]

The quality of the entries varies considerably, presumably depending on the particular enthusiasm of the respective surveyors for each area. There is a lack of address information or details on the types of retailers, other than in Glasgow. Nonetheless, they do indicate the numbers of shops which existed and allow comparisons to be made between different towns. For example, in 1785, the City of Edinburgh had the most shops at 626 and Glasgow had a similar number at 600 shops. Aberdeen is the next largest centre with 149 shops but smaller centres like Perth (59), Inverness (23) and Stirling (20) had considerably fewer. Ayr, Dumfries, Montrose and Falkirk all had around 30 shops indicating their status as centres within their districts and counties. The only indicator of retail types is from Glasgow where the highest category was for grocers at 157 shops with the general term of merchant second at 105.

Figure 17: The Village Shop, New Lanark, c1880 showing the wide bow windows
© Courtesy of RCAHMS. Licensor www.rcahms.gov.uk (facing page)

Hanging Signs and Development of the Fascia

The Shop Tax records give an indication of the numbers of shops in existence but do not tell us about the architecture. The late eighteenth century represents a watershed when shop design changed dramatically and permanently. Two different elements, notably the banning of hanging signs and secondly the fashionable stimulus of classical architecture were highly influential in this period.

Due to the high level of illiteracy in the population, traders from the seventeenth century were identified by the use of hanging pictorial signs.[41] These large and decorative sign boards were more akin to what we might see today on a public house or inn. Quoting from Topham's "Letters from Edinburgh" Graham states *"High up in front of the houses were the strange signs, painted in colours on black ground, each tradesman picturing thereon the article in which he chiefly dealt".*[42]

These large boards, with a black or dark background onto which the emblem of the trader was painted, were hung on a bracket outside of the shop. Although the emblem used by a trader should have been directly related to his business, such as a wheatsheaf for a baker or boot for a shoemaker, the reality was rarely as clear. Part of the problem with this was that over time, the original meaning of a sign was sometimes lost in obscurity and confusion could also arise with some designs such as "Whale & Gate" or "Bull & Bedpost". There were a number of possible explanations for this. First, a new shop owner may have incorporated an existing sign, possibly forming a landmark in the area, into his own sign when he moved into premises. Secondly, two tradesmen may have amalgamated their business and therefore the emblems in their two separate signs were combined. Thirdly, an apprentice may have used his master's sign and combined it with a new one of his own and finally, the congregation of particular trades in an

Figure 18: Drawings of old Glasgow shop signboards, for Old Glasgow Club, 1911 © Glasgow City Archives and Special Collections, Mitchell Library

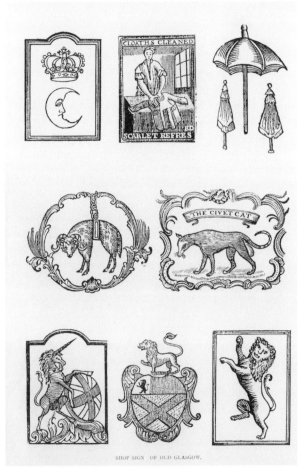

Fig: 18

Figure 19: Three dimensional shop signs in the collection of The Museum of Edinburgh

Figure 20: Advertisement for Mrs Hamilton's Nursery Shop, West Bow Edinburgh, 1757 © Edinburgh City Libraries. Licensor www.scran.ac.uk

Fig: 19

MRS HAMILTON, at her shop in the West-bow, first turn on the left hand going up, at the sign of the gardiner, has just now imported an assortment of fresh GARDEN SEEDS, GRASS SEEDS, sundry sorts of FLOWER SEEDS, and TREE SEEDS, particularly very good BEECH-MAST, all of last year's saving. ANEMONIE's and RANUNCULUS roots, either common or fine kinds may be had at the same shop.
*** As also, a choice collection of double blue white and rose coloured hyacinthus's, polyantho's and narcissus's blowing in water glasses: Likewise continues to sell all sorts of garden utensils, green and white split pease, anise, caraway and coriander seeds, seeds for birds, &c.—Such as please to favour her with their orders, may depend on punctual service, and charged at the lowest prices.
N. B. Any who want collyflower, cabbage, asparagus plants, &c. may be served at the lowest prices.

Fig: 20

area may meant it was difficult to identify individual shops so a trader may have added a personal emblem to help customers find his premises.[43]

Street numbering had not yet been introduced so shopkeepers had to describe where their shop was located. A Broadside Advertising sheet probably dating to the eighteenth century includes an advertisement for a shop which states *"There is to be sold at easy and reasonable rates by Andrew Gardner, at his shop at the Golden-Key, opposite to the Cross-Well, North-side of the Street, Edinburgh, the following Goods, in Whole Sale or Retail"*.[44] The advert therefore provides the name of the shop owner, his signboard (a golden key) and the location in the street. Other examples indicate the importance of signifying the location of the shop like Mrs Hamilton's Nursery Shop which is described in a mid eighteenth century advert as *"in the West Bow, first turn on the left hand going up at the sign of the gardiner"*. Her sign depicts a person equipped with a spade and a rake.[45] (Figure 20)

Over time the signs became larger and a dangerous nuisance in the public street. It was felt that they blocked air and sun and their poor maintenance became an increasing concern. Following deaths in London in 1718 when a large sign fell and killed four people, efforts were made to remove them.[46] Paris led the way and banned hanging signs from her streets in 1760. A proclamation was subsequently issued in 1762 that all hanging signs within the City of London and soon after the City of Westminster, were to be removed. Other towns and cities then followed, such as Bath in 1766. Hanging signs were banned by the Town Council of Glasgow in 1772 because they were obstructing the view along the streets. Graham summarises the position stating that the streets *"broke out into an eruption of signboards, and there dangled and creaked in the air from poles, red lions and blue swans, cross keys, golden fleeces, golden breeches, golden gloves, till the magistrates, in course of time, ordered their removal, as obscuring the light of their new lamps at night"*.[47]

An Edinburgh by-law of 1839 states that all signs are to be *"placed or affixed close on or flat to the wall or front of the houses, shops, warehouses or other buildings situated close upon streets or within areas whereunto they shall respectively belong"*.[48] Despite these regulations, old habits died hard and there were some traders who continued to refer to their sign. For example, an advert in the Glasgow Post Office Directory of 1853-54 for Mrs Geo. Thomson, outfitter, where her shop address is given as *"No 32 Candleriggs, Observe- Sign of the Golden Fleece"*.[49]

While Glasgow led the way banning the use of hanging signs in 1772, in other Scottish towns the practice

of hanging signs would have been banned at different dates depending on the enthusiasm of the local Town Council for their removal. For example, it is clear that trade signs were still in use in Dumfries at the end of the eighteenth century because in 1797, a Mrs May Dickson complained to the Provost that her sign had been pulled down despite being fixed to the wall by iron clasps and *"carried off to the new bridge where a decent man saw a parcel of boys about to thro' it and some others over the bridge"*.[50]

Although the banning of hanging signs was significant for the general streetscape, it had a much more fundamental impact on shop design. Effectively, the banning of these signs was a catalyst in shopfront development as Morrison explains:

> *"The fascia came into its own after 1762, when a law was enacted in London prohibiting the hanging of signs, although innkeepers, pawnbrokers and barbers usually persisted in using them. The legislation was not implemented immediately, but the switch from hanging signs to fascias proved pivotal in the development of what is now regarded as the 'traditional' shopfront."*[51]

Shop design therefore had to adapt to meet the needs of retailers but without the crucial hanging sign. Classical architecture offered a design solution and became central to shop architecture; the arch, the pilaster, the console bracket and the entablature (fascia). The fascia became the element most important for the sign. The early fascias tended to be modest and narrow with painted lettering but during the nineteenth century as shops became taller and fascias deeper, the lettering and sign writing associated with shops became considerably more elaborate.

Figure 21: Chemist's Mortar and Pestle

Fig: 21

Hanging signs were not totally forgotten as three dimensional signs re-gained popularity during the nineteenth century. Fixed above the shopfront, these substantial signs were often gilded or painted different colours to make them visible so they could be seen from a distance. The most common surviving example is the mortar and pestle which still graces many pharmacies. Others were associated with certain trades such as a Highlander or a Moorish figure, both generally associated with tobacco and snuff merchants. A bear with a red and white pole indicated a barbers as bear oil was traditionally used to grease hair in the eighteenth century. These signs have enjoyed a further revival in recent years and some signs, such as the pawnbrokers three golden balls have survived remarkably well, often in poorer districts.

Shop Design in the Eighteenth Century

The association with fashionable classical architecture and the banning of hanging signs were an impetus for design improvements. No longer were shops a simple opening with a sign hung above; instead the move to formalise shopfronts emerged, reflecting the fact that shop numbers and therefore competition were increasing. Change was gradual with different types of shops emerging at the end of the eighteenth century and existing alongside each other. These included bow-fronts, fixed enlarged openings and larger, formal schemes.

Bow-fronted shops

The style which we most strongly associate with the Georgian period is the bow-fronted shop. This is where the window has been enlarged with the addition of a timber, bow-shaped window which may take the shop beyond the building line. These Georgian shops were characteristically small-paned because of the limited size of glass that was

Figure 22: Old wooden-fronted houses, High Street, Dunfermline by William Thomson around 1902 © Dunfermline Carnegie Trust. Reproduced with thanks to Fife Council Libraries and Archives

Fig: 22

affordable. Although technically it was possible to make larger sheets of glass, these were generally beyond what a shop owner could reasonably afford and the majority had to accept the limitations of small panes of Crown glass.

The bow has several advantages over a flat window, notably that it allows in more natural light, it offers improved display opportunities and perhaps most importantly, it makes the shop highly visible in the street, marking it out from surrounding properties as a retail outlet.[52] It therefore became an important fashion statement for the retailers who could afford the expense of improving their shop in this way.

The earliest examples of this form of shopfront probably existed in the mid eighteenth century in England, pre-dating their arrival in Scotland. In London, for example, Fribourg and Treyer at 34 Haymarket dates to circa 1740 and a surviving bow-fronted shop in Bath dates to the 1760s. Its lack of a fascia suggests that hanging signs were still in use at its time of construction. However, by the 1790s the shops had developed a narrow fascia designed to accommodate lettering.[53]

In Scotland, the idea gained popularity from the 1780s onwards and by the 1790s they were becoming established certainly in the larger centres. Glasgow burgh records of 1793 report "*the improvements lately made in constructing shops with large bow windows and elegant and spacious entries, have drawn haberdashers and deallers in fashionable and valuable goods to shops in parts of the town where these improvements can be made*".[54] Although the implication from this is that there is a novelty about these designs, the statement also suggests that they are both fashionable and popular, particularly with certain types of retailer such as drapers and haberdashers. The idea would have gradually dissipated through the country as retailers appreciated the potential advantages of the design and sought to be more fashionable than their neighbouring shops in order to attract in customers.

Bow-fronted shops were extremely varied in their execution. There was no template for these shops, and they varied from place to place depending on particular local circumstances but driven by certain determining factors such as the aspirations of particular retailers, local topography and the craft skills available. Some may have been quite vernacular in inspiration as depicted in a drawing of old wooden houses in Dunfermline with small-paned, flat-roofed projecting bows which are square in plan. (Figure 22) Others were perhaps more formal in design and considered in the approach to their design. Certainly the earliest examples may well have been simple bow-windows created by slightly widening the existing opening and inserting a timber bow but over time the

Fig: 23

Fig: 24

Figure 23: Deuchars, South Street, Perth

Figure 24: Post Office, Sanquhar

designs became more sophisticated. Increasingly elaborate designs were created, such as the use of a barrel shape or serpentine arrangement.[55] However, perhaps these were less practical as they do not appear to have been widespread and it may be that these more fanciful types were confined to small numbers of shops.

Local geography and architecture also appear to have been determining factors. In Edinburgh, for example, there developed a high bow front which although not exclusive to the capital, seems to have been a prevalent style of bow-front here. This bow comprised a high, shortened bow window, typically three panes of glass deep, with a door to the basement situated immediately below the window. This arrangement with the basement access below the bow forces it to be high and shortened. The result is that although the bow is visible in the street as a shop it is quite impractical to see in given its height above the pavement. This perhaps suggests a naïve if pragmatic solution to the local constraints but one which is still trying to incorporate the fashionable style of the time.

An example survives at 515 Lawnmarket, Edinburgh and it is particularly notable because there is a large pillar inside the window indicating that this improvement was much more about the outward shopfront appearance than the practical aspects such as improving display and light. (Figure 213) Making a statement was as important as solving daylight or display problems. Although this is the only surviving high bow-front, images of Edinburgh indicate they were once numerous, albeit there was considerable variation in their styles.[56]

Descriptions of shops in Dundee in 1820 suggest a similar arrangement existed there. Here, small-paned bow windows had steps leading up to the shop which project into the street (perhaps like a fore-stair) and other steps leading down into the cellars. Like Edinburgh, these basements were used for retailing and storage and their stair entrances were covered at night with sloping wooden covers to prevent pedestrians from falling down the steps.[57]

By the early nineteenth century, the simple bow window had evolved into a more formal and architecturally elaborate style. The shop formerly at 58 High Street, Perth for Barlass ironmongers probably dates to around 1810 when Barlass was first established. This incorporated two bow fronts either side of the door with a serpentine fascia above and slender fluted pilasters. It maximised light and display with the minimal stallrisers, the window being six panes deep.[58]

Geographically, bow windows would have been found almost anywhere in Scotland although the dissemination of the style would have been both erratic and unpredictable, as retailers chose to invest or not in this design. It was perhaps a case of the particular economic prosperity of a place at the height of their fashion which determined whether they were popular. It may also have been the case that the adoption of the design by one or two shopkeepers encouraged others in the area to have their shops remodelled in this way rather than be left looking unfashionable and potentially losing customers.

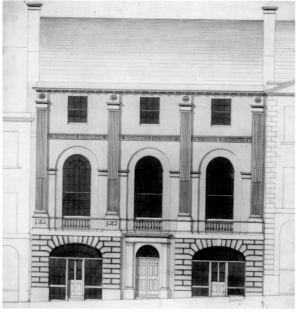

Fig: 25

In Scotland today very few of these early bow-fronted shops survive although examples can be found in Perth, Edinburgh and Sanquhar as well as one in a derelict building in Glasgow. (Figures 23 and 24) In other places there may be a suggestion of where a bow front previously existed, as in Campbeltown and Sanquhar where a curved sill and lintel suggests a bow window was once there. Some are also associated with other types of use such as public house in Jedburgh and a residential property in New Galloway. The Post Office, Sanquhar is the oldest continuously occupied Post Office in the world having existed since 1712.[59] Here the bow is supported by a bracket below because it is more deeply curved. Other bows were quite shallow in their curvature and are referred to as '*suppressed*' bow fronts.[60]

In Nicholas Street, Glasgow, close to the High Street, a derelict building retains a bow-fronted window and which was presumably a shop. Situated in the angle of the building, this very shallow and barely discernible bow has an unusual glazing arrangement with 7 high and 3 across, the panes sitting horizontally like lying panes.[61] The number, size and orientation of the panes varied although the most usual arrangement was for glazing to have a vertical emphasis rather than lying.

These surviving examples indicate how varied the styles of these shopfronts were reflecting not only their time of construction but also other factors such as affluence of the shop owner, architectural fashions and the skill of local craftsmen. Although in the late eighteenth century and early nineteenth century they were the most fashionable design for a shopfront, other more practical designs became available and they soon appeared old fashioned by

comparison. The obsession of shop owners with modernity means that these bow-fronts were gradually replaced in the nineteenth century as they became old fashioned and impractical in the face of plate glass.

Fixed enlarged openings

While some shops certainly had bow-fronts, it may be that they were only fashionable in certain towns or localities. There must have been an expense involved which was probably beyond the means of some shop owners but, as shop owners recognised the advantages of having greater light and display, some merely enlarged the existing window opening to achieve this. It was presumably a cheaper alternative than a bow-front although would certainly not have been as fashionable. Enlarged fixed and bow windows are therefore merely variations on a theme; the improvement of light and display combined with the opportunity to make the building distinct from domestic design; a combination of fashion and practical necessity.

As well as square headed openings, the influence of classical architecture encouraged the use of arched openings in purpose-built buildings. This combined with the heavy rustication of ground floors found in neo-classical buildings lent an austere appearance to shopfronts. Early designs incorporated a flattened arch such as in Trades Hall, Glasgow (Robert Adam, 1791-94) and Hunter Square, Edinburgh. The Edinburgh Merchant Company built 3 and 4 Hunter Square, Edinburgh in 1788-90 designed by John Baxter. The elliptical arches and rusticated stonework make for an elegant form of shopfront.[62] (Figure 25)

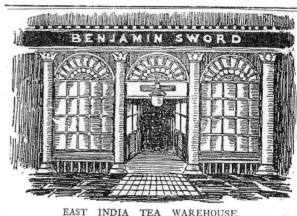

Fig: 26

Fig: 27

Fig: 28

Figure 28: West Nicholson Street, Edinburgh showing the regularity of arched openings

A nineteenth century letterhead for Perth drapers H Mitchell & Co features a shopfront with a substantial arched opening suggesting that these designs were not confined to main centres like Edinburgh but retailers with money and vision were also seeking beautiful shopfronts. However, it is likely that such properties were confined to the most affluent retailers such as drapers and silk mercers and would have been beyond the means of many small retailers at this time.

An impressive early and very fine example is Benjamin Sword's 'East India Tea Warehouse' located in Trongate, Glasgow. It was part of a magnificent tenement built in 1784 in an *elegant and substantial manner* and known as Spreul's Land. The shopfronts incorporated arched windows with fanlights, columns with a narrow fascia for the name and a dentilled cornice above.[63] The construction of such a shopfront must have been a significant statement at the time, reflecting the affluence of Mr Spreul who erected the tenement. (Figure 26)

Fig: 29

Figure 29: 5 Bridgend, Perth, late 19th century, with arched openings framed by plain pilasters © Courtesy of Perth Museum and Art Gallery, Perth & Kinross Council

The use of a series of arched openings for shop doors and windows presents a unified scheme but also allows flexibility; the tenement may be large or small and the shops can be single or double-fronted. The adoption of arched ground floor openings offered a flexible but formal design for shops which was fashionable in the early nineteenth century in many Scottish towns. Architects Thomas Fletcher, John Smith and Archibald Simpson designed King Street, Aberdeen, the original intention being for buildings of uniform appearance to create "*a street which shows the character of diversity within uniformity*".[64] Numbers 36-40, built around 1810, have two shops with arched openings and a fanlight arrangement for the glazing. Similarly, West Nicolson Street, Edinburgh which also dates to the early nineteenth century features a long colonnade of arched shopfronts. The fanlight arrangement to the glazing and the band course indicate the typical form type for these buildings.

The ideas also permeated to smaller centres like Perth where arched openings with pilasters formed part of a design for tenements with shops at Bridgend. Similarly in Jedburgh, a three-storey tenement built in 1825, Abbey Place, has a ground floor with arched openings. One shop is double-fronted, the other single-fronted and they both have high stallrisers indicating their early date. These also use pilasters to frame the openings, a fashionable development in the 1820s which made the shopfront appear more formal and dignified.

Figure 30: Drawings for Reform Street, Dundee, 1841, by William Scott © Courtesy of RCAHMS. Licensor www.rcahms.gov.uk

Purpose-built major schemes

Although conversion to retail of existing buildings was underway in the late eighteenth century, the construction of major purpose-built schemes also made an important contribution to shopfront design. In the late eighteenth and early nineteenth century, Scottish burghs were breaking the confines of their medieval street patterns and in some cases, punching entirely new streets through the medieval fabric. These substantial redevelopments in Edinburgh, Perth, Dundee, Glasgow and many other towns included accommodation for retail premises.

One of the earliest examples is probably Robert Adams plans for South Bridge, Edinburgh. The idea for a multi-level concept which Adam had executed in the Adelphi redevelopment in London (1768-71) was transferred to a 'viaduct street' for South Bridge in 1785. This was to have "*colonnaded shops and housing to a unified design*" but it was never built.[65] Instead a less elaborate design by Robert Kay was built 1786-88. The scheme executed featured series of arched shopfronts at ground floor, the openings providing classical regularity for the shopfronts linking the Old and New Towns.

Elsewhere in Edinburgh, retail in the first New Town was initially resisted, the buildings being entirely residential. However, by the early nineteenth century, some street designs did include purpose built shops such as William Street, built c1825. Here the pilastered shops

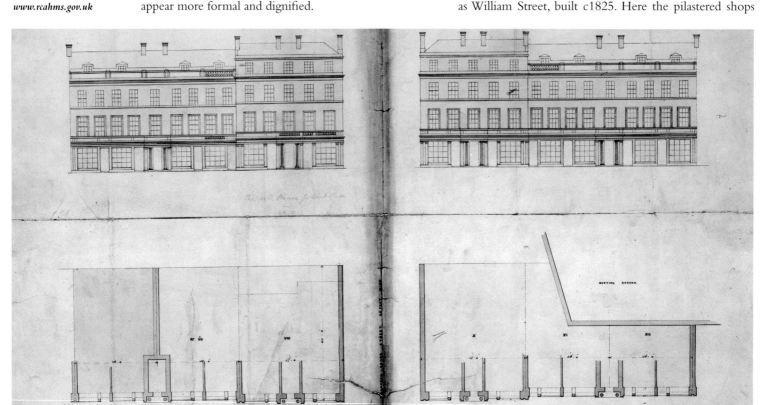

Fig: 30

are accessed via a stone platt and a small iron platform and railing allows potential customers to view goods in the window. This regularity creates a simple but effective scheme along the length of the street.

The vision for a unified and dignified scheme in Dundee formed part of William Burns 1824 improvements. Construction was underway from 1830, the architect being George Angus of Edinburgh. On completion in 1832, the street was named after the Reform Bill of the same year. (Figure 30) The double-fronted shops had pilasters with a balustrade running above the cornice although gradually over time some of these original elements were removed or lost. In recent years some of the architectural detail has been reinstated, albeit in man-made materials rather than stone, but this has allowed the original vision for the street to be appreciated once more.

Pattern Books

Pattern books were catalogues of architectural designs which in their finest format were produced by Palladio (Four Books of Architecture) and James Gibb (A Book of Architecture) but were also available in a more populist form produced by builders such as Batty Langley and William Halfpenny. Although these were generally concerned with domestic architecture, the steadily increasing numbers of shops meant that there was sufficient demand for publications associated with retail architecture. I and J Taylor published *Designs for Shop Fronts* in 1792 which included around 20 designs. John Young produced *A Series of Designs for Shop Fronts* in 1828 and Nathanial Whittock published very elaborate designs in his 1840 *On the Construction and Decoration of the Shop Fronts of London*. Whittock advocated '*stylistic association*' where particular retailers should adopt certain architectural styles such as use of Gothic for goldsmiths and jewellers.[66] However, this was not a fashion that proved to be particularly popular with retailers.

Some of these designs were extremely elaborate and decorative. Materials included 'compo' and imitation finishes of marble and gilt which were popular in the Regency period.[67] These drawings heralded a new era in shopfront design which was taken to elaborate extremes in the Victorian period.

Figure 31: Jack Cleland, Paterson & Co, Trongate, Glasgow, 1812 showing the elegant interior of this upholsterer's warehouse © Glasgow City Archives and Special Collections, Mitchell Library

Fig: 31

Shop Interiors

The improvement in shop design was not just confined to the exterior and by the early nineteenth century there is some evidence for grand shop interiors, designed specifically to appeal to the upper classes. Drapers and furniture dealers were the predecessors of the department stores which emerged in the later nineteenth century. These retailers were central in developing new designs and techniques in building design. They were also appealing to a certain class of customer and had to accommodate their expectations displaying modernity and style in their shops. With the increase in depth of shops, lighting became an issue and this was overcome through the use of top-lit saloons. Here, a cupola or similar arrangement allowed a substantial area to be naturally lit and would also have provided a sense of opulence and quality to the premises that could afford such an elaborate structure.

A Gradual Process

Although some of the historical records and contemporary accounts hint at dramatic change in retailing, it is unlikely that the architectural response was immediate. Instead, the formalising of shop architecture in Scotland was a slow and gradual process, particularly in provincial towns and rural areas. Ideas emanated from London and other fashionable centres like Bath. Scotland's main cities of Edinburgh and Glasgow gradually adopted these styles, adapting them to fit in with their own architecture. Other

HIGH STREET 50 YEARS AGO

Fig: 32

Figure 32: High Street, Haddington, 1836
© East Lothian Council Library Service. Licensor www.scran.ac.uk

These books are significant not just for the ground-breaking and sometimes exotic designs which they promote, but like William Creeche's observations on the changes in retail establishments, they are indicative of the changes happening in shops and shopping. These highly ornate shopfronts therefore reflected the increasing importance of shopfronts and the wider aspirations of shopkeepers to have a decorative front which discerned them from their neighbours. Shopfronts were, for the first time, architectural statements.

Fig: 33

Provost Stewart's Land

towns like Dundee, Perth and Aberdeen as well as smaller burghs would have been slower to take up the ideas although it is possible in any place that an enterprising and perhaps wealthy retailer would have had a new shop designed in the latest fashion. There is also evidence that even the smaller places had surprisingly sophisticated retail architecture. Sanquhar, for example, had numerous bow-fronted shops, perhaps reflecting a period of prosperity in this Dumfries village.[68] An image depicting Haddington in 1836 also shows rows of fine shops. (Figure 32) It is therefore likely that the fashions dispersed unevenly and unpredictably and the full pattern or reasons for the development are difficult to discern.

Even once plate glass was widely available, smaller panes of 2 ft, 3 inches were still commonly used perhaps because of the exorbitant cost of plate glass.[69] The improvements would also have at least initially, been confined to certain types of retailers; the fashionable and affluent drapers, silk mercers and goldsmiths tended to lead the way in shop design before these ideas emanated to other retail sectors. As shop numbers continued to increase, owners were encouraged to improve their shops in order to attract customers. The steady march of retail is particularly evident in Princes Street in Edinburgh. Built as a residential street, gradually through the early nineteenth century shops began to become established in the ground floors. Youngson states:[70]

"Princes Street was one of the first to show signs of that social decay which has since overwhelmed it and turned it into little more than a shopkeeper's parade. In 1799, a quarter of a century after building began, it was still very largely a residential street. The non-residential intruders were comparatively few in number and confined almost entirely to the east end of the street, where the first twenty or so numbers were mostly of a non-residential character."

The late eighteenth and early nineteenth century can be seen as a period of transition and experimentation in shop design. The gradual adoption of classical features, the influence of pattern book designs and the impact of increased wealth together with a recognition of the importance of the shopfront all evolved during this time. By 1850, shops were numerous and had become an established part of Scottish town centres from Edinburgh to Elgin but the face of shopfronts was changing once again. The bow fronted shops were no longer in vogue and were being superseded by larger, more open shopfronts. The Industrial Revolution, the availability of cast iron and plate glass and an affluence which allowed retailers to indulge in a degree of elaboration never seen before awaited the shoppers of the late nineteenth century.

Figure 33: West Bow, Edinburgh, 1830 by Thomas Hamilton © Courtesy of RCAHMS (RIAS Collection). Licensor www.rcahms.gov.uk

Old Assembly Rooms.

GLASS AND IRON:
SHOPS FROM THE MID NINETEENTH CENTURY

"Whose magnificent emporium in Sauchiehall St unquestionably forms one of the 'lions' of the city, and an unending source of delight to brilliant assemblages of the fair sex who frequent the establishment."
On Copeland & Lye, Glasgow Warehousemen[71]

The second half of the nineteenth century represented a time of dramatic change in all aspects of society, not least in shopping and its associated architecture. Innovation aided progression from the restrictions of the Georgian bow-fronted shop to light and airy premises in a matter of a few decades. This period proved to be highly influential in shop design and many of the ideas are embedded in retail architecture.

The changes in retailing can be attributed to a combination of rising incomes and increasing urbanisation with a continued move towards fixed shops and corresponding decline in the use of markets. Shops were also no longer confined to the central areas of cities but gradually began to be established in the high density and generally poorer urban areas. Shopping had also developed beyond the need for everyday goods and become a fashionable pastime, its popularity encouraged by the expansion of the railway and tram networks as well as the establishment of holiday locations particularly spa towns, which offered real opportunities for retailers. As a result, the 1880s and 1890s witnessed an explosion in shop numbers and retailers had to respond to the ever-increasing competition by improving their premises. With shops more numerous, design gained importance as the advantages associated with having an attractive and fashionable shopfront became evident. (Figures 35 and 36)

Such advances were achieved through the highly innovative nature of the Victorians who embraced new products and materials, many of which were mass-produced and therefore affordable. These materials transformed shops into welcoming places where business could be conducted in a pleasant and inviting atmosphere.

Glass and Iron

Undoubtedly the most powerful influence on late nineteenth century shop architecture was the availability of new materials particularly plate glass and cast iron. This combination allowed retail architecture to shake-off its Georgian restrictions of small-paned windows, limited-sized openings and low ceilings. In their place came shops of a previously unimaginable height, flooded with natural light, designs beyond the wildest dreams of any Georgian shopkeeper.

Glass production improved significantly with the invention of plate glass by the Chance Brothers in 1834. Initially, this major technological advancement was restricted by the application of excise duty to glass which penalised glass by weight so it remained an expensive product still beyond the financial reach of ordinary shop owners and therefore perhaps reserved for the more affluent retailers like drapers and for those in prime retailing locations. London was therefore the first to embrace the possibilities of plate glass, a design for John Harvey in 1841 depicts a cavernous-like entrance with improbably high walls of glass.[72] The significant expense and bravery in investing in such a shop, pre-dating the lifting of the Glass Tax, can only be guessed at.

Figure 34: Gardner's Warehouse, Jamaica Street, Glasgow (facing page)

Figure 35: 35-41 Low Street, Banff, c1890 with arched openings to ground floor shops © Courtesy of RCAHMS. Licensor www.rcahms.gov.uk

Figure 36: 35-41 Low Street, Banff, 1965 showing how the arched openings have been replaced by tall, square shopfronts, probably around the turn of the twentieth century © Crown Copyright: RCAHMS. Licensor www.rcahms.gov.uk

Fig: 35

Fig: 36

Fig: 37

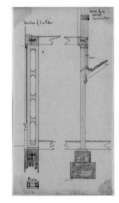

Fig: 39

More modest attempts to take advantage of improvements in glass technology resulted in a move to reduce the number of panes, a horizontal arrangement of two or three panes being favoured.

The Glass Tax was finally repealed in 1845 which meant that glass was not only available in larger sheets, but it was also cheaper. Eldridge says that the lifting of this tax burden *"removed a serious constraint on the use of plate glass"* and ultimately the size of the glass *"became the influential factor in shopfront design"* by allowing shops to become taller with larger windows.[73] Victorian shops were gradually released from the confines of a multi-paned fenestration.

The development of plate glass and removal of the Glass Tax went hand in hand with the mass production of cast iron. The Crystal Palace of 1851 demonstrated what was achievable and encouraged these materials to become fashionable. As demand rose, iron foundries sprang up across the country particularly in the Glasgow area. Walter MacFarlane's Saracen Foundry, George Smith's Sun Foundry and the Lion Foundry all grew on the back of the seemingly endless Victorian demand for mass produced architectural ironwork including railings, bandstands and shopfronts.

This versatile material offered considerable design opportunities because of its ability to be cast into so many decorative shapes as well as the more functional structural columns and lintels. The foundries were quick to take advantage of the potential market for retail buildings and included pages in their catalogues depicting entire shopfronts. It was from the 1850s that ornamental columns and lintels specifically designed for shops were first included in foundry catalogues. Frew describes the cast iron shop frame as *"cheap, easy to assemble, supposedly fire-proof and immensely strong. It was also capable of resolving the period's characteristic fondness for decorative effect with structural economy, the latter permitting the full exploitation of continuing advances in glass technology"*.[74]

Fig: 38

Cast iron therefore served a dual purpose. First, it allowed the shop to be opened up through the use of structural lintels and columns in the frontage and interior, removing heavy masonry piers so that the shop was lighter and airier.[75] (Figure 39) Second, the decorative nature of the material was an added advantage and it was used for pilasters, cresting, signage, balconies and columns. This meant that although some functional elements were hidden from view, columns could be used within the shop and for the front in a structural and decorative way. It was even used for entire façades and made possible two-storied shopfronts where the amount of glass could be maximised to allow in natural light at both the ground and upper floor levels.

St Andrews' architect John Milne (1823-1904) designed Foote's drapery in Cupar in 1861. It epitomised the use of plate glass and cast iron with extensive sheets of plate glass more than six feet across and a large hall "*supported by two rows of cast metal pillars of a chaste ornamental design from Shotts Foundry, Leith*".[76] Only five years later the transformation of shops in Montrose was being welcomed by Mitchell stating: "*The shops below are of a new and improved construction, besides being large and spacious and having in connection with them rooms and places behind adapted for carrying on a large and extensive trade. The metal pillars below are a great improvement, and give the shop windows a large frontage, and light and elegant appearance to the whole*".[77] At this time there were three iron foundries in Montrose employing over 100 men and these may well have supplied local shops with the columns they needed to improve their premises.

The decorative cast iron elements were not only related to function, they were also about raising the status of the shopfronts and in an age of increasing competition this was of great importance; having a distinctive shopfront whilst making use of cost-effective, mass-produced materials. Identical elements were typically used in different combinations allowing shops to be individual or were used in deliberately matching pairs or rows of shops offering a uniformity of design. The same elements are therefore evident from Lerwick to Dunbar with certain styles or patterns used repeatedly.[78] This also reflects the fact that foundries plagiarised each others designs so very similar patterns may be found in different foundry catalogues. Cast iron was also favoured by certain types of retailer, notably ironmongers reflecting their own trade and some also had a small foundry associated with the business.

Certain geographical locations show a significant concentration of cast iron shops which may reflect associations with a particular foundry or architect. St Andrews, for example has almost thirty examples mostly

Fig: 40

dating to the 1880s and 1890s. (See Survey Case Study 5: St Andrews, Fife in Section 2) This reflects both a boom time in the development of the town and the preferences of local architects who designed these shops. Crieff and nearby Comrie, Perthshire also have cast iron shopfronts, many of the same design which may reflect the preference of local architects or builders and the columns which were available locally.

Although smaller foundries contributed to many shopfront designs, undoubtedly the greatest cast iron shopfronts were designed by the large Glasgow foundries. Around 1900, a grocer in Cromarty chose Macfarlane's Saracen foundry to transform his traditional looking building with a magnificent new shopfront using cast iron pilasters and spandrels and complete with elaborate crests. Applied to the front of the building with little alteration, this shopfront is a statement not a structural necessity. It signifies a fashionable shop in the latest style, a brave and what may be considered by some at the time to have been an unnecessary investment for a shop in a small rural Scottish town. (Figure 40) Status was clearly important to shop owners, not just in the fashionable streets of Edinburgh but also in the towns and villages across Scotland. Iron foundries local and national were able to indulge their desires.

Iron Warehouses and Emporia

The immense possibilities of plate glass and cast iron are evident in the iron warehouses and emporia of the mid nineteenth century. These were Scotland's first large, purpose-built retail buildings but were less sophisticated than the later department stores with their elegant interiors and saloons. Nevertheless, they were pioneering in their designs as they attempted to sell goods on a larger scale than had previously been undertaken.

Figure 40: Cast iron shopfront, Cromarty by Saracen Foundry, Glasgow

Figure 41: New Iron and Glass Warehouse, Glasgow, Illustrated London News, *March 15, 1856* © *Mary Evans Picture Library*

NEW IRON AND GLASS WAREHOUSE AT GLASGOW.

Fig: 41

By the mid nineteenth century, a few retail businesses were expanding sufficiently that they required larger premises to display and sell their goods. This generated considerable difficulties in trying to light such a large internal space but which could be partly overcome by the construction of buildings using the new materials of cast iron and plate glass. The iron warehouses of Glasgow are of special interest in terms of the architectural, technological and retailing history of Scotland. These revolutionary buildings were popular for a short period in the mid nineteenth century and utilised the expertise of some of the country's leading architects, Thomson, Baird and Lochhead.

The first iron-framed warehouse of any significance was erected for Wylie & Lochhead in Argyle Street in 1850, pre-dating the Crystal Palace. Gomme & Walker describe it as *"remarkably advanced for its time"* outlining its architecture as *"having a tall narrow frontage with an immense window covering the entire upper storeys, the glass being divided by two very slender iron mullions. Above was a fairly heavy attic with its own cornice, and at ground level a three-bay arcade whose shouldered lintels gave a somewhat Moorish appearance"*.[79]

Internally it had a central well surrounded by galleries, the premises filled with furnishing fabrics, paper hangings and furniture.[80]

Although Wylie & Lochhead had started out as feather merchants and cabinet-makers, they soon expanded their business into a number of lines including carpets and paper-hangings. As their business flourished, they moved to a new building erected in Buchanan Street by Lochhead in 1855. However, this suffered a fire in 1883 and was rebuilt to a design by architect James Sellars. This building was constructed with an iron frame but incorporated a fire-proof ornamental terracotta façade and an arched glass roof. This innovative company were the first British store to install a passenger lift at their premises in Buchanan Street.[81]

Inspired by Wylie & Lochhead's building, a number of similar designs followed in Glasgow. The peak period of building in cast iron and glass façades was in the period 1853 to 1859 although they remained popular until the 1880s. Gardner's, Jamaica Street, was built 1855-56 by John Baird (1798-1859) who also designed the Argyle Arcade

Fig: 42

in 1827. Gomme & Walker describe Gardner's as *"a lovely example of the functional use of a visually simple principle derived from a relatively sophisticated method of construction, carried out with a taste and restraint which make it appear nearly, but not quite, anonymous"*.[82]

In nearby Gordon Street, the Ca' d'Oro building was designed by architect John Honeyman in 1872 for F & J Smith as a furniture warehouse. Like many others it combines stone and cast iron for a highly effective façade with maximum natural light.[83]

Although these early and substantial retail buildings were often connected with sale of large goods like furniture, they represent the first changes in the transition to new retail practices and the establishment of large, purpose-built and multi-storied buildings to accommodate retailing. Their embracing of the new materials of the age demonstrates how retail buildings were emerging as vital elements within the townscape with Glasgow leading the way in embracing these designs and materials.

The ideas used in these early buildings were then developed through the nineteenth and early twentieth century and in some cases produced an entire façade of cast iron. The Alexander's Stores in Ayr had a cast iron façade produced by the Lion Foundry of Kirkintilloch. The shopfront even included the name of the business impressed into the front of the building with the title 'The Popular Supply Stores'. Such entire cast iron façades were rarer in Scotland than the use of columns, but demonstrate the great versatility of this material.

Innovations and Practical Solutions

The Victorians were a highly innovative society and constantly sought to improve the design of their buildings. They introduced practical features and these remained integral to the basic form for shopfronts into the twentieth century.

Ventilation, for example, was regarded as of great importance to ensure a good supply of fresh air into properties, partly because gasoliers produced combustion products and excessive condensation. Ventilation could be introduced through various design features including hopper opening fanlights, window head ventilators and fretwork to doors and stallrisers. They introduced simple methods to control the flow of ventilation such as 'hit and miss' ventilators and fanlights with a ratchet system to allow the size of the opening to be moderated.

Shop owners were also concerned with the practicalities of security for their premises, not least because glass was such a precious element. The earliest

types of protection were offered by wooden shutters or boards which were lifted into the shop each morning and replaced at night. Set into a shutter slot or groove and held in place by an iron bar or by metal pins, these were a heavy and cumbersome way of protecting the shop and so other more innovative types were developed such as slatted wooden or iron roller shutters. The *Illustrated London News* of 1856 provides a detailed account of a new type of shutter used in Gardner's Warehouse, Jamaica Street, Glasgow:

> *"They are made in two pieces in the height, of plate iron, and extending the whole width of each compartment. The upper portions of the shutters run up into a recess behind the frieze cornice and dado over the shop windows; while the lower portion runs down the stone pier, and being hung by pulleys and chains, so as to balance one another, are opened and shut with remarkable ease and expedition."*

The article goes on to say that the girders and the shutters were invented by the contractor for the iron work, Mr Robert McConnel and have been patented.[84] A similar principle was used for timber rising shutters which operate on a counter-weighted pulley system, similar to a sash and case window system, stored in the basement area then pulled up into position when the shop is closed.

Protecting goods from the sun required further innovation through the development of different types of blinds. This was particularly essential on streets which faced south into the sun and for fresh produce retailers. Retractable roller blinds on a spring mechanism were introduced in the early nineteenth century.[85] These blinds were of canvas and on a metal frame which was pulled out from the casing. Aprons hung at the sides offering additional protection and sometimes the blind incorporated a design or name of the shopkeeper as additional advertising. They had the added advantage of allowing shoppers to stand under cover while inspecting the shop displays. However, in some towns the excessive number of blinds located

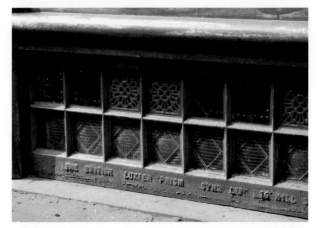

Fig: 43

along the street made it difficult for pedestrians to make their way along and the wing blinds in particular came to be regarded as a street nuisance.

Although natural light was considerably improved through the availability of plate glass, the ineffectiveness of the artificial lighting systems available meant that shops, particularly basement areas, remained a problem to illuminate. Pavement lights and stallboard lights originated from 1883 and comprised square 'prismatic' glass tiles.[86] Smooth on one side, they incorporated a series of prisms which refracted the light allowing it to pass deeper into a room in a more predictable way making them ideal for basements.[87] The glass blocks were set into cast iron frames integral to the stallriser and sometimes complemented with pavement lights which offered additional light. (Figure 43)

The British Luxfer Prism Syndicate was set up in 1898 to promote this innovative product and it was widely used for stallrisers and also in the clerestory of shop windows. However, the popularity of prismatic glass dwindled in the early twentieth century as electricity became increasingly available.[88] By the 1930s it was no longer being manufactured although they remain as a visible architectural link with the past on some Victorian and early twentieth century shopfronts.

Decorating the Victorian Shopfront

Where Georgian shops were restrained and refined, Victorian shops were bold and exuberant. Embellishment was a key feature, achieved by the application of various forms of decoration, many derived from classical elements. However, while classical architecture remained the basic inspiration for many shopfronts, the strict rules were rarely adhered to: *"proportions were no longer governed by classical rules, and its architectural elements were progressively transformed, often being overlaid with ornament and becoming more an aspect of decoration than of structure".*[89]

One of the features we most strongly associate with Victorian shopfronts is the console bracket. In classical architecture these were a decorative form using volutes or scrolls used to support a cornice and also known as *Ancones* derived from the Greek word for elbow or hollow.[90] Their main purpose in shop design is to balance the shopfront and mark the end of one shop and the beginning of another. Although apparently structural supporting the cornice, they do not generally perform this function and are merely applied to the fascia as a decorative element.

One of the earliest examples of their use for a commercial frontage was by architect Joseph Papworth in 1829-30 for a Gin palace in London.[91] (Figure 44) Although console brackets are evident in Dean of Guild drawings for South Bridge as early as 1841, it was really the later nineteenth century before they became fashionable and were then widely used. Of either timber or stone, console brackets were made locally or pre-fabricated elsewhere and could be a simple scroll or incredibly elaborate. In some cases they were carved in stone forming an integral part of the building. It is not uncommon to see several of the same console brackets in a street or adjacent streets which suggests the same builder, architect or a fashion for particular consoles, perhaps relating to a period of development.

Figure 44: Design for a corbel or bracket by JB Papworth, c1828
© RIBA Library Photographs Collection

Figure 45: Bookend Console incorporating human figure, Crieff

Fig: 44

Fig: 45

Figure 46: Ironwork used in St Stephen Street Shops, Edinburgh

Fig: 46

In the late nineteenth century, fascias became much deeper and also angled which meant that the traditional shape of console bracket was not appropriate. This encouraged the development of so-called 'book-end' consoles which were deeper in shape and tended to be more elaborate than their earlier counterparts. The outer face, which is highly visible, is typically carved decoratively and the console bracket may use figures or animals as part of the design. (Figure 45) Shops with book-end consoles will generally date to the 1880s and 1890s in what was a fairly short-lived fashion.

The other applied decorative features most commonly used on Victorian shopfronts are pilasters which are non-structural supports applied to the front of the shop, either side of openings. They may be constructed of various materials including timber, stone and cast iron. Their designs changed progressively; Georgian pilasters tended to be slender but sometimes with decorative moulding. Early Victorian ones are quite plain and were used either singly or as pairs. Fluting or half-fluting was a popular finish or decorative panelling, sometimes in geometric patterns which could also match the design on the stallriser. There were no set designs or patterns and each shopfront designer probably favoured particular styles depending on the fashion at the time. Their prominence in Scottish burghs may relate to periods of development such as in Kelso, where there are over twenty pilastered shops, many dating to the mid nineteenth century when the railway arrived in the town encouraging economic expansion.

Victorian shop owners sought other decorative ways to embellish their shopfronts. Cast iron brattishing was used as cresting on cornices to create a formal and expensive image. It also had practical applications such as for railings and cast iron balconies, often associated with shops with a platt access in the Edinburgh New Town as well as for lettering on fascias.

Figure 47: Victorian Ceramic Tiles

Fig: 47

Ceramic materials were now mass produced for the first time and this offered great possibilities for both interiors and for the shopfront. This clean and hygienic material had numerous practical uses including floors, walls and stallrisers and raised the quality and status of shopfronts. Lobby floors were enhanced with the use of geometric or encaustic tiles. Hard wearing and attractive these became immensely popular from the late nineteenth century onwards and despite their mass-production, shop owners could seek their own styles or patterns or personal designs which gave their shop the individuality that many owners sought.

Advertising the Business

Victorian shopkeepers recognised the importance of advertising and promoting their business in an increasingly competitive market. The most obvious way to advertise was using the fascia of the shop. Initially simple and narrow in design, the fascia in the later nineteenth century became angled, curved or S-shaped rather than flat to the face of the building and much deeper in profile, partly to accommodate the integral roller blinds which were now proving popular. As shopfronts became taller, perhaps the increasing height of the fascia from the pavement meant that it was desirable to have a larger and more noticeable fascia.

Lettering was painted by a skilled signwriter but during the later nineteenth century different techniques for fascia lettering were introduced such as timber cut-out letters and gilded signs with plate glass coverings. These gave a high class appearance to a shopfront and became very fashionable in the later decades of the nineteenth century.

The considerable competition for customers meant that, in some shops the advertising was taken to extremes. Late Victorian photographs typically show buildings with the whole of the façade or gable-end painted with the name of the proprietor and the goods he purveyed as the shop owner attempted to attract maximum attention for his shop.

The latter half of the nineteenth century proved to be one of the most dramatic periods in shop design. For the first time there was a significant recognition of the importance played by the design of the shopfront by all retail sectors. The greatest opportunity came from the technological improvements made during the nineteenth century and the development of new materials like plate glass and cast iron had a significant impact on shop design. They transformed shops from small dark rooms to lofty and welcoming places which became fashionable places to visit. Shopping was no longer just a matter of necessities, it had become a leisure activity for middle and upper class people and the shops reflected the status of their customers, a trend of opulence that continued into the Edwardian period and was displayed at its best in the department stores of the period.

Figure 48: Norwell's Boot Shop, 45-47 High Street, Perth, late nineteenth century showing the use of many different advertising mechanisms to attract business © Courtesy of Perth Museum and Art Gallery, Perth & Kinross Council

Fig: 48

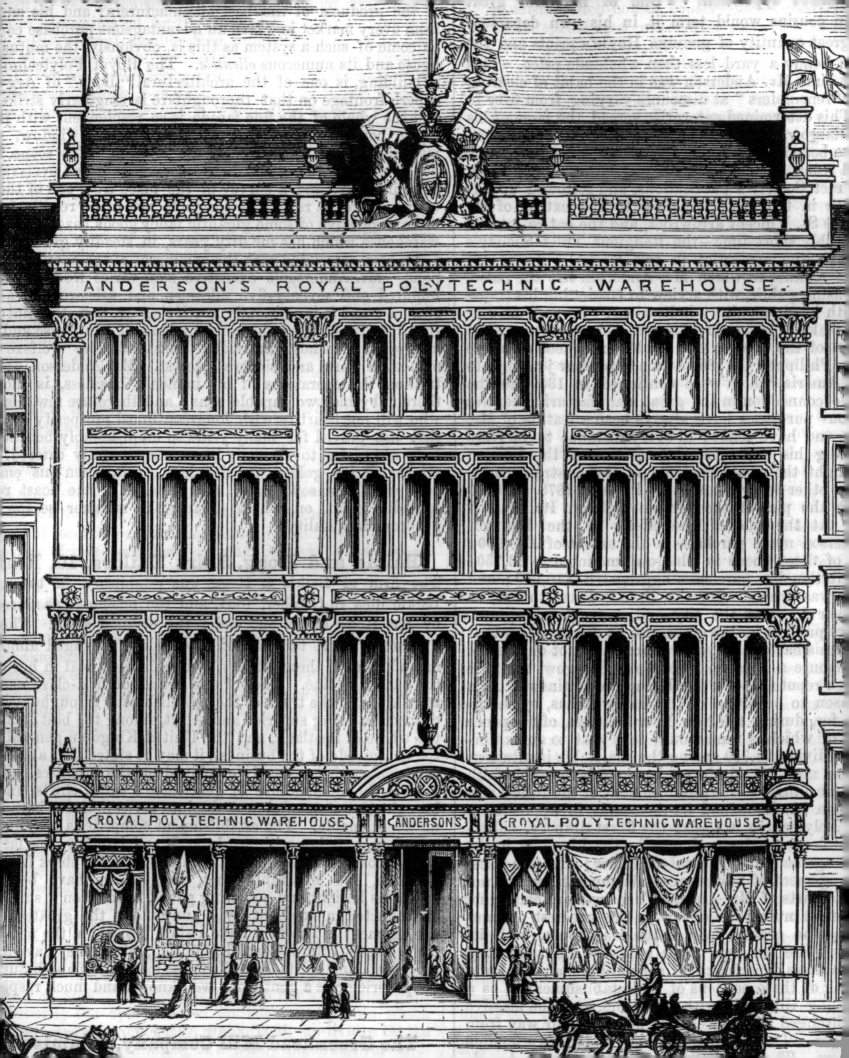

SCOTTISH DEPARTMENT STORES

"Shoppers, attracted by their palatial buildings and novel facilities, were then tempted to spend by seductive display." Moss & Turton[92]

Department stores emerged during the nineteenth century and have their origins in the wealthy silk mercers and drapers of the late eighteenth and early nineteenth century. It may be difficult to define exactly what a department store is, but may be considered as a large retail building where there are at least four different departments including children's wear and women's wear as well as other types of goods.[93]

The first department stores in the United Kingdom are believed to be Bainbridge's of Newcastle (1830) and Kendal Milne of Manchester (1831). In Scotland, it seems that J & W Campbell was one of the first, together with Stewart & McDonald and Anderson's Royal Polytechnic. J & W Campbell & Co was founded by two brothers James and William first in the Saltmarket in 1817 then Candleriggs and finally to a substantial building on the corner of Ingram Street and Brunswick Street in 1856. They sold drapers goods including hosiery, silk and ribbons. John Anderson was from Perth but moved to Glasgow in 1835 where he set up a drapers shop in the Gorbals. He subsequently moved to Clyde Terrace then Argyle Street having created a store which became of great renown in Glasgow. An advert for the store in *The Scotsman* 20 March 1899, says *"Unprecedented success of an enterprising policy brought home to your own doors. Great Victory of Cash Trading versus Credit"*.[94]

By the middle of the nineteenth century there were established, certainly in Edinburgh and Glasgow, firms who were operating on a much larger scale than before and introducing new retailing practices, breaking away from the traditional credit-sales, low turnover approach where customers had to haggle for goods. Fixed, low prices with stock on display and no obligation to purchase was the new approach adopted. The improving retailing opportunities available in the nineteenth century allowed these firms to expand, particularly with the ready access to Edinburgh and Glasgow through the expansion of the train and tram networks.

In Edinburgh, the firm of Kennington and Jenner opened at 47 Princes Street in May 1838. Like other department stores, they advertised profusely in newspapers such as *The Scotsman*. Their adverts in editions in 1838 promoted their wide range of drapery goods including laces, gloves, linens, silks, ribbons and fabrics. A new department for furniture and carpets was opened in 1867 for their premises at 47 and 48 Princes Street. By 1874 they were

known as Charles Jenner & Company and their store on the corner of Princes Street was, by 1890, the largest retail store in Scotland. This building, like many other department stores was subsequently destroyed by fire in 1892 but it was rebuilt with a fire-proof method of construction in 1893–95 designed by William Hamilton Beattie.

In Glasgow, Arthur and Fraser first established in 1849 and by 1865 was Fraser and McLaren then by 1875 was Fraser & Co. They were based at 8 Buchanan Street, Glasgow but suffered two major fires in 1872 and 1888. Despite these set-backs, the firm grew to become Scotland's most successful department store and subsequently acquired many other smaller companies. Some of these traded under their original name such as Arnott's but eventually House of Fraser became the established name.[95]

The department stores which emerged were therefore of two main types. The first were long-standing firms who gradually developed their business and expanded such as Anderson's Royal Polytechnic and Jenners. However, there were also firms who came into the business as department stores and these included the Army & Navy Co-operative Society (1871) and Civil Service Supply Association Ltd (1866).[96] The traditional style drapers-cum-department stores traded on the longevity of their firm and had an established and often middle-class customer base. Some of the newer firms, however, targeted a lower priced market and gained considerable success.

The Architecture of Department Stores

By their very nature, department stores broke new ground in terms of their internal layouts and in their external appearance. Shops were established and then gradually evolved, consuming neighbouring properties as the business grew. By the later nineteenth century these rambling inter-connected buildings were no longer suitable and department stores were being built specifically for the purpose, inspired by their iron warehouse cousins of the mid nineteenth century. Design and appearance were of great importance to their customers, especially where they were aiming to appeal to a higher class of customer. The purpose built stores of the late nineteenth and early twentieth centuries were grand in design reflecting their special status in the retailing hierarchy. Selfridges in London is one of the most famous, erected to an American model in 1909 on eight floors with 130 separate departments and inspired a new approach to department store design.

Figure 49: Anderson's Royal Polytechnic Warehouse, Argyle Street, Glasgow, 1888, as depicted in Glasgow of Today *© University of Strathclyde - ABACUS. Licensor www.scran.ac.uk. (facing page)*

Fig: 50

However, the increasing depth of stores caused by the sheer size of these premises introduced a number of problems such as access, lighting, fire risk and dealing with cash transfers.

As these shops grew in size access through the building proved problematic. Technological development including lifts and escalators aimed to improve access to every floor for goods and people and encouraged shoppers into all parts of the building. The first passenger safety lift was invented in America in 1853 by Elisha Otis. Early lifts were steam or hydraulic powered and installed in department stores and hotels from the 1860s although Wylie & Lochhead had a 'crude lift' in their Buchanan Street store in 1855. From the 1890s electrically operated systems were available following the invention of the electric motor by Werner von Siemens at the end of the nineteenth century. It was the enterprising owners of Harrods of London who installed the first 'moving staircase' in 1898 which popularised the idea of escalators for department stores.[97]

Electric light was not available until the end of the nineteenth century so shops sought various ways to maximise natural light into these substantial premises. The architecture incorporated large windows to increase daylight and top-lit galleries and light wells were utilised to flood light into areas located away from the front of the building. (Figure 50) Mirrors also helped to reflect light into darker areas. Artificial lighting was primitive and took the form of coal-gas chandeliers or gasoliers or paraffin lamps and lights such as the Bude light, invented by Gurney and Rixon in 1839. Gas lighting was introduced in the early nineteenth century and was generally available in the large stores by the mid nineteenth century. Electric lighting was not provided by Glasgow Corporation, for example, until 1893 although Walter Wilson did introduce it in his Colosseum in 1882. Perversely, once electric light became available, the stores seemed reluctant to let go of their light wells. Morrison states that *"As light wells were no longer a practical necessity, their wastefulness in terms of space now carried connotations of luxury, and implied the preservation of traditional service".*[98] For example, Liberty's Tudor Block in London had three light wells and an intimate and domestic atmosphere.

The threat of fire was a serious and ongoing problem for department stores. Many early department stores were destroyed by fire, sometimes on more than one occasion. (Figure 51) The large premises with numerous goods and hazardous lighting with candles, gas and early electricity meant that fire was real hazard. This encouraged the development of fire-proof construction in some of these stores.

The size of these premises with numerous cash registers on several floors posed problems for cash retrieval. To solve this, cash railways were introduced to transfer cash and receipts around large shop premises, having been first created in America in the 1870s and 1880s.[99] Numerous types were developed including a wire system, cash ball and particularly popular in the UK, a pneumatic system, the main manufacturer being Lamson. The first store in Scotland to invest in an automatic cash carrier was Arnott & Co in Jamaica Street, Glasgow who installed a Lamson Cash Railway in 1885. The pneumatic tube had been first introduced into department stores in America in the 1880s by John Wanamaker, usually operated by an electric fan which created a vacuum in a series of tubes allowing the carriers to travel through the system. Smaller systems used a foot pedal which operated bellows to create the vacuum.[100]

Over time till systems were modernised and the need for a cash office was reduced leaving the systems obsolete. They were also probably viewed as unsightly within the shop premises and perhaps interfered with displays. Ultimately, the majority were removed from the stores and only a handful remain, some only partially. Despite the loss of older systems, Lamson continued to manufacture modern pneumatic systems and these proved popular with large supermarkets to avoid the tills having large quantities of cash at any one time.

Although department stores were largely found in Edinburgh, Aberdeen and Glasgow, they were also located in Dundee (Draffens), Perth (Wallace's and McEwens) and even smaller centres like Crieff, Stonehaven and Peebles. These smaller department stores were really large drapers and did not have the facilities, technology or impressive size of the city stores. Despite this, they were economically important for their areas, often fondly regarded by residents and were aesthetically important in the townscape. Veitches in Peebles commanded an important corner site in the Borders town, in a Scots Baronial style of architecture. In recent times it has been hard for stores like these to be viable and many have been redeveloped for other uses. The former Ramsay's department store at 12-16 Market Square, Stonehaven is now a small grocery supermarket. Again in a prominent corner position, this 1920's shopfront has an unusual survivor of a glass showcase in the corner using curved glass for maximum effect. The store also had upper floor display windows with a fascia advertising the millinery and drapery goods above. (Figure 52)

Fig: 51

Department stores were important in the history of retailing because they were the first to adopt innovative techniques, not just in selling but in their architecture, lifts, cash railways, lighting and fire-proof construction. These affluent businesses were at the cutting edge of retail design and Scotland has an auspicious history in terms of its department stores and can claim one of the most important retailers in this field, House of Fraser. Department stores have had to change and adapt like all types of retailer in order to satisfy continually changing customer needs. The legacy of buildings, largely from the turn of the twentieth century is an important element in our streetscapes.

Figure 51: Jenner's Department Store, Edinburgh destroyed by fire in 1892
© Courtesy of RCAHMS. Licensor www.rcahms.gov.uk

Figure 52: Ramsay's Drapery, 12-16 Market Square, Stonehaven
© Crown Copyright. Licensor www.rcahms.gov.uk

Fig: 52

NINETEENTH CENTURY
MARKET REFORM

"The nineteenth century market hall partakes of the Victorians obsession with comfort, cleanliness and efficiency. Until the later appearance of the co-operative store, the department store and the twentieth century supermarket, the market hall was the pioneer in creating an environment which maximised comfort and service for both customer and consumer. Schmiechen and Carls[101]

While shops were expanding and department stores were being erected, the traditional shopping of the markets was gradually being altered through laws to control their location. Reform of market trading was deemed necessary during the nineteenth century given the considerable demand on public space and improving requirements for hygiene. The Burgh Reforms of 1833 and 1834 introduced sanitary improvements such as street cleansing and control over slaughterhouses and shambles. The location of butcher's shambles had been an ongoing issue, particularly in large towns and cities. Although slaughterhouses were erected at the Nor' Loch in Edinburgh in 1621, the first public slaughterhouse was not built in Edinburgh until 1850. However, throughout the nineteenth century regulations increased such as the keeping of stall-fed cattle which were inspected after 1865 and further by-laws which gradually pushed the unpleasant trades away from their traditional

sites.[102] This meant the erection of purpose-built market halls and slaughterhouses. In Britain by 1866, around half of all towns had moved their traditional street markets to an enclosed space which meant that the way in which food was purchased altered rapidly from street purchases to buying from fixed shops or covered markets.[103]

Planned towns like Thurso and Stonehaven were given a formal market place to encourage trade. Stonehaven built a grand classical market building in the Market Square in 1826 designed by Alexander Fraser. The 130 foot spire was subsequently added in 1857. This grand building which oversees a substantial square in the centre of the planned layout of Stonehaven was where the local markets were held. It functioned as a Market House until 1897 but produce was also sold from stalls within the arcaded ground floors, harking back to the piazzas of the seventeenth and eighteenth century.

Figure 53: Great Hall, Aberdeen New Market, built 1842. It was destroyed by fire in 1882 and then rebuilt in 1883 Courtesy of Aberdeen Library and Information Services (facing page)

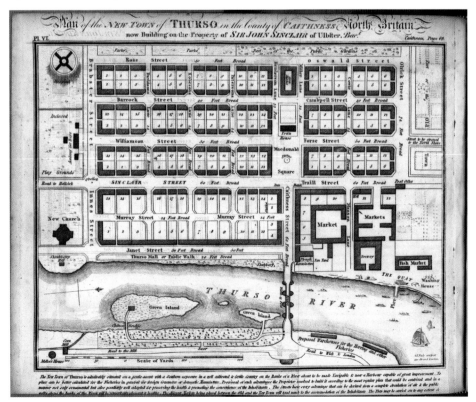

Figure 54: Plan of the New Town of Thurso, 1801 showing the location of the markets © Courtesy of RCAHMS. Copied from A general view of the agriculture of the county of Caithness. Licensor www.rcahms.gov.uk

Fig: 54

Fig: 55

In the larger towns and cities the move was towards covered or partially covered central markets which sold a variety of goods. In Glasgow, The Bazaar at Candleriggs was originally laid out in 1817. The city was one of the first to segregate its markets into an enclosed space, Candleriggs being the largest in Britain when erected.[104] It grew over time into an even larger building, eventually being roofed over. Initially it had a variety of goods on sale from fresh produce to books and toys. However, the market gradually became more specialised which was attributed by the Glasgow Corporation to the growth of retail shops and the availability of large provision stores.[105]

Instead, purpose-built stores were erected in more suitable locations and which were fit for purpose. *'These central, enclosed markets were revolutionary, for they freed the market from the non-marketing activities of the traditional market place. Public access was usually limited to a number of carefully selected points for pedestrians and one for carts, thus giving the town officials greater control over who and what passed through the market. Some enclosed markets had separate roofed spaces for shops and stalls, and often the market was divided into speciality areas.'*[106]

Having long had battles over the location of the numerous markets in the city, Edinburgh also took on board the nineteenth century reforms. A purpose-built market was erected at Stockbridge, designed c1825 by Archibald Scott. It was modelled on Liverpool market and sold a variety of fresh foodstuffs but, like many others of its type, it closed in 1906. The building was demolished leaving only the entrance arch remaining as a reminder of the fashion for purpose-built market halls.

In Glasgow, specialist markets included the City Clothes Market. Originally in Bridgegate and known as 'Paddy's Market' on account of the Irish immigrant traders, a proper building was erected in Greendyke Street in 1875, designed by John Carrick, City Architect but it was demolished in 1922. The Bridgegate or 'Briggait' became the site for the purpose-built Fish Market in 1874 designed by Clark and Bell in a French Renaissance style.[107] Other markets included the Bird and Dog Market, Cattle and Horse Market and Dead Meat Market. All Glasgow markets had originally been part of the common good of the city but with various Acts between 1845 and 1905, they were all transferred to Glasgow Corporation control.

In Aberdeen, a new market was built in 1842 designed by Archibald Simpson. It had a large meat and poultry hall, a basement for fish sales and a gallery selling fancy goods. It suffered a major fire in 1882 but was rebuilt in 1884. The building survived until 1971 when it was demolished for the redevelopment of the site for British Home Stores.

From the 1880s onwards the street markets for animals gradually declined, being viewed as a street nuisance and environmental health concern. Increasingly purpose-built animal and wholesale markets were erected, sometimes run by the Town Council as in Glasgow. These tended to move away from the central locations where the markets had been previously held, particularly those with animals. However, there was often resistance to this. The town authorities of Arbroath erected a new fleshmarket in Hill Street but it failed.[108] Similarly, they tried to move the fishwives from their position 'hunkering' in the High Street and selling their fish to a new position in Market Place. However, it also failed because of the "*fishwives persistently preferring to continue squatting on the High Street*".

In the early twentieth century, these markets were still generally thriving, although were perhaps becoming more wholesale dominated than they had in the past with the gradual increase in retail premises. In their purpose-built buildings they were well set out but often away from the main retail areas. With changes in standards and requirements these too became redundant and were either demolished or converted into other use such as leisure or retail. Despite this, finding a successful alternative use can be a challenge.

Likewise, annual fairs which were a tradition in many areas remained but gradually changed during the twentieth century developing more into Fun Fairs and amusements rather than for trading.

Scotland differed from England in that only the large towns of Edinburgh, Glasgow, Aberdeen, Inverness and Dundee had covered market halls. However, smaller towns retained their markets and fairs although in an increasingly altered and diminished way. It is possible that the more rigorous control over Scotland's market management together with slower commercialisation meant that the situation differed from that in England.[109] Ultimately however, these markets moved to a solely wholesale basis as retail premises began to dominate towns of all sizes.

Figure 56: Glasgow Fruit Market, Candleriggs, Glasgow. The market hall was built in 1852-3 and extended in 1907. © RCAHMS. Reproduced courtesy of J R Hume. Licensor www.rcahms.gov.uk

Fig: 56

EDWARDIAN SHOPS

"Edwardian buildings.… had ceased to be merely examples of the constructor's art. They had incorporated mechanical and power systems, the prime aim of which was to control environmental conditions and communication. It was as though a nervous system was at last integrated into the body of the building."
R. Fellows[110]

The Edwardian era was an exuberant period of shop design reflecting a wider affluence and enthusiasm for erecting public buildings, tenements and department stores. Architecturally the period is complex with influences from the Victorian period, including the Gothic Revival, Baroque, the Arts and Crafts Movement inspired by William Morris and the Art Nouveau style which emerged at the turn of the century.

The Edwardian shopfront galvanised these styles with its innovative adoption of new products and high quality materials. Shopping had become as much a past time as a necessity and the style and design of the premises reflected the desire to attract middle-class shoppers who sought additional services like restaurants, tea rooms and home delivery.

Edwardian shop architects and architecture

The continuation of Victorian themes into the early twentieth century makes it difficult to differentiate between the periods and the Edwardian era should therefore be viewed as a continuation of the late nineteenth century. Grundy[111] observes that at the beginning of the twentieth century there were two main types of shopfront. First, one displaying *"flamboyant Victorian showmanship, with gaudy fittings and decoration, reminiscent of fairground craftsmanship"* and secondly more refined, Arts and Crafts influenced shopfronts with more restrained decorative features.

Although during the later nineteenth century architects had recognised the potential of shops as a source of work, this was largely from locally-based architects, albeit their contribution is significant. These include architects like David Smart (Perth), J P Allison (Hawick), James Gillespie (St Andrews) and James Thomson (Bo'ness). Within their localities they designed shops, tenements and other buildings and in many cases made a significant contribution to these towns.

However, there is also evidence of architects who are recognised as of national importance like Charles Rennie Mackintosh and George Walton (1867-1933) designing shopfronts. Mackintosh's contribution to shop architecture

is small but his friends, Brough and Macpherson of Comrie owned a drapery business and he designed new shop and house premises for them following a fire which had destroyed their shop. The shopfront is deceptively simple in design but the interior retains shelving and long counters typical of Edwardian draperies but bearing the distinctive hallmark of its innovative designer.

Walton, a contemporary of Charles Rennie Mackintosh, designed shops in the early twentieth century for Kodak in a nostalgic style. He designed showrooms for the photographic company in London, Brussels, Milan and Dublin as well as a Scottish branch at 72-74 Buchanan Street, Glasgow in 1901. This marked a new creative approach both in terms of the corporate ideal but also the new importance now placed on shopfront design. Walton, like Mackintosh, designed not only the shopfront, but also beautifully detailed interiors with stencilled friezes and

Figure 57: James Flett & Son, grocer and ironmongers, Bridge Street, Orkney, 1910 © Orkney Library and Archive (facing page)

Figure 58: Kodak shop, 72-74 Buchanan Street, Glasgow by George Walton © RIBA Library Photographs Collection

Fig: 58

Figure 59: Hoarding
for Kodak shop,
West Strand, London
designed by George
Walton
© RIBA Library
Photographs Collection

fittings graced with stained glass. Walton even designed elaborate hoardings which were painted with Edwardian street scenes for protecting the shop during work. The first time he used this was in 1896 for the work to Miss Cranston's tea rooms at 91 Buchanan Street, Glasgow and it is possibly the first time that a hoarding was treated in such an aesthetic way.[112] The same idea was adopted for the new Kodak shop at 40 West Strand, London and here the upper section of the hoarding was filled with tinted canvas and illuminated at night for maximum publicity.[113]

The availability of particular materials also allowed Edwardian shops to excel in quality. Joinery was of a particularly high standard making use of exotic hardwoods such as mahogany which allowed the creation of high-class shopfronts. Slender cast iron or timber colonnettes maximised the amount of glass possible in a decorative way. The elaboration of doors with pediments, dentils and panelled soffits to the lobby entrances all indicated

superior quality and brass ironmongery completed the opulence found in many shops.

Plate glass was the material of choice for the majority of shopfronts although its use was not universally welcomed. Writing in 1906, Ellis [114] disparagingly refers to the "*modern shop front*". He states that there tends to be no vertical division bars and instead a huge expanse of plate glass:

> *"The paucity of any woodwork renders it almost*
> *impossible to design shop fronts with any pronounced*
> *individuality in their treatment, the supposed requirements*
> *of the shopkeeper over-riding all considerations of*
> *architectural effect. The result is the monotonous repetitions*
> *of big sashes mounted on narrow strips of framing*
> *and surmounted by heavy name boards which line the*
> *thoroughfares."*

Figure 60: Drawing
for Fletcher's Music
Shop, 121 South Street,
St Andrews by James
Gillespie & Scott
© James Gillespie and
Scott, supplied courtesy
of University of St
Andrews Library

Figure 61: Art Nouveau
stained glass, South
Street, St Andrews

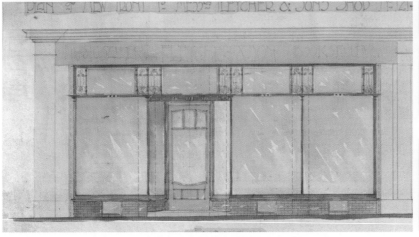

Fig: 62

However, this criticism is perhaps excessive as many Edwardian shop windows made use of other glass products to enhance their appearance. The clerestory became an important decorative feature, particularly through the use of stained and leaded glass, sometimes Art Nouveau inspired. Small panes in the clerestory could be coloured or plain a nostalgic link with Georgian small-paned windows and perhaps reflecting an Arts and Crafts style backlash against the plate glass to which Ellis refers.

However, the improved technologies could also significantly enhance shopfronts. Curved glass was particularly fashionable and was used to great effect in shop entrances with curved and bell-shaped lobbies. The shop entrance gained considerable significance and became deeply recessed and elaborately detailed with decorative pediments, dentils, panelled soffits and mosaic tiled floors to draw the customer in, attracted by the extensive array of goods on display in the windows and lobby showcases. The mosaic lobby floors sometimes incorporated the name of the shop owner or perhaps their business, lending an air of permanence to the retailer. The Victorian rectangular

and dark lobbies with double storm doors had been superseded by a more welcoming and transparent entrance with maximum display opportunity.

The fascia was often elegant and carefully proportioned with the shopfront usually slightly angled giving better visibility for passers-by. Use of dentils on the cornice was common and lettering was tasteful with timber V-cut and gilded lettering or hand-painted signage.

The interiors of Edwardian shops reflected the high quality of the exterior, demonstrating opulence with grand staircases, timber panelling and ornate plaster ceilings. Natural light flooded down from the expansive light wells although the steady introduction of electric lighting made such structures superfluous. Despite this, they remained fashionable and saloons with their elegant ceilings were often a showcase for these shops. The utilitarian interiors had become much more welcoming and open.

Department stores became particularly fashionable at the beginning of the twentieth century with several

Figure 62: Mosaic lobby floor, David Irons, Forfar

Fig: 63

notable stores constructed at this time including Harrods in Knightsbridge, London. The firm was founded in 1849 although the present London building is 1901-05 created by the shopfitters, Frederick Sage & Company. Scottish companies like Jenners, Wylie & Lochhead and Frasers continued to expand their retailing empires.

The grocery and provision trade expanded exponentially from the late nineteenth century into the early twentieth century. Jefferys states that by the outbreak of World War I "*the grocery and provisions trade from being a purveyor of luxuries to the rich had been transformed into a trade catering for all classes*". However, he also points out that there remained variety in terms of pricing and retail style although less significant than had been in the late Victorian period. More goods were imported and improvements made in manufacturing goods.[115] There was a shift as long-established retail types like Italian warehousemen and specialist tea and cheese dealers declined and in their place came new grocery retailers like Thomas Lipton and Andrew Ewing of Buttercup Dairy. They took advantage of new products like margarine and canned products as well as the opportunity to brand goods with their own name.

Their shops also reflected branding and each company developed its own corporate style and colours. One of the most enduring is the Buttercup Dairy Company which utilised Art Nouveau influences and tiles by Glasgow tile firm, James Duncan Ltd.

Edwardian Technology

Like their Victorian predecessors, the Edwardians developed new technology including reinforced concrete and structural steel which proved fundamental in allowing new types of buildings to be created.[116] Selfridge's department store in London (1907-09) had a ground-breaking design which was not compartmentalised for fire protection in the normal way. Its innovative construction methods allowed London County Council to pass an Act in 1908 allowing for increased continuous internal volume ultimately changing the way store design was approached.

Technology also improved life within buildings, electric light being a crucial development. Although Thomas Edison had invented light bulbs in 1879 that were of practical use, adoption was slow because they were both expensive and inefficient. From 1910, the much improved tungsten filament bulb was available and as these became cheaper and more readily available electricity became the favoured method of lighting buildings.

Ultimately, the widespread availability of electricity had a profound and lasting impact on retail design as shops were no longer reliant on natural light or inefficient gasoliers. As a result, shop entrances could now be deeper and this was a feature which was further developed in the inter-war period with complex arcaded entrances. It also transformed window displays as these could be lit at night. Selfridges led the way in window-dressing by employing specialist staff who prepared the displays and having the window displays lit until midnight for full effect.[117]

Even some modest-sized shops installed lifts although generally for moving goods rather than passengers. David Irons in Forfar is a traditional ironmongers and has a very early hydraulic lift (1896 although the building at the front dates to 1909) installed to move goods from the basement into the upper floors of the shop which is still in working order.

These technological improvements contrast with the more traditional style of Edwardian retail architecture. This interesting and complex period represents a continuum between the Victorian elaboration of the nineteenth century and the minimalist architecture of the inter-war years. They borrowed ideas from many sources including Art Nouveau and Baroque but some of the features which were prominent in this era, notably the use of a decorative clerestory and the significance of a deep and elaborate entrance remained central to inter-war shop design.

The Edwardian period may be regarded as a time of innovation in materials particularly the use of steel to open up shopfronts. Cast iron remained popular although in a more modest and refined way than during the Victorian period. Curved glass products were also in vogue and remained so into the inter-war years. With the vast extent of the British Empire and the availability of exotic hardwoods and similar foreign materials, shops made extensive use of high-quality timber. There was attention to detail with panelling and showcases and curved glass, all lending a high-class elegance to many Edwardian shopfronts.

The period was also one of transition in terms of technology. New possibilities were offered to retailers through the development of electricity and more specialised equipment like lifts and escalators. Retail buildings were at the forefront of the adoption of these, grasping the opportunities to make their shops the most modern and the best. However, progress was abruptly halted in 1914 when World War I started and it was the 1920s before shop design and innovation were revived.

Figure 63: Longrow, Campbeltown by TL Watson, 1909, 'Glasgow Style' tenement with tall ground floor shops maximising the use of plate glass © Argyll & Bute Council Library Service, McGregory Collection (facing page)

Projet pour une parfumerie

RENÉ PROU, arch.

INTER-WAR SHOPS 1920-1939

"The commercially acceptable Moderne style of the 30s was a 'marriage de convenance' between Art Deco and Modernism. Figured veneers, tinted mirrors, neon and fluorescent lighting fixtures, Bakelite, Formica, Vitrolite and chromed metal were amongst its principal ingredients, and it was seen at its best in cocktail bars, smart restaurants and expensive shops." R. Kenna[118]

The inter-war period was revolutionary in terms of shop design and transformed the whole approach to shopfront construction. This was in spite of, and perhaps even encouraged by, the considerable economic uncertainty which plagued much of the inter-war years. Shop architecture abandoned its classical roots in favour of minimalist designs with smooth, reflective surfaces and embraced with gusto the new materials of the age, manufactured glass and metal products which could transform a shopfront, literally overnight, typically undertaken by a team of shopfitters. The period is short, a mere twenty years, but the surviving shops reflect this highly progressive and innovative architectural era. This period was "*as short-lived as a dandelion puff ball. Yet its seeds, like those of the dandelions, were to prove vigorous and widespread*".[119]

Economy and Retailing

Following the end of World War I, the subsequent two decades proved to be an economically volatile period with significant fluctuations in the building cycle. The situation in Scotland was less favourable than in England as, for example, during the depression years of 1931-32 unemployment was at twenty percent in England but twenty-seven percent in Scotland and although those in employment were enjoying a rising standard of living including a greater availability of cheaper consumer goods, those who were unemployed suffered hardship.[120] Following this period of economic depression, there was growth from 1932 onwards with a peak in this boom time in 1937 [121] and McKean suggests that the imminence of war in the later 1930s provided an impetus for growth in Scotland stating that "*the majority of the projects date from the short period of 1935-38*" including commercial premises like shops.

Choice improved and as demand for consumer goods grew the individual producer/retailer "*virtually disappeared*" although the quality and range of goods improved.[122] New products were now available including electrical goods like the radio as well as packaged and tinned goods. Chain stores like Lipton's and Ross's Dairies branded their goods with their own corporate logo and sought to establish brand loyalty in their customers. The growth of national chains

meant that local companies were being squeezed out as these firms established stores throughout the country and developed national marketing schemes for the first time. The result was a noticeable decrease in local influence and an increase in homogeneity.[123]

This enthusiasm for a national approach was also reflected in the approach to shopfront design. Chain stores adopted a strategy of corporate identity and branding of stores, a trend which had its roots in the late nineteenth century. Some firms were now sufficiently large to employ their own architects to produce designs for shops that would be the same regardless of location or size including Burton's, Marks & Spencer, Woolworths and many others. This approach would ultimately have a significant impact on shop design across the country as designs were created in a head office, remote from the location of the shop.

Despite the economic depression, the period was innovative and embraced new ideas and materials. Grundy suggests that post-1914 there were changes in retailing including the fact that price was not the most important aspect and there was an increasing importance of non-food items. "*Selection and fashion became more important, encouraging window shopping which emphasised the value of display space.*"[124] With considerable competition, retailers had to impress shoppers by modernising their premises. Shops needed to be clean and hygienic as well as being more attractive in terms of display and the goods available. Services such as home delivery, credit and promotions helped to boost sales.[125] Beeching's contemporary *The Modern Grocer and Provision Dealer* advocates good quality finishes and also taking the advice of a shop construction expert stating that "*the shopfront in its entirety is the frame for the setting of the goods, and harmony and perfect blending is essential*".[126] Certainly post-1914, window display became a more important way of enticing the customers to part with their money, particularly as non-food goods were now more readily available.[127] This meant that the shop design of the inter-war period became increasingly competitive and the designers turned to a combination of new styles and new materials to make their shops stand out.

Figure 64: Violet Parfumerie by René Prou (1889-1947) featured in Devantures de Boutiques *by L-P Sezille, 1927 © RIBA Library Photographs Collection (facing page)*

Fig: 65

Shopfronts in the early 1920s

Shops in the first years of the 1920s represent a transition period between the traditional appearance of Edwardian shops and the Art Deco/Moderne influences which emerged later. Although more conservative and 'traditional' compared to those of the 1930s, they were still a source of criticism for their use of modern materials like plate glass. Architects became increasingly concerned about the extensive use of plate glass and the fact that the upper storeys of buildings appear to 'float' above the shops below. Burford describes a glass corner as "*fatal to good design"* and suggests a number of "*devices"* to "*counteract the menace of disaster consequent on an effect of structural impossibility"*. His "*devices"* include use of upper floor projecting balconies and canopies, series of vertical supports or increasing the number of smaller vertical supports. However, Burford does acknowledge that there is a difficulty in maintaining architectural integrity whilst meeting the needs of client's requirements although he considers the design to be of prime importance stating that it is "*difficult to conceive where good design will not give an added distinction"*.[128]

Despite these concerns, the shops dating to this time are typically elegant, reflecting sophisticated Parisian influences and making use of bronze, hardwoods and curved glass. One of the most notable examples of a 1920s bronze shopfront is the former Ciro Pearls shop at 95 Buchanan Street, Glasgow. Designed by Glasgow architect, George Arthur Boswell (1879-1952) in 1926, the French-inspired design included not only the shopfront but also the interior fittings.[129] The elegant clerestory with the fascia and script writing above presents a high-class shopfront reflecting the expensive goods to be found inside. (Figure 65)

Influence of Art Deco and the 1925 Paris Exhibition

Art Deco had its origins in the first decade of the twentieth century, but it was following the 1925 *Exposistion Internationale des Arts Decoratifs et Industriels Modernes* in Paris that the style was catapulted into the architectural world. This impressive international fair was "*the premier showcase of Art Deco"*.[130] Shops were part of the exhibition and a number of the designs feature in *Devantures de Boutiques* by L-P Sezille. This collection of drawings of shopfronts by French architects includes a selection from the Paris exhibition of 1925. These radical and experimental designs were often minimalist and angular with the effective display of goods of prime importance in these set pieces.[131] These demonstrate the continued importance of France as a leader in shopfront design with architects like Sezille, Siegel and Chanut.[132] (Figure 64 and 66)

Fig: 66

Fig: 67

As a style Art Deco was complex, drawing on many different sources for inspiration including Egypt following the discovery of Tutankhamen's tomb in 1922. Kenna states that towards the end of the 1920s the designs were largely "*quasi-Egyptian motifs and hard angular shapes, derived from Cubist and Abstract paintings and the chevrons and zig-zag patterns of the American skyscraper style (itself deeply influenced by Colombian art)*". Certainly geometric patterns like chevrons featured strongly in many shop designs.[133] The use of this can be seen in Matthew Steele's design for a department store in Bo'ness. This white cube erected in 1926 is of a striking design and which hints at Czech cubism. This daring architecture must have caused considerable discussion at the time.

The first examples were undoubtedly revolutionary, and the designs gradually dispersed as architects experimented with the ideas promoted at the Paris exhibition. A design for Lotus and Delta shoes in Princes Street, Edinburgh in 1928 shows an early example of Moderne influenced design by James Emberton (1889-1956).[134] Its deep entrance, chrome blind box and flush fascia is a precursor to the 1930's shops which followed. (Figure 67)

The following year, Erno Goldfinger designed what has been described as "*the first undecorated modern shop front in England*" for Helena Rubinstein in London.[135] Goldfinger states that he was aiming for a '*decoration-less*' shopfront.[136] The contractor was the famous high-class shopfitters, Frederick Sage & Co of London and the interior was similarly minimalist and somewhat clinical in design.

Although these ideas were adopted quickly for elite shops in prime retail locations following the Paris exhibition, it took longer for the impact to reach the provinces although shops certainly played an important role in helping to disseminate the ideas associated with the Modern Movement.[137] By the 1930s the formulative ideas of the mid-1920s were being adopted with confidence in shops throughout Scotland.

Influence of New Materials

Within the wider economic trends and emerging architectural styles, the impact of new materials in inter-war shop design cannot be underestimated. The move to mass-produced glass, metal and ceramic products transformed shop design introducing glossy surfaces, reflectivity and use of contrasting colours like black and white. The options for the modern shop keeper of the 1930s were apparently limitless; bronze for windows or decoration; chrome for windows, blinds and decoration; ceramics with white or coloured finishes; numerous glass products including etched and sandblasted glass or Vitrolite, a coloured structural glass; polished stone including marble and granite.

These materials were destined for a new type of shopfront where reflection and strong visual impact were paramount. Bands of chrome and black emphasised the horizontal designs and evoked ideas of streamlining. Mass produced, these materials were widely available and affordable and in sufficient variety, colours and types to offer shopkeepers that ever important individuality of design.

Figure 66: Jean Luce Ceramics Shop by L-P Sezille in Devantures de Boutiques, 1927
© RIBA Library Photographs Collection

Figure 67: Lotus and Delta Shoe Shop, Princes Street, Edinburgh by Joseph Emberton, 1928
© RIBA Library Photographs Collection

Figure 68: 1930s materials

Fig: 68

Metals proved popular because of their glossy, smooth and reflective qualities. Bronze was favoured for the sashes of windows and also could be used decoratively in the clerestory and for air vents. A quality material, it also complements the other materials used such as marble and Vitrolite. Chrome, a plated metal, was widely used in 1930s shopfronts, often in combination with Vitrolite and marketed under the name of 'staybrite'.

Shop designers continued to take advantage of the developing market of new glass products, both for glazing and for re-fronting. Shops made extensive use of plate glass for the shopfronts, high visibility of the interior being part of the design ethos combined with the ability to internally illuminate premises. McKean says that customers were "*lured in by the transparency of glittering windows, showcases and clever lighting, enhanced by the use of glass block*" and the "*illuminated interior shining through a transparent façade*".[138] The decoration of the glazed clerestory became an integral part of the overall design, particularly as a way to emphasise the horizontal lines. This was achieved through the use of sand-blasted or acid-embossed glass with sun-ray motifs or geometric designs including chevrons and wavy lines. Simple leaded glass was also used to where a more traditional appearance was sought.

One of the materials we most closely associate with the period is Vitrolite. This coloured structural glass was originally produced in white, but by the 1930s numerous colours were available including green, yellow and pink although black remained the most popular colour for shopfronts.[139] It proved to be a highly desirable material with shop owners because of its smooth and reflective properties, low maintenance and the ability to modernise a shopfront quickly.

Part of its success can be attributed to clever promotion notably the 1935 '*52 Ways to Modernize Main Street*' competition initiated by the Libby-Owens-Ford Glass company which manufactured Vitrolite. It was also widely promoted through the use of travelling salesmen who took samples of different colours and types of Vitrolite to demonstrate the material to potential customers.[140] However, the material must have been a great self-advertisement. The overnight transformation from traditional timber to a sleek, Moderne shopfront must have made any adjacent shops seem drab by comparison.

The smooth and glossy theme was also achieved through the use of ceramics and polished stone cladding. Brightly coloured tiles were popular for Victorian shops, but by the inter-war period there was a move to plain coloured ceramics and most notably the use of faience, an architectural ceramic. Available as a facing material or more

Fig: 69

structural sections, it was often white or cream and gave the architecture clean and clinical lines. It was used widely by Burton's the tailors in the 1930s purpose-built stores as well as other multiple retailers including Woolworths. As a country of stone, polished granite was widely used as well as other imported materials like marble and terrazzo. These offered a variety of colour choices although black and green proved the most popular.

1930s Signage and Lettering

During the 1930s, lettering and signage became an integral part of the shop design; the shops were so minimalist that the lettering played a significant role in the overall appearance. The availability of new materials and the opportunity to have signs which were illuminated at night for the first time offered a new realm of possibilities.

Again, the innovative designs at the Paris Exhibition inspired architects and shopfitters. The Moderne shop had a fascia flush with the building and considerably deeper than previous shop styles. Some were set in a stepped Art Deco fascia or others made use of chrome and bronze to form the sign.

New font styles were also introduced. More stylised lettering was adopted sometimes in a Hollywood Moderne style or in other shops script writing was popular. Although in some cases the lettering is very bold, in other shops its effectiveness is in its simplicity and perhaps subliminal nature.

Neon lighting played a significant role in shop design in the 1930s. Neon is a gaseous element which glows when an electric current is passed through it. The gas was developed into practical use for lighting by the French engineer and chemist, Georges Claude. The first shop to

Figure 69: Burnett and Forbes, 36–38 High Street, Nairn, c1930 with its black Vitrolite frontage and bronze windows
© Highland Photographic Archive, David Whyte Collection

reputedly use a neon sign was a barber's in Paris in 1912 and the following year the Champs Elysées was graced with a substantial neon sign depicting the word 'Cinzano'. Claude patented the neon lighting tube in 1915 and through his company Claude Neon promoted its use particularly in America in the early 1920s. Neon has a reddish-orange glow but other colours are available when it is combined with other gases. The availability of electricity and desire to maximise advertising opportunities meant that neon signs were visible both during the day and at night with their eye-catching colour schemes contrasting with the more austere and minimalist shopfronts.

Neon was at the heart of Art Deco emblazoned on cinemas, shops and the glass box pavilions at the Glasgow Empire Exhibition of 1938. It remained a popular lighting product into the post-war period and it is only in more recent years that it has lost favour and unfairly became associated with poorer and undesirable districts.

Shopfitting

Historically, shops had been designed and constructed by local joiners and builders. During the later nineteenth century, architects had begun to take an interest in shop design but there was also the emergence of a new breed of shop designer, the shopfitter. They were almost unheard of until the end of the nineteenth century but the increasing opportunities in shop work became evident to builders and joiners and they gradually chose to specialise in this area of work. The design and construction of shops offered both interior and exterior work, including the production of specialist showcases. Many of these firms also undertook fit-outs for ship interiors and had a background in this type of specialist joinery interior fitting and design. Gradually through the early twentieth century, shopfitters increased in number with the 1930s being a period of great expansion and prosperity for such firms.

The reluctance on the part of some architects to be involved in shopfront design persisted into the twentieth century. In 1924, A J Davies presented a lecture to the RIBA titled *"Shopfronts and their Treatment"* proposing ideas on colour, lettering and lighting as well as adapting shop design for particular businesses, but Grundy states that he *"failed to shift the entrenched attitudes of the architectural establishment"*.[141]

Figure 70: The Clydesdale Supply Co Ltd, 2-12 Bridge Street, Glasgow, 1932 showing how the availability of electricity was used, sometimes to excess, in retail buildings © Glasgow City Archives and Special Collections, Mitchell Library

Fig:70

Figure 71:
Advertisement from
The Scotsman, *29 April*
1938 promoting the
importance of new
shopfronts
© The Scotsman

Fig: 71

However, architects perhaps also failed to recognise that they now had significant competition in the field of shopfront design as shopfitters rose to prominence. Shopfitters created daring, modern designs and Grundy suggests that the architects had serious competition from shopfitters suggesting that *"While architects were worrying about plate glass to the exclusion of a positive approach to shop design, shopfitters were getting on with the job"*.[142]

London's two most prominent firms offered highly-specialised shopfitting services. E. Pollard & Co specialised in jewellers shops and Frederick Sage & Co secured the contract for Harrod's shopfront in London in the early 1900s. This confirmed Sage's reputation as a superior shopfitting firm and they went on to establish branches in Paris, Berlin and Buenos Aires.[143] In Birmingham, Harris & Sheldon were responsible for the high-class shopfronts of the Maypole Dairy Company. Such lucrative contracts ensured a steady flow of work for these shopfitters and helped their businesses to flourish.

These companies were highly innovative. Pollards, for example, sought to improve the glass products for shopfronts. Powers states that *"the enterprising shopfitters, Pollards, took out a licence for a French system of non-reflective glazing which became popular in the 1930's, using curved plate glass in various combinations"*.[144] McGrath also notes their use of specialist glazing techniques in their shopfronts and the introduction of the *'invisible window'* which he describes as a *'highly specialised installation'*.[145]

Although these English shopfitters did establish branches in Scotland, they were competing here with well-established firms including Archibald Hamilton and

A McEwan & Co of Glasgow and Donald Grant & Sons, Heggie & Aitchison and Adam Currie of Edinburgh. Shopfitters were rarely based in smaller centres like Perth and Stirling although undoubtedly local joinery firms would have undertaken this type of work and some retailers sought the services of shopfitters from Glasgow and Edinburgh, seeking their specialist skills. Some of the larger firms had contracts with the national chain stores and therefore worked throughout the country.

Shopfitters treatment of shops differed from the approach taken by architects because they were less concerned with architectural purity and more focused on providing a shopfront which was distinctive and noticeable. This led to criticism from the architectural profession. Grundy explains that *"shopfitting, as a trade rather than a profession, had little concern for ideology but a keen interest in men and materials, wages and prices"*. She goes on to point out that:

> *"Consideration of the complete façade was rather academic as much shopfitting was mere cosmetic treatment, amply demonstrated by the frequent refronting and refitting of shops, especially multiple stores. A succession of different shopfronts could be applied to the same superstructure."[146]*

Shopfitting firms wisely used their own premises to showcase their work. McEwan & Co had a traditional style pilastered shopfront with an elliptical fascia typical of the early twentieth century located at 98 Glassford Street in 1931. However, a move to a new showroom at 203 Hope Street in 1932 indicates a dramatic new approach with a completely flush, sleek frontage with no decoration other than an unusual circular sign; a square display window and entrance complete the ultimate picture of shopfront modernity. No customer visiting this showroom could have failed to have been impressed by this sleek modern design. (Figures 72 and 73)

Fig: 73

The different focus of shopfitters compared to local architects who were aware of local styles and influences clearly has implications for the style of a shopping street because they were not concerned with maintaining a local identity. Instead they sought to provide their client with a shop that would stand out, available in the latest materials and fashionable styles and presumably the retailers sought their advice because of this. However, in some cases, the shopfitter was contracted to carry out a design prepared by an architect and it was not always the case that shopfitters were responsible for the design. The 1935 shopfront for John Kirsop, hatter, at the corner of 133 West George Street and 25 Renfield Street by prominent architects, Burnet, Tait and Lorne exemplifies the elegance and simplicity of a high-quality inter-war shopfront. Its clean lines and grand entrance with a canopy and curved glass, reminiscent of a cinema, make a strong statement in its corner position.

Arcaded Entrances

The shop entrance gradually gained importance from the turn of the twentieth century and by the 1930s it was taken to extremes through the adoption of arcaded entrances. These were deep and complex entrance arrangements made possible through the wider availability of electricity; shops were no longer reliant on natural light and the entrance could therefore be heavily recessed. Arcaded entrances were particularly favoured by drapers and shoe retailers because they allowed them to display their vast array of goods successfully. A central showcase island was also occasionally adopted to complete the arcade allowing 360 degree viewing of the goods.

One of the first references to a Scottish shop with an arcaded entrance features in an article in the *Glasgow Herald* newspaper entitled *An Example of Modern Shop Design*.[147] It discusses the opening of the reconstructed McLaren & Son, hatters and tailors at 42 Gordon Street designed in 1886 by George Bell II of Clarke and Bell.[148] The article describes the new frontage installed in 1921 as follows:

"The main feature in the external arrangement is the manner in which the entrance to the shop has carried back from the pavement, providing for a great increase in window space. This permits a more effective display of goods and at the same time allows prospective customers to inspect them under cover and clear of the pavement."

There is also a discussion of the light and spacious interior fitted with mahogany and special lighting and a large selection of stock on display to the customer. By later examples it is not particularly deep and still retains elements of great elaboration that were later swept away in the 1930s.

Fig: 74

Figure 74: D Thomson, watchmaker and jeweller, 131 High Street, Dunfermline. Inter-war shopfront with an arcaded entrance, an arrangement popular with jewellers © Fife Council Library and Archives

Writing in 1922, Burford states that the setting back of window and door of the shopfront in this way *"forms a vestibule or lobby which provides protection for the window and extends an ever-open invitation to prospective patrons. Drapers… recognise the arrangement as a method of enticement"*.[149] During the late 1920s and early 1930s elaborate and complex arcaded shop entrances were considered to be highly fashionable. The plan form could be a straight but recessed entrance, but more often was complex in layout with zig-zags, in-and-out or 'Y' or 'U' shaped, sometimes of considerable length (Figures 75).

Their extravagance is highlighted by the materials used in their design including terrazzo, mosaic, bronze and plate glass with polished granite for the stallrisers and mahogany showcases graced the entrances. The cost of installing such a frontage would presumably have been considerable and not all retailers would have been able to fund such an elaborate alteration. Such designs were not popular with all shopkeepers because they tended to create a cavern effect which meant that goods were not readily visible unless close to the shop.[150] The arrangement was really only practical for large premises which could afford to give up the space to an entrance and for circulation.

The popularity of these entrances was short-lived and by the early 1940s they were no longer in vogue and many were removed, their space seen as too valuable to use for circulation and overly time-consuming to maintain the displays.

Figure 75: Arcaded entrance for J & R Allan Ltd, 74–84 South Bridge, Edinburgh, 1932
© RCAHMS (Dunn and Findlay Collection). Licensor www.rcahms.gov.uk

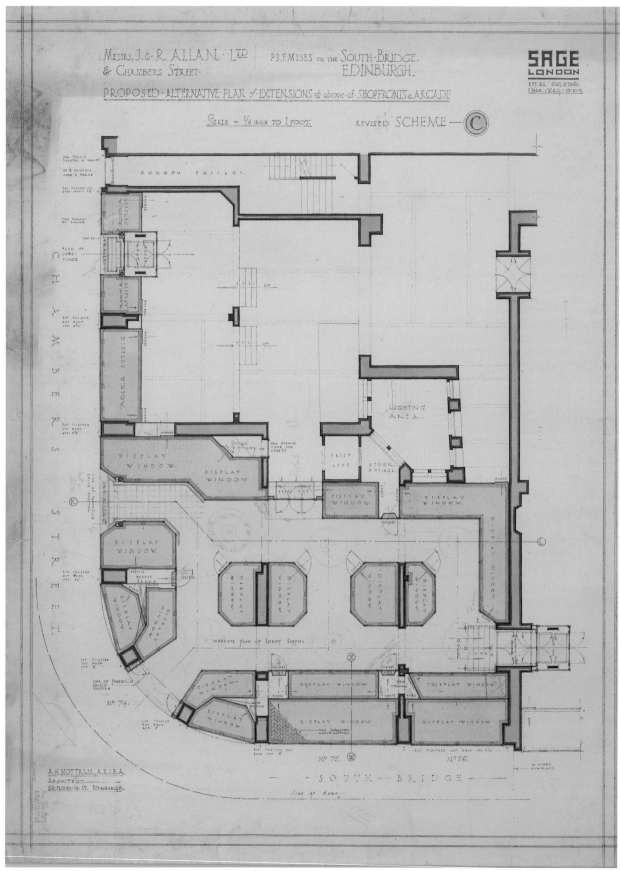

Fig: 75

Glasgow's Inter-war Retail Revolution

What is particularly remarkable about the 1930s is that despite a severe economic depression, shop owners seemed to have gone out of their way to modernise their shops. It appears that shopkeepers recognised the importance of investing in a modern shopfront in order to attract customers.

Glasgow, like no other Scottish city, embraced wholeheartedly the idea of Moderne shopfronts. While other towns tinkered with Vitrolite and chrome, Scotland's Second City took these materials to her heart. The long arteries of Great Western Road, Maryhill Road, Paisley Road West and Kilmarnock Road were a mass of Vitrolite, shiny chrome, flickering neon and an explosion of sunrise motifs. Glasgow became Scotland's Art Deco capital and the shopping streets must have been a magnificent sight, particularly when illuminated at night. Their enthusiasm for renewing shop frontages therefore appears to contradict the general trend. The streets of central Glasgow were "*enlivened with a mass of Art Deco-style shopfronts, some decorated with zig-zags and sunburst motifs, their names spelled out in stylish letters; others with streamlined corners and shiny Vitrolite surfaces*".[151] The sun-rise motif is one of the most enduring designs from this era and featured on signs, windows and doors.

From large chain stores to the smallest tobacconist, the march of new shopfronts continued through the 1930s, not confined to any particular locality or retailer type. All shopkeepers were prepared to invest in their future; being left behind in a drab Edwardian or Victorian shopfront was not an option.

In celebration of this era, Glasgow hosted the Empire Exhibition in 1938 in Bellahouston Park which, according to Kenna "*epitomised the romantic side of Thirties Moderne and also reflected the somewhat woolly, 'pie in the sky' social idealism of the late-Thirties*".[152] The immaculate white buildings, lit up at night promoted the ideal of the Art Deco period but were demolished soon after the exhibition ended as war loomed in 1939.

The inter-war period was one of innovative and rapid progression in shop design. Despite an uncertain economic climate, shops abandoned the well-established materials of hardwood and cast iron in favour of new products like Vitrolite and chrome. The Art Deco Movement was embraced by shop owners and their shopfitters who designed and executed sleek and glossy shops in the latest fashions and materials.

In many ways the beauty of these shops is in their simplicity of design. The minimalist architecture

Fig: 76

is however, carefully planned and executed from the facing in Vitrolite to the dome-headed chrome screws in the stallriser vents. Where there is little elaboration it is the small elements which combine to make a successful whole.

Of all of Scotland's urban areas, it was Glasgow which adopted the Moderne shop as its own. The city blazed like a comet of modernity with other towns hanging on its tail. The endless renewal of shops using Vitrolite, chrome and bronze must have transformed the shopping streets of Glasgow particularly with the illumination of shops at night.

The ethos of the era is summarised by Robertson and Yerbury in their 1928 pictorial appreciation of French architecture. They state:

> "*It is in the shops, the homes, the hotels, the cafes, the buildings sheltering activities which lie at the door of everyday existence, that we find the reflection of a desire for new expression. These buildings make no claim as regards posterity; they are buildings of today for modern people. They reflect what modern people think and do and want.*"[153]

In many ways, the shop architecture of the inter-war period was brutal in its approach having little regard for either the existing shopfront or the parent building. Historic fabric was frequently swept aside in favour of a completely new shopfront which bore no resemblance to what had been there before. Despite this, the shopfronts of this period should be admired for their bravery of design and innovative use of materials resulting in some of the most striking shopfronts of our entire retailing history.

Figure 76: Café Moderne, 1012 Pollokshaws Road, Glasgow © Glasgow City Archives and Special Collections, Mitchell Library

SCOTLAND TOMORROW

POST-WAR TO PRESENT DAY

"Although an atmosphere of fake history is undesirable, shop fronts should not disregard the architecture above and around them. Diversity, colour and even vulgarity are part of the tradition of shop front design and should not be swamped by corporate good taste any more than by the shopfitter's lowest common denominator." A Powers[154]

World War II largely halted the construction of shop buildings and re-fronting of existing premises. However, in the immediate post-war period there was considerable rebuilding and shops formed an integral part of the extensive redevelopment which occurred across the country. The 1960s and 1970s witnessed demolition of many historic buildings in town centres and the introduction of traffic management schemes which drastically altered traditional town layouts. Further changes to retailing practices in the 1980s, 1990s and post-millennium meant a shift to out-of-town retailing and the dominance of large supermarkets. This has had a significant impact on traditional retail patterns and locations resulting in the closure of many independent shops as multiple stores and supermarkets have continued to dominate the retail sector.

Post-war shops tend to be less architecturally distinctive than their predecessors with a visible homogeneity to designs. This reflects a wider trend in architecture in this period, such as in house-building where the same design can be seen across the country and where local influence is largely absent. The quality of materials and workmanship used in post-war shop architecture has also deteriorated with wide use of man-made products like fibre-board and plastic which have a poorer life expectancy compared to traditional materials like well-seasoned timber.

In the post-war era, occupation of shop premises has probably been more short-lived than in the past. Historically businesses would have remained in premises for many years, particularly when associated with a family firm and this tended to prevent or at least restrict change. In contrast, where there is a turnover of occupiers, change tends to occur more often as new occupiers will generally want to alter the shop to suit their particular retail business. This encourages a short-term or more temporary approach to investment in the shop design and execution with a corresponding reluctance to invest heavily in expensive materials.

The 1950s and 1960s

In the immediate post-war period, styles tended to echo the later inter-war period. Materials like marble, chrome and stained timber finishes remained popular and Vitrolite continued to be used for shopfronts. However, they rarely matched the stunning designs evident in the 1930s and Powers states that 1950s shops tended to be simple in design but were generally '*drab*' and largely '*ignored both the decorative style of the Festival of Britain and the stylish modern designs of Italy*'.[155]

The redevelopment of town centres focused on purpose-built blocks with either entirely commercial use or a mix of residential and commercial. Post-war purpose-built premises were generally substantial, square retail blocks erected in town centres, often in stark contrast to the surrounding older buildings. Typically plain in detail with large square windows dominating upper floors and ground floor windows of plate glass, the simplicity of their design and their very regular form perhaps brings them in for unfair criticism as some are undoubtedly a strong presence.

The typical 1950s shopfront has an angled window and slightly recessed entrance, a feature that continued into the 1960s. Other shops incorporate a square 'showcase' at the front of the shop. These were popular with shoe shops as offered good display opportunities. These are generally flat topped and project almost like the showcases of the inter-war arcaded shopfronts but remain integral to the shop itself.

Figure 77: 'Scotland Tomorrow', Princes Street, Edinburgh. This was one of 14 displays in shop windows for the 1947 Enterprise Scotland Exhibition © University of Brighton Design Archives http://www.brighton.ac.uk/designarchives/ (facing page)

Figure 78: Norwell's Shoe Shop, High Street, Perth, 1956. This square three storey block utilises marble for the shop façade, a material popularised during the 1930s © Courtesy of Perth Museum and Art Gallery, Perth & Kinross Council

Fig: 78

Fig: 79

Figure 80: Paynes Hair Stylist, King Street, Dundee c1960. This shop design has reduced the windows to small octagonal panes of glass. The contrast with the more traditional parent building is striking © The Trustees of the National Museums of Scotland

Figure 81: Walker's Shortbread shop, Aberlour

The 1950s shops were therefore generally modest but into the 1960s, a few more quirky and inventive shop designs emerged. Some made use of the idea of windows as a 'fish tank', reducing the glazed areas to small shapes, focusing the attention onto the window. (Figure 80) For others, the design of the shop remained of importance in reflecting the status of the retailer. This is evident in the shopfront for Joseph Walker in Aberlour installed circa 1960. The shortbread manufacturer has a long association with the town and the shopfront is executed in bronze and travertine marble. The quality of the finish is exceptional and it is a truly outstanding post-war shopfront. (Figure 81)

Despite some daring examples, on the whole the standard of shops of this period was not notable. Powers is scathing of 1960s shops stating

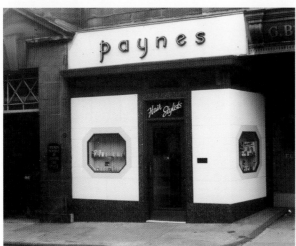

Fig: 80

Fig: 81

"The legacy of the Sixties which still afflicts us is the standard aluminium shop front with an internally illuminated plastic box sign, usually with lettering in a crude sanserif, placed without regard for scale or spacing. Shopfronts like these contribute to the sense of indeterminate squalor in so many British streets." [156]

For some areas, reconstruction continued to be viewed as a suitable alternative for the lack of consistency in certain streets. This was most famously considered for Princes Street, Edinburgh. Redevelopment was first proposed by R Furneaux Joradan in 1938 replacing the existing buildings with distinctive steel and glass prisms and then further criticism was levelled in the Abercrombie Plan of 1949 which suggested a more unified and cohesive approach to the street. The 1958 Princes Street Panel then proposed that the street be redeveloped and the new buildings were to have first floor walkways which would connect the shops.

Although some redevelopment occurred with seven Panel Buildings erected, the vision for a unified street was subsequently abandoned in the 1970s and although initially criticised, these buildings are now being recognised in their own right for their architectural merit. Number 64 Princes Street, occupied by BHS (British Home Stores) was listed Category B in 2008. Designed by Robert Matthew, Johnson-Marshall and Partners in 1964-68, this four storey building was the first of the Panel Buildings to be erected and had an unusual layout with the main circulation stair and escalators at the centre of the plan. The only other panel building to be listed is 84-87 Princes Street which is listed Category A having been designed in 1966-69 by Alan Reiach, Hall and Partners. It retains its first floor walkway. [157]

Elsewhere in post-war Scotland, the government initiated the construction of New Towns across Scotland to cater for families living in slum housing in Glasgow and

Figure 82: Design for Cumbernauld Shopping Centre, 1964 © Courtesy of RCAHMS (RIAS Collection). Licensor www.rcahms.gov.uk

Fig: 82

for people displaced by bombing during the war. Spread across Central Scotland, these new communities were located at Glenrothes in Fife, East Kilbride, Cumbernauld and Irvine in Ayrshire. It was necessary to provide residents with other services including shopping centres. At the forefront of modern design, these towns adopted new and innovative shopping centres with concrete as the primary construction material. Cumbernauld constructed the first multi-level shopping centre in 1964. (Figure 82)

The 1970s onwards

The 1970s continued the trend of redevelopment in town centres and erection of new purpose-built shops and shopping centres. During the 1970s and 1980s indoor shopping malls were viewed as the way forward with purpose-built centres like The Thistle Centre in Stirling and Wellgate Centre in Dundee. These indoor centres offered shoppers a new experience of being out of the weather with parking integral to the complex. There was also a dominance of multiple retailers compared to independent retailers with key retailers like Debenhams and Marks & Spencer courted to fill the large anchor units as an incentive for other retailers to lease units.

The concept of speciality centres gained favour in the 1980s, such as Princes Square in Glasgow designed to offer high-class and speciality shopping and restaurants. Located in a renovated Listed Category B building which was formerly a merchants' square it focused on specialist and designer retailers and it remains a success more than two decades later.

This period also witnessed the move to out-of-town retail parks where warehouse type premises with free on-site parking offered customers a large range of goods in an accessible environment. Initially favoured by DIY retailers and those selling furniture and white goods, gradually the market has moved to other consumer goods with companies like Boots, Next and Marks & Spencer now occupying units in these centres. The convenience of endless free parking adjacent to the stores makes them very attractive to shoppers, sometimes combined with leisure outlets such as cinemas or restaurants. The dominance of the large supermarkets has increased dramatically in recent years with most towns having a variety of supermarkets from small, central units to substantial edge of town or out-of-town stores. Many of these stores retail not only groceries but white goods, gardening and DIY equipment and clothes. They aim to provide one-stop shops and to supply as many of their customers needs as possible.

Current Shopfront Design

It could be argued that recent retail architecture lacks the distinct identity which we associate with some earlier architectural periods. Like the 1960s, there are occasional examples of quirky and appealing shops such as the Fringe Shop in Edinburgh which was designed for a specific retailer. It has a totally unique design which is different and successful. Other modern shops seek inspiration from historic detail but if not well executed these can fail to be successful. Powers describes 44 George Street,

Edinburgh as 'one of the best modern classical designs…using subtle modification of the Ionic capital to suggest spectacles'.[158] This example demonstrates that the premises which work well are those which make use of a combination of good and sensitive design with high-quality materials.

There is no doubt that the post-war era in Scotland is a disappointing period in terms of shopfront design. Townscape redevelopment, lack of sensitive design approaches and perhaps above all, use of poor-quality materials has contributed to an era where there is no discernible shopfront style for the first time in over 200 years. There has been a focus on pastiche 'Victoriana' style shopfronts which can sometimes reduce a town to a recreation or stage set rather than enhancing its local identity. Compounded by the influence of large corporate retailers and supermarkets who have pushed their brand at the expense of local identity and the loss of many independent shops because of their dominance, traditional shops have undoubtedly suffered. Despite this, a few good examples of post-war architecture survive. Those that remain, such as Walker's shop in Aberlour, are as precious as shops from earlier periods and should be conserved wherever possible.

Summary

Scotland's rich retail heritage stretches back to the medieval burghs and their early trading rights. Booths and stalls were the precursor to fixed shops, some of these were located under the arches of piazzas as burgh authorities sought to have grand colonnades of arched buildings made of fire-resistant stone.

As fixed shops increased in number in the late eighteenth century, there was a greater focus on design, particularly associated with classical architecture. By the late eighteenth century we see the emergence of fixed shops and the use of classically inspired detailing such as pilasters and fascias. Small paned windows prevailed until the development of plate glass and the lifting of the Glass Tax in 1845 which had severely restricted the designs possible. From then shopfronts were transformed into light and airy places, made possible by cast iron columns and beams from Scotland's numerous foundries. This allowed shops to break free from their previous constraints and to be highly ornate and also to meet many practical requirements.

The twentieth century opened with high-class and elegant Edwardian shops using curved glass and mosaics to create elegant and distinctive entrances. They also had innovative technology, using steel and concrete for the first time and developing lifts and lighting. The trend for deeper entrances continued into the inter-war period with the creation of arcaded entrances. Art Deco and the Paris Exhibition of 1925 had a significant and lasting impact on shopfront design in the 1920s and 1930s. Like the impact made by plate glass and cast iron, the use of bronze, chrome and Vitrolite transformed inter-war shops into sleek and minimalist frontages, illuminated at night by the now widely available electricity.

The post-war period has seen a decline in quality of materials and design and the legacy of shops from the 1950s onwards has been disappointing. Despite this, Scotland's shopping streets remain distinctive and retain the character attributable to the regional or local architecture as well as to wider trends in retail architecture.

Scotland's towns reflect these hundreds of years of layering of retail architecture, of materials and of the people who designed these shops. This amazing legacy is evident in towns and villages and cities across Scotland.

Retail Buildings:

STRUCTURES AND TYPES

"Shopfronts vary in all manner of ways, but in all cases it will be found that each type of front has a characteristic of its own, according to the kind of trade carried on." Perry, 1933[159]

Scotland has a myriad of different types of retail building. Some may be associated with particular periods of development or may even prevail in certain locations. This variety of building types contributes to our townscapes.

In their most basic form, shops have in common an entrance door and a window offering some kind of display and typically a sign advertising the location of the shop and its business. There may be architectural detailing, either integral to the structure, such as stone pilasters or applied, such as timber consoles. The materials used are closely related to the age of the shop and the design adopted.

In very general terms materials used can be summarised as:

- Pre-1850: largely stone with some timber detailing, crown glass but plate glass slowly being adopted after 1830;
- 1850-1900: use of stone, cast iron, plate glass, timber, decorative ceramics;
- 1900-1920: use of stone, cast iron, plate glass, timber, decorative ceramics and introduction of steel;
- 1920-1940: use of new materials like Vitrolite, chrome and steel as well as marble and bronze and ceramics (faience). Extensive use of plate glass;
- Post 1945: use of marble, steel and aluminium and manufactured timber such as plywood. More recently use of MDF and PVCu.

The materials used were also closely related to the occupying retailer. Some favoured a traditional image but others sought clean and modern lines available through the use of new materials. This is typified in an image of two Glasgow dairies in 1938. Maypole is trading on their traditional image with an almost Victorian style shopfront with dark stained timber, cast iron frames and cut and gilded lettering to the fascia. This contrasts strongly with the new shopfront for Ross's which is white Vitrolite with chrome frames and sans serif lettering embracing the Modern Movement (Figure 121). Certain retailers may therefore reject the latest fashions and materials in favour of a style that reflects their particular business image.

While we tend to think of shopfronts independently and in isolation, it is vital to consider them within the wider context of their parent building and also the townscape in which they are located. This requires a consideration of the architecture of the very varied retail building types that exist. These broadly may be considered as:

1 Domestic style: little adaptation, limited signage
2 Purpose built shop and tenement: normally Victorian, Edwardian or other twentieth century
3 Kiosks and small shops: including those of timber and corrugated iron
4 Built-out shops: those projecting from the front of buildings
5 Bungalow shops: single storey lock-up shops with no living accommodation
6 Purpose-built commercial premises and showrooms
7 Located within covered shopping arcade
8 Shops belonging to chain stores: early corporate identity
9 Co-operative stores: erected by local or regional co-operative societies

These shops contribute to the huge variety of our townscapes in terms of their scale, architecture, materials and also for the retail economy.

Figure 84: Macpherson's Pharmacy, Kyle of Lochalsh © Duncan Macpherson Collection, Dualchas Heritage Service (facing page)

TYPE 1: DOMESTIC STYLE

Figure 85: William Ward's Shop, Merrybar, Orkney: This conversion of a cottage by simply adding an external sign was typical of many rural shops © The Trustees of the National Museums of Scotland

Figure 86: Benbecula Post Office, 1903: Traditional thatched dwellings served as shops in rural and island communities. Little adaptation or signage was required in these locations ©The Trustees of the National Museums of Scotland

The first fixed shops, other than small timber booths, would have been simple adaptations of domestic properties. Through time they became more formal in style, but there remain, particularly in rural or fringe shopping areas, shops which are essentially domestic in appearance. Despite their limited adaptation, they represent an important part of retail history.

The main architectural features are:

- Buildings are domestic in scale and appearance;
- Typically retain original house window, or this may be slightly enlarged. They may have a sash opening but are usually fixed;
- Signage painted onto stonework or a simple timber board;
- Entrance sometimes via a lobby which may also be shared with the house entrance;
- The shop may not be fully separated from the house itself;
- These shops may also have a cottage appearance with dormer windows to the upper floors.

These shops are therefore rather vernacular in inspiration and proportion with features which are derived

Fig: 86

largely from the architecture of the parent building. They are found in various locations but usually in villages or rural settings although may also be in some small towns. Given their location, their retailing potential may be restricted by their small size and fringe location where footfall is limited. However, in tourist locations such as Falkland and Glencoe their attractive appearance is probably viewed as an advantage. Their appeal is in their simplicity and visually, they integrate well to the townscape.

Despite their attractive appearance, these shops may have particular drawbacks, including the access into the shop as the door may be narrow with level changes

Fig: 85

involving steps. This can pose problems for customers and compliance with the Disability Discrimination Act may encourage owners to alter the traditional door arrangements. Internal natural light may be poor and generally the display and advertising opportunities will be limited. In some cases, the sign may sit vertically above the eaves level to make it more visible or because there is insufficient room on the building frontage. The small size of these shops will also restrict the type of retailer likely to occupy these premises.

It is likely that many of these buildings are listed or located in conservation areas and therefore have the benefit of statutory protection. However, many are under pressure because they are struggling for financial viability.

With changes in consumer habits and a more mobile population, people are less reliant on rural shops and instead will travel significant distances to visit larger shops and supermarkets. This may be seen as a natural cycle of economics; a house which was converted to commercial use and then eventually reverting back to that use. However, although shops like these may be overlooked, they do make an important contribution to townscapes and to their local economy. It is therefore important that they are not all converted as the loss, particularly of rural shops, has a significant impact on the local economy and vibrancy of villages. However, they will often be under threat from conversion because of their location and their relative ease of conversion to residential.

Figure 87: Donald MacGregor's Tweed Shop, Main Street, Kyle of Lochalsh: Displaying goods in the street is a way of overcoming limited display © Duncan Macpherson Collection, Dualchas Heritage Service

Fig: 87

Figure 88: Glencoe: In scenic areas the vernacular quality of domestic style shops is appropriate

Figure 89: Sash window, Falkland: Some shops retain their domestic sash and case window

Fig: 88

Fig: 89

TYPE 2: PURPOSE-BUILT TENEMENTS WITH SHOPS

Tenements with ground floor shops are the building blocks of Scottish townscapes forming the back-bone of their central districts. The flexibility of this model means that they are found in towns and villages of all sizes and feature great variations in style.

The main architectural features are:

- Building purpose-built with shops on ground floor and domestic accommodation above;
- Two, three or four storeys, or occasionally higher;
- Ground floor shop or shops with door leading to building above;
- Flexible pattern allowing for changes in shop size as well as location of the stair access;
- Constructed in architectural periods from Georgian to post-war.

The idea of living over the shop dates back to medieval merchants. The earliest buildings for merchants would have been a fore-booth and loft onto the front street of a 'land' and this developed into a larger building with a fore-stair onto the street.[160] Tenements as we recognise them today existed from the latter sixteenth century and

Figure 90: Designed in 1907 by Perth architect James Walker Smart for Peddies ironmongers, this red sandstone Edwardian tenement is of Glasgow Freestyle. W & D Peddie remain in the premises today © Courtesy of Perth Museum and Art Gallery, Perth & Kinross Council

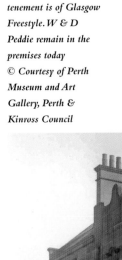

there would have resided merchants who also traded from their premises. The Scottish tenement was different from the type of housing found in England because typically it contained all manner of social class and occupations within one building. Shops and stores were on the ground floor with the residents above occupying part or all of each floor.[161]

Although during the Georgian period there were some purpose-built shops, it was really during the later nineteenth century that this type of shop became well established as central to retail design. They proved to be a highly adaptable and flexible model which could be altered to accommodate the requirements of the proprietor. For example, Wordsall suggests that working-class tenements in Glasgow had an "*interchangeable ground floor - a two-apartment house being readily convertible into a shop with a back room or vice versa*". However, sometimes the tenements were designed with shops in mind and here "*the ground-floor ceiling is abnormally high, to allow for storage space and adequate ventilation*".[162]

Architecturally, there are significant variations depending on the locality, period of construction, materials used and the prevailing architectural fashions. Many of these shops were designed by local architects and pre-date the influence of shopfitters who were merely concerned with the shop and its interior, not with the building as a whole. Local architects, with their knowledge of the particular needs and circumstances of their local area designed buildings which fitted in well to the townscape. There may also be a sense of continuity through a town where a local architect has designed several buildings within a district and which display similar characteristics.

What they all have in common is that they have been designed as set pieces, that is, the shops are a unit with the building above and features in the shop architecture will generally mirror the details of the rest of the building such as dentils and the shape of openings. This makes these buildings powerful in the townscape and their integrity is dependent on retaining the original proportions and features.

They are found in all retail locations from city centres to small rural towns and villages. Twentieth century designs from the inter-war and post-war periods may be located in suburban shopping districts.

Fig: 90

Fig: 91

Figure 91: York Corner, Perth designed by GPK Young, 1907. This impressive Edwardian Baroque building has delicate cast iron shopfronts and matching Art Nouveau inspired mosaic lobby floors. The blocking up of windows loses the overall impact of the shopfronts

Figure 92: 101 High Street, Dunbar is a good example of a purpose-built tenement and shop which is designed as a singe unit. The cast iron shopfront is by MacFarlane's Saracen Foundry

Fig:92

TYPE 3: KIOSKS AND SMALL TEMPORARY SHOPS

The smallest shop types are referred to as kiosks but other small shops are found in a variety of rural and urban situations. They may be of a temporary construction such as of corrugated iron or timber boarding and although largely unnoticed in many urban situations, these tiny premises do make a contribution to the townscape.

The main architectural features are:
- Usually timber or sometimes corrugated iron construction;
- Small size with limited storage;
- Typical retail use is for small goods like confectionary or newspapers;
- Located in rural areas, gap sites or in railway stations.

Kiosks are most commonly associated with railway stations. John Menzies and WH Smiths both had shops on railway station platforms from the mid-nineteenth century and these were an integral part of their stationery businesses, particularly in the early days of their development. The first Scottish railway bookstall is believed to have been opened by David Robertson of Perth at Dunkeld Station in 1849. John Menzies opened his first railway bookstall in 1857 in an agreement for stations at Perth, Bridge of Allan and Stirling. In the subsequent years they acquired the vast majority of the bookstalls in Scotland.[163] By 1920, W H Smith, John Menzies and Wyman & Sons operated almost 1000 newspaper stands across UK railway stations. [164]

These kiosks were purpose built on the platform and could be quite elaborate in design. Their shapes vary from half moon to rectangular or circular with wooden lifting or slatted shutters which when removed leaves the shop open to the platform. Storage is very limited although these shops make the most of their display and typically sell small goods like confectionery, newspapers and books. Others, like Malcolm Campbell, sold fruit and vegetables.

Although kiosks were located on railway station platforms, small shops of a 'temporary' or vernacular nature were built often in rural areas. These could be of timber and/or cast iron and usually small with limited display. These buildings while perhaps humble in appearance, are part of the rural landscape in many small Scottish villages.

Timber shops may also be found in urban situations typically as infill development. They tend to be in fringe or neighbourhood shopping districts and are certainly unlikely to be located in prime retail locations. These small

Figure 93: Post Office, St Kilda: A corrugated-iron shed was built in 1913 on Hirta, St Kilda to host the local Post Office. It remained in use until the island was evacuated in 1930
© The National Trust for Scotland

Fig: 93

shops have a variety of retail uses but their very small size makes them most likely to be used for newsagents or confectioners although some may end up in alternative commercial uses such as offices.

All of these types of shops are vulnerable. They are unlikely to be listed and may not be located in a conservation area. Given their small and apparently temporary nature they are generally viewed as insignificant and the sites they occupy may therefore be regarded as suitable for development. Within railway stations, many are no longer regarded as economically viable and have been replaced with vending machines.

Figure 94: Timber shop, Scalloway, Shetland
© Shetland Museum and Archives

Figure 95: Barber's Shop, Pitlochry: kiosks are often found in small gap sites

Figure 96: John Menzies Kiosk, Central Station, Glasgow, 1936
© Glasgow City Archives and Special Collections, Mitchell Library

Fig: 94

Fig: 95

Fig: 96

TYPE 4: PROJECTING SHOPFRONTS

A projecting shop is one that is essentially an extension at the front of a building taking it beyond the original building line. In this way they maximise the use of valuable space to the front of the building for sales use. They have various names including 'built-out' shops and 'pop-out' shops.

The main architectural features are:
- Usually a flat roof often with decorative balustrade of stone or cast iron;
- Building behind is typically residential other than ground floor shop;
- Location may have originally been a more residential district (and may still be predominantly so) which has been gradually converted to commercial use.

Projecting shops are found in a variety of locations but can only be sited where there is room at the front of the building to accommodate them; where the

building line fronts the pavement it does not permit such development. They are therefore located where there was formerly a garden or basement to the front of the building, dating usually from the mid-Victorian period onwards. The shop then takes the original building forward to the street level, again bringing the shop nearer to the public. Once one shop has altered its building line, the adjacent premises are almost forced to follow in order to keep up with their neighbours and not be left partially visible. However, sometimes those in domestic use remain true to their original building line which can result in an uneven townscape pattern. They are often located slightly out of the main area, related to historical building patterns which were different away from the more congested town centres where every piece of ground was highly valued and built upon.

In the New Town of Edinburgh, the buildings were set back and accessed via a platt across the basement below. This provided an opportunity for expansion across the gap to extend the shop and a drawing of Princes Street in 1847 indicates the gradual process of shops being extended over the basement.[165] These therefore evolved out of the desire for greater space and light and improved display. Attracting customers in the mid to late nineteenth century became much more important than it had ever been before.

Although some were additions to existing buildings, later examples may be purpose-built and integral to the design of the parent building. These will often exhibit matching features such as doors, entrance lobby tiles and console brackets.

Projecting shops are relatively widespread but they vary considerably in style. Some may not have any distinctive architectural features being essentially a box on the front of a building. Others may be heavily embellished including a balustrade or cast iron brattishing. These architectural elements tend to be vulnerable and their loss may be detrimental to the appearance of the building so their reinstatement should be considered.

In some cases, the addition of projecting shops may now be considered inappropriate and there may therefore be a desire to remove them and restore the building to its original footprint and elevation. Such action is only likely where the retail use is marginal but was undertaken, for example, at Laurieston Place in Edinburgh in 1989-92.

Figure 97: Dundas Street, Edinburgh: In Edinburgh's New Town, many shops were extended over the basement area to create projecting shopfronts. Some were square in form but others much more elaborate

Fig:97

Fig: 98

Fig: 100

Fig:99

Figure 98: High Street, North Berwick: projecting shops are also found in smaller centres

Figure 99: High Street, Newburgh: the projecting shop can add significantly to the display opportunities of a retail building

Figure 100: High Street, Dunbar: although many projecting shops were later additions, some were purpose-built. This row are all linked by common architectural features like doors and tiled lobbies

TYPE 5: BUNGALOW SHOPS

Figure 101: Station Hill, North Berwick: This row of Edwardian shops is located on a sloping site. Some rows are infills on more difficult sites

Figure 102: George Street, Oban: the use of cast iron brattishing is a common feature on many bungalow shops

Bungalow shops are single-storey rows of shops which are purpose-built as lock-up shops rather than converted. They may date to the end of the nineteenth century and early twentieth century but numerous examples were erected during the inter-war years. Occasionally they may be an individual shop rather than a row and these generally date to the inter-war period, sometimes constructed by retail organisations such as the Co-operative Societies.

Main architectural features:

- Single-storey row of two or more shops although some are for a single shop;
- Roof is usually flat or hidden behind a parapet or brattishing or roof may be of pitched slate;
- Common architectural detailing found in each shop such as doors and entrance tiling which links the shops.

Bungalow shops tend to be found on arterial routes out of a town, away from the main centre, although occasionally will be found in the centre. They are generally not located in prime retail areas because of the pressure to maximise development of such sites. There may also be difficulties associated with the location, such as a sloping or narrow site where there are more limited opportunities. An advantage of these rows of shops is that their low profile may allow a view through to another building, such as a church or other town landmark.

Fig:102

Their striking element may be the use of common architectural features or decoration. They will typically have the same door styles, entrance floors or mosaic or encaustic tiles and a parapet detail of cast iron or stone which links all the shops together. Inter-war shops may have features typical of the period such as a stepped fascia or use of Vitrolite cladding whereas late nineteenth century buildings more commonly use cast iron brattishing.

A particularly good example is located in the Ayrshire village of Cumnock. A row of bungalow shops at 38-42 Ayr Road are exceptionally decorative with Gothic double doors, encaustic tiles and pierced decorative work around the openings. This low rise building is in contrast to the adjacent, significant taller Crichton Church. The church was designed by Duncan Menzies (1837-1901) in 1897 and it is believed he also designed this unusual row of shops.[166]

The small shop size means that the type of retailers who will take this type of unit will be limited and their location in non-prime positions further restricts their appeal, particularly for retailers who rely on passing trade. This can lead to high vacancy levels and a consequent loss in confidence in the location. However, the rental levels of such premises will be correspondingly lower than the main locations so may appeal to certain types of retailers, often those providing a service and who may be less reliant on passing trade.

These buildings are generally not listed because they may not have sufficient architectural merit to warrant listed status and their location on the fringes may also mean that they are outside of conservation areas. They may therefore not be within the umbrella of statutory control and can be vulnerable to alteration or redevelopment because the site may be perceived as being under-developed.

Fig:101

Figure 103: Friars Street, Stirling: This 1930s row of shops largely occupied by one retailer have curved glass entrances and stepped fascias typical of the period

Fig: 103

Figure 104: Northgate, Peebles: The low-rise nature of bungalow shops permit views to buildings or landscapes beyond

Fig: 104

Figure 105: Ayr Road, Cumnock: This elaborately detailed row has Gothic features reminiscent of the adjoining church

Fig: 105

TYPE 6: PURPOSE-BUILT COMMERCIAL PREMISES AND SHOWROOMS

While initially buildings were adapted to accommodate shops, from the mid nineteenth century onwards, purpose-built commercial premises were erected. The early cast iron warehouses in Glasgow are early examples of purpose-built premises. These buildings differ from the tenement and shop arrangement in that they do not include domestic accommodation but are entirely commercial including retail, storage and office space.

The common architectural features are:
- Built from mid nineteenth century onwards;
- Often innovative in use of materials and design;
- Premises are entirely retail and commercial with minimal or no domestic accommodation;
- Located usually in prime or main shopping centres but may also be found in smaller towns;
- Retailer types vary but typically are drapers, furniture stores and those requiring larger premises;
- Showrooms are generally associated with utility companies such as gas showrooms.

While some perhaps followed the model of tenement and shop and appeared outwardly in that vein, others were more daring in their design, particularly in the inter-war and post-war period. Certainly many of the Edwardian buildings are constructed of stone and slate and their tenement-like appearance fits into the townscape well with their tenement-like appearance such as D Irons the ironmongers in Forfar. This conservative Edwardian approach contrasts, for example with the daring design found at East Parting in Bo'ness which is a cube-like structure with large proportions of glass. Designed by Matthew Steele in 1926, it hints at Czech cubism.

Chain stores developed their own 'house style' for these buildings and their designs are considered under Type 8.

During the 1930s, there was a vogue for constructing specialist showrooms, particularly by gas and electricity boards. Reflecting the appliances found within the stores and their modernity, these showrooms were inspired by the latest architectural designs and sought to convey the spirit of the age. Good surviving examples can be found in Dunfermline of both former gas and electricity showrooms.

In their grandest form these purpose-built premises are department stores. Many of these date to the late nineteenth and turn of the twentieth century. They are the most opulent of purpose-built premises and were at the leading edge of technological improvements. In city centres these stores are generally substantial, such as Jenners in Edinburgh, Draffens in Dundee and House of Fraser in Glasgow. However, they also feature in smaller centres such as Veitches in Peebles (now being redeveloped).

These purpose-built shops and showrooms make a significant contribution to the townscape because of their substantial size and sometimes innovative design. Many are listed and they are often located within conservation areas. However, their original design may not be compatible with modern retail requirements and the future of these buildings may be under threat. This has been shown with Draffens in Dundee. It was occupied for a number of years by Debenhams but when they moved to the new Overgate Centre nearby this store became vacant. This tall 1930s building with its bronze shopfronts by high-class London shopfitter, Frederick Sage & Co has struggled since to find an occupier.

Figure 106: Gas Showroom, 522 Sauchiehall Street, Glasgow: Designed in 1935 by A McInnes Gardner (1878–1934) this stunning shopfront is executed in a Parisian style with bronze frames © Glasgow City Archives and Special Collections, Mitchell Library

Fig: 106

Fig: 107

Fig: 108

Figure 107: East Parting, Bo'ness: Designed in 1926 by local architect Matthew Steele (1887-1937) this white Modernist cube designed for a drapers is in stark contrast to more traditional buildings in the town

Figure 108: Veitches, Peebles was typical of the purpose-built small department stores found in provincial towns

Figure 109: Dean of Guild drawing for Gas Showroom, Canmore Street, Dunfermline: This showroom for the Burgh of Dunfermline Gas Department was designed in 1937 by Robert Henderson Motion. It was fitted out to a high standard and included a lecture theatre on the first floor Reproduced courtesy of Fife Council Archives

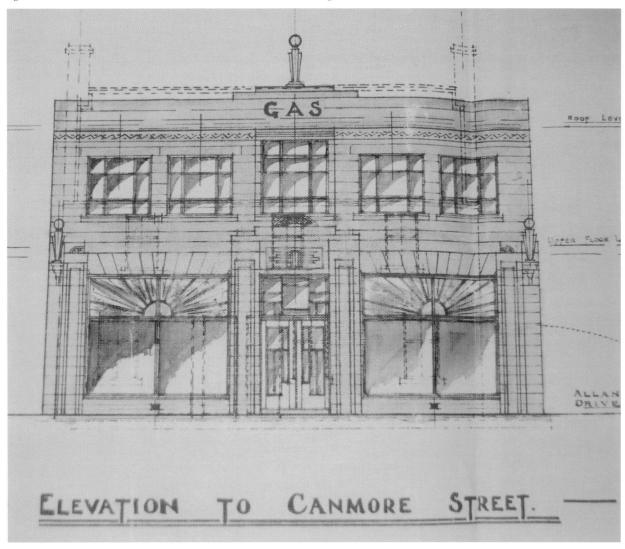

Fig: 109

TYPE 7: SHOPPING ARCADES

Figure 110: The Argyle Arcade was Scotland's first, built in 1827. Its iron hammer-beam roof floods light into the arcade which is now occupied largely by jewellers

Figure 111: The opening of DM Brown's shopping arcade at 80 High Street, Dundee in 1908 attracted considerable crowds. The arcade included shops, restaurants and other facilities
Photograph courtesy of University of Dundee Archive Services

Arcades have their origins in the twelfth century in the Middle East where covered bazaars were developed as a response to the hot climate.[167] In Britain, exchanges developed as places for merchants and traders, the earliest being Sir Thomas Gresham's 1568 Royal Exchange in London. In Edinburgh, the Royal Exchange on the High Street was built 1753-61 by John Adam and John Fergus. This U-shaped building featured a central courtyard where shops, offices and coffee houses were located.[168] These exchanges were the first to experiment with the idea of formally designed shops within a covered area and may be regarded as the precursor to later shopping arcades.

It was the Parisians who saw the advantages of arcades and at the end of the eighteenth century up to forty were built in the city. Mackeith states that *"they were extraordinarily successful, taking the role of the market place as a cultural, social and retail centre under glass, contributing an air of novelty and unreality"*.[169] Britain's first covered arcade with skylights was the Royal Opera Arcade by Nash and Repton built 1815-17.

Fig: 111

The opportunity to shop under cover in comfort also appealed in Scotland. Although none of those constructed in Scotland were as grand as the London or Parisian examples there are some notable arcades. The most famous and probably the first to be constructed in Scotland is the Argyle Arcade built 1827-28. Designed by John Baird Primus (1798-1859) with the developer was James Robertson Reid, it links Buchanan Street and Argyle Street via an L-shaped, 450 foot long glass-covered arcade.

Fig:110

Fig: 112

Fig: 113

Figures 112 & 113: North Bridge Arcade has a magnificent mosaic ceiling and stained glass cupola. These help to encourage light through what is otherwise a dark space

It is very light inside with a glazed hammer-beam roof of cast iron construction. When it first opened there were a variety of shop types but today the arcade is mostly occupied by jewellers. Alterations and additions were made in 1933 by Miller & Black and today the ground floor shopfronts are largely modern in style with only some of the original pilasters and the upper Georgian timber casement windows surviving. Linking two prime shopping streets and with a reputation for specialist shops, the arcade has prospered in almost 200 years of use, and its role as Scotland's first shopping arcade makes it of special significance.

Located in the centre of Inverness is a more complex arcade which leads to a former market hall. It has multiple entrances and was added to over a period of years so the architectural style varies within the building. The arcade to Academy Street was designed by Matthews and Lawrie 1869-70, together with the markets. Here the shopfronts are brick-arched and the roof is of cast iron. The markets were then altered and extended by the Burgh Surveyor in 1890 and the Union Street Arcade added in 1890 by Ross and Macbeth. In 1897 the Queensgate Arcade was designed by Duncan Cameron and has various shop styles. There is a series of arched fronts similar to the rest of the building, but these have stained glass to the arches. In the same arcade there is a row of pilastered shopfronts which have faience by Doulton of Lambeth (stamped on the side) and polished granite pilasters. These tall and elegant shopfronts have a central recessed door with a tall fanlight.

The Crawford Arcade in Stirling was erected 1879-82 by John MacLean (1854-1950), for William Crawford, china merchant. The original design had 39 shops, a 1200 seat theatre and two hotels, the Douglas Hotel on Murray Place and McDonalds Temperance Hotel on King Street. There were also six residential dwellings. The building is two or three storeys high with a timber and glass roof and there is a central square with classical facades. No original shopfronts remain in the arcade although they all have a similar style of modern frontage.

A later construction in Edinburgh, the North Bridge Arcade links Cockburn Street and North Bridge. It was erected in 1899-1902 by Dunn & Findlay and forms part of the Scotsman building on North Bridge and Cockburn Street. This small, dog-leg arcade has a central rotunda crowned with a dome of stained glass and shops below with curved glass incorporating delicate mullions. The opulent interior of marble pilasters with a ceiling of gold and turquoise mosaic is impressive. The building was renovated recently with funding assistance from Edinburgh World Heritage.

These arcades were typically constructed as an investment and funded either by an individual or a company rather than as a public enterprise although some, such as the Inverness arcade, were built as part of the market site development.[170] The Crawford Arcade in Stirling indicates an attempt to maximise the site with a diverse range of properties including hotels, residential and a theatre in addition to the thirty-nine shops. Put up for auction around 1920, the rent from this arcade and associated premises was £1820 10s. Tenants at this time included grocer William Low & Co as well as the long-established Stirling drapery, Thomas Menzies & Co who occupied the 'draper's saloon'.[171] The Cockburn Arcade and Argyle Arcades are likewise part of larger developments which include not just shop premises. This variety of style and property types was to be typical of arcades which evolved from the earlier Parisian and London examples, the idea being adopted by "*provincial builders who developed the building type and produced it in great numbers and in a wide variety of styles.*"[172]

Traditional arcades have, in many cases, been superseded by modern, climate-controlled malls and they can seem drab, dimly lit and cold compared to their modern counterparts. The lack of pedestrian footfall affects the viability of shops causing a downward cycle within the arcade. The small size of the shops combined with challenging viability within some arcades means that tenants may change quite frequently. This can result in changes to the shopfronts as occupiers attempt to adapt the shop to their own needs and requirements and perhaps to modernise it in an attempt to attract custom. However, in spite of their apparent disadvantages, arcades are both an important part of retailing and architectural history but also remain interesting and attractive places to shop. In the case of the Argyle Arcade, arguably Scotland's most successful traditional shopping arcade, it is its speciality focus on jewellers shops which attracts customers. Recent renovations to the Cockburn Arcade

in Edinburgh including improved lighting and specially designed iron gates at the entrances to prevent the area being used inappropriately when the shops are closed. This demonstrates that quite small measures can have a significant impact on the attractiveness of an arcade and maintain it as a place suitable for modern retail use.

Fig: 114

Figure 114: Market Arcade, Inverness 1870 © Highland Photographic Archive, Joseph Cook Collection

Figure 115: Flower Shop, Queens Arcade, Inverness. The repetitive use of arched openings are livened with coloured glass

Fig: 115

TYPE 8: SCOTTISH CHAIN STORES

Chain stores are those where a retailer has a number of premises spread either over a regional area or nationally. They have been defined as a retail firm with ten or more branches.[173] The shops are generally of a similar style, using the same materials and design to present a particular image to customers, one that is instantly recognisable as the brand of that retailer. The initial focus for the development of chain stores was in the grocery and then the dairy trade although it later expanded into confectionery, clothing, footwear and variety stores as well as pharmacies.

During the late nineteenth and early twentieth century, Scottish retailing was transformed by the emergence of companies like Lipton's, Massey's, Templeton's and Buttercup Dairy. These were the first shops to develop a corporate identity and leave a small but important legacy of shops, mainly dating to the inter-war period.

Main architectural features:

- Standard design used across the country although style varies over time;
- Innovative use of materials and design;
- Limited regard for local identity, materials or styles;
- Use of corporate images such as vent grilles, tiles and other signage;
- Interiors of interest with tiles, counters and shelving.

Thomas Lipton pioneered the idea of a corporate identity as he particularly favoured advertising gimmicks as well as brand image for his shops. Lipton's shops had black and white chequered floor tiles, tiled walls, a horseshoe counter and a butter window and a ham window. Shops were brightly lit with gas lamps and staff were expected to be smartly turned out. Shop numbers grew exponentially in the last three decades of the nineteenth century, from one in 1871 to 500 by 1899.[174]

The idea of having a familiar identity for shops was adopted by other retailers during a highly competitive time when shop numbers were quickly expanding. Companies developed their own livery, tile schemes, signage and identity so that their shops were instantly recognisable in the street. Grocery chains like Massey's (1872), Templeton's (1870s), Cochrane's (1881) and Galbraith's (1884) all originated in Glasgow. These companies all had similar beginnings in that they were "*clustered within a few years of each other, established by poor but enterprising young men having either a family apprenticeship in the trade or being sent to an established Glasgow tradesman as a first job*".[175]

Although Glasgow proved to be a hub where these firms started out, one of Scotland's most important dairy firms, the Buttercup Dairy Company, originated in Leith, Edinburgh around 1908. Set up by Andrew Ewing, the company had at least 250 shops, located particularly in the east of Scotland. This dairy company was particularly at the forefront of egg production and at one point had the largest egg production in the UK and possibly in Europe.

Fig: 116

Fig: 117

Figure 116 & 117: Lipton's, 184 Paisley Road West, Glasgow, 1930. These two images show the modernising of a Lipton's to be remodelled in the latest corporate style. The tiled frontage has been replaced with bronze and marble, the fashionable materials of the period © Glasgow City Archives and Special Collections, Mitchell Library

Figure 118 & 119:

Lipton use a distinctive

tile scheme of

shamrocks and thistles

intertwined and an 'L'

for Lipton. Many of

their tile schemes were

installed by James

Duncan Ltd

Fig: 118

Fig: 119

Following Lipton's ideas for a corporate identity, Ewing sought to brand his company using the buttercup to signify fresh and natural products. His enigmatic image of a small girl holding out a buttercup to a brown cow endured beyond 1949 when the company began to decline, selling off stores to some of the managers.

While Scottish companies dominated the market here and gradually in England, similar companies also emerged from south of the border including Maypole Dairy Co (Birmingham), Home and Colonial Stores (London) and Meadow Dairy Co (Newcastle-upon-Tyne). They

all established branches here but Scotland was clearly a formative heartland for many of these retailers. Their success was through building up their businesses on key items like tea, butter, ham and eggs which were imported and sold primarily to the mass market of the working-class urban populations although a small number did favour a more middle-class market. It was the changes in consumer behaviour which offered opportunities for these companies. Beer consumption as a main drink, for example was reducing and in its place people were drinking large quantities of tea, something which had formerly been a luxury item. Ham and bacon as well as eggs were also staple foods of the working classes which were typically cheaply imported from Ireland and the Continent.

The typical chain store grocery or dairy had a double-fronted shop sometimes with a lifting window on one side and fixed window on the other to allow a ham window and a dairy (butter and cheese) window. Entrance lobbies usually had the name impressed into the mosaic reinforcing the corporate message. The frontage was in the corporate style of the time, for example, Lipton's favoured green marble in the inter-war period with bronze window frames. Signage was also extremely important to impart the corporate brand. Maypole Dairy and Lipton's favoured cut and gilded lettering which gave a traditional and quality image. Lipton also had bronze signs fixed to the stallrisers with the name 'Lipton'. Massey's favoured red shopfronts with gilt lettering and Galbraith's of Paisley had a standardised approach from early in the firms business using black and red decoration, standardised frontages and signs and green tiled interior with floral decoration.[176] Others like Ross's Dairy of Glasgow sought the clean and clinical lines of Vitrolite for their signage, embracing a more modern image.

Figure 120: Birrell

confectioners, 46

Kilmarnock Road,

Glasgow, 1933. The

Scottish confectioners,

Birrell had high

class shopfronts and

interiors with bronze

and marble shopfronts

and mahogany interior

shelving. Here the

fashionable sunrise

motif has been used in

the shop fascia

© Glasgow City

Archives and Special

Collections, Mitchell

Library

Fig: 120

The interiors were also important with substantial counters, sometimes marble-topped, hardwood shelving and use of tiling to floors and walls. Some, such as Maypole Dairy made use of mirrors particularly in the windows to help reflect light into the shop. Floors in Lipton's stores were black and white chequered geometric tiles whereas Maypole had green and white. Wall tiles were also specially commissioned with the Maypole Dairy using an image of children dancing around a Maypole and Lipton's had shamrocks and thistles reflecting Thomas Lipton's Irish and Scottish roots.

Like the grocery trade, confectionery chain stores also became an important part of Scottish retailing. R S McColl, Birrell and McMillan & Munro all originated in Glasgow, specialising both in retail sales but also in manufacturing. In 1920 around twenty percent of multiple confectioners were in Scotland, rising to forty percent in 1930, their clean and well-stocked shops located in the prime shopping districts.[177] Birrells were high-class confectioners and their shops reflected this quality with marble and bronze shopfronts and beautifully finished hardwood interiors.

These designs were rolled out across the country so that the same shop style was present in every town. As some of these companies owned hundreds of shops the corporate identity was widespread. These stores were often at the cutting edge of design, adopting the newest and most daring materials for their shops. Being at the forefront of retail architectural fashion was of great importance.

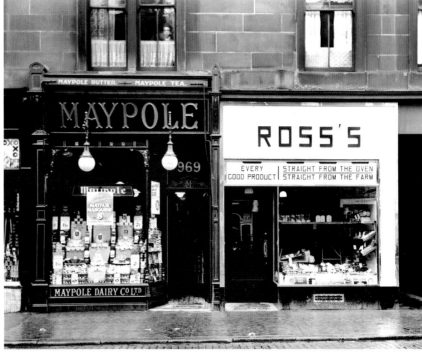

Fig: 121

Fig: 122

Although many started off employing a local architect, as their firms grew they could justify having their own architects departments. These were usually located in their head office and designed the styles to be executed across the country. This centralisation of design had a considerable impact on local areas by introducing architectural design in the latest fashion but with little regard for the local materials or identity. This was particularly the case in the inter-war period.

During the twentieth century many of these companies re-branded or were merged with other organisations. Shops were also continually updated and rebranded to keep up with the latest architectural fashion. As result, very few of these original chain stores survive intact making those which retain a large degree of original features of considerable importance. The smaller shops survive in varying degrees with occasional good survivors such as a former Lipton's in Arbroath and a number of good Buttercup Dairy shops remain although surviving interiors are extremely rare.

These shops represent an important development in the architectural history of shops. They also occasionally have fine tiled interiors which are worthy of conservation. The lack of recognition of these shopfronts and their associated history means that they are often overlooked. However, they deserve to be conserved for their contribution to retail and architectural history.

Figure 121: Maypole Dairy and Ross's Dairy, 969 and 971 Maryhill Road, Glasgow, 1938. The traditional style used by Maypole Dairy contrasts with the modern image presented by Glasgow Dairy Company, Ross's © Glasgow City Archives and Special Collections, Mitchell Library

Figure 122: Buttercup Dairy Company tiled mural. The powerful image of the small girl holding out a buttercup to a brown cow was an enduring image for this firm. The association with a traditional farm scene contrasted with its high intensity production methods, particularly for eggs

TYPE 9: SCOTTISH CO-OPERATIVE SOCIETY BUILDINGS

Figure 123: Wigtown Co-operative Society, c1920: Co-operative stores often had more than one shop in a town, serving different retail requirements such as a boot department, bakery and grocers © Whithorn Photographic Group. Licensor www.scran.ac.uk

Figure 124: The City of Perth Co-operative Society, Scott Street, Perth. This impressive purpose-built store was erected for Perth Co-op in 1883 and features the clasped hands, a symbol of unity on the front of the building © Courtesy of Perth Museum and Art Gallery, Perth & Kinross Council

The Co-operative Movement emerged during the nineteenth century in response to the considerable poverty experienced by the working classes. They were a large, if low-paid section of society who represented a steady demand for food, clothes, newspapers, tobacco and newspapers and their demands were "*homogenous, predictable, concentrated, and, in the mass, enormous*".[178] In 1844, the 'Rochdale Pioneers' (a mixture of Chartists, Owenite Socialists and temperance campaigners), invented both the idea of branches and also vertical integration through a Wholesale Society based on philanthropic rather than commercial motives. Although the Rochdale Society is recognised as the beginning of the Co-operative Movement, at least fourteen societies in Scotland pre-date the 1844 establishment in Rochdale, Fenwick Weavers Co-operative Society and a society in Bridgeton in Glasgow having formed in 1769 and in 1800 respectively.[179] The industrial working class areas formed the basis for the co-operative movement and it then spread throughout the United Kingdom. In Scotland, the mining areas of the Lothians, Fife and Lanarkshire were co-operative strongholds.

These Co-operative Societies adopted a philosophy which mirrored other philanthropists of the nineteenth century, they established shops, particularly in less wealthy areas as well as providing delivery services to serve outlying areas. They supplied their shops from their own purpose-built bakeries and dairies. The Scottish Wholesale Co-operative Society also had factories manufacturing goods like footwear and furniture and provided banking, finance

and funeral services. Within a town, the Co-operative could own several premises each devoted to a specific retail purpose such as a shoe shop, a butchers and a bakers. Later, department stores and supermarkets were constructed.

Societies were local to their own area where members could vote on activities. Each society had specific rules which were to be followed by their members. Importantly, members received a 'dividend' based on their spending at the branches. The Rochdale principles for example state that "*the profits should be divided pro rata upon the amount of purchase made by each member*".[180] The idea was a phenomenal success and by 1914, the Scottish Co-operative Wholesale Society had expanded with sales of £9.5 million.[181] Their philosophy was very different from those of the chain stores which were emerging at the same time. Their motive was not profit but was based on self-help and efficient wholesaling and retailing systems which could provide members with suitable quality services at as low cost as possible. They increased their trade by expanding the services they offered and by increasing the intensity of trade within a district, not by expanding its boundaries.[182] Many of their buildings retain symbols of the Co-operative Movement such as clasped hands or beehives indicating their origins of co-operation. (Figure 124)

Some societies were quite modest but others were substantial, such as the St Cuthbert's Society in Edinburgh. This was one of the most successful companies which, in 1923, was not only the fifth largest but had

Fig: 123

Fig: 124

the highest turnover. They established their first shop in Fountainbridge in 1859 but 100 years later they had almost 300 outlets and covered everything from laundries to butchers and provided services such as coal merchants and a firewood factory. This Society merged with Dalziel and West Lothian Co-operative Societies in the early 1980s to form Scotmid.[183]

Despite their humble beginnings serving the working classes, the architecture of some of the buildings for the Co-operative Societies reflected the latest architectural fashions. During the 1930s their shops were fronted in modern materials including Vitrolite and chrome such as a former co-operative shoe shop in Peebles executed in black Vitrolite and a yellow Vitrolite store in Nursery Street, Arbroath.

Fig: 125

One of the greatest Art Deco co-operative designs was for the Northern Co-operative Society in Stonehaven. Like many other Scottish seaside towns, Stonehaven enjoyed immense popularity during the 1930s and this building reflects this period of relative prosperity. The Carron Tearooms, 20 Cameron Street and shops at 26-34 Evan Street formed a shop and tearoom complex built in 1936 and designed by Colonel H S Tawse of Tawse and Allen with the tearoom interior designed by MacDonald and Cresswick of Edinburgh.[184] The builder for the project was Messrs Hall.[185] In typical co-operative style there were individual shops for each retail trade of butcher, baker, grocery and pharmacist. The shops feature bronze Art Deco

geometric glazing patterns to the clerestory and each shop has a medallion depicting its purpose such as a wheat-sheaf and a bulls head. (Figure 125) The tearoom was an extension to the rear of the shops which sits above the garden frontage onto Cameron Street with its magnificent bow window.[186]

Architects chosen to design the shops were often local to the area. For example, Matthew Steele of Bo'ness was chosen to design premises for the Bo'ness Co-operative Society in 1923 and the Cowdenbeath Co-operative Society appointed Dunfermline architect Andrew Scobie to design new premises for Cowdenbeath High Street in 1891. J P Allison (1862-1932) of Hawick was the architect appointed to create a daring design for premises at 11 Exchange Street, Jedburgh for the local co-operative society in 1899. The building cost £2105 to construct and is exceptional for its glazed wall creating exceptionally large expanses of plate glass for such an early date. The building is Listed Category A.[187] (Figure 126)

However, perhaps the most stunning example of modern co-operative architecture and use of glazing was the extension to the St Cuthbert's Society premises at Bread Street, Edinburgh in 1936 to a design by Thomas Waller Marwick (1907-1971). The first curtain-wall construction system in Scotland was used on the upper floors to create a breathtaking wall of glass adjacent to the store's earlier, elaborate Edwardian façade. Together with its deep arcaded entrance, this building demonstrated how innovative the co-operative societies were not just in their approach to retailing but also in the architectural styles

Figure 125: Window detail of former Co-operative, Evan Street, Stonehaven

Figure 126: Report and Balance Sheet for Jedburgh Co-operative Society, September 1942. Co-operative stores maintained excellent records and their history is therefore well documented. This image on the left depicts the store in Jedburgh designed by JP Allison © Co-operative Group Archives, image supplied by Scottish Borders Council Archives and Local History Service

Fig: 126

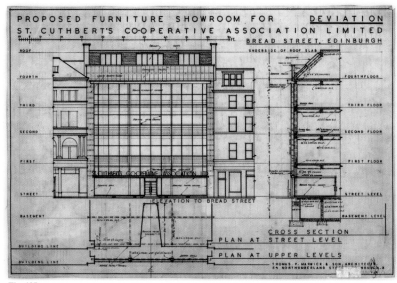

Fig: 127

Figure 127: Design for St Cuthbert's Co-operative Store, 28-32 Bread Street, Edinburgh, 1936 by Thomas Waller Marwick (c1901-71), this was Scotland's first 'curtain wall' building © Courtesy of RCAHMS. Licensor www.rcahms.gov.uk

Figure 128: Entrance to St Cuthbert's Co-operative Store, 28-32 Bread Street, Edinburgh © Courtesy of RCAHMS. Licensor www.rcahms.gov.uk

they adopted. This building is now the Point Hotel having been converted in 1999.

Interiors were also of a high standard and occasionally opulent. As tiling was a favoured material of the late nineteenth century, the butchers and other shops were often beautifully tiled. Scottish tile firm, James Duncan Ltd were responsible for several co-operative tiled interiors including at Maybole, Camelon and Paisley. While the mural of the Forth and Clyde Canal at a former co-operative butcher's in Camelon is impressive, the most magnificent scheme is at the former Paisley Provident Co-operative Society building at Causeyside Street. Dating to 1907-08, the tiles were supplied by T & R Boote of Burslem and incorporate an elaborate interior to the grand Edwardian building with a mosaic floor and lobby entrance panels on a nautical theme. The tiles up three flights of stairs have roses reminiscent of the 'Glasgow Style'.[188] Such schemes indicate that the co-operative societies were prepared to make their buildings both functional and beautiful and their co-operative foundations did not prevent them from experimenting with the latest styles or materials.

Many of the original co-operative societies had to merge and amalgamate in order to survive. As a result, numerous buildings have become redundant. Their extensive premises, erected in the late nineteenth and early twentieth century, are now often surplus to requirements. While some remain occupied as co-operative shops, others have new occupiers, changes of use or are vacant. Few have retained their original ground floor shops as numerous changes over the years have resulted in regular re-fronting. Despite this, like the chain stores, these represent an important development in retailing history and their contribution is therefore of significance. Any shops which do survive with a high degree of original fabric are of importance.

Fig: 128

Figure 129: Entrance, 25-29 Causeyside, Paisley: Designed in 1907-08 by Robert Miller, this impressive building for the Paisley Provident Cooperative Society has a magnificent tiled entrance by Glasgow tile firm, James Duncan Ltd

Fig: 129

Technical Background:

SHOP ELEMENTS AND MATERIALS

"The shopfront may possess architectural or historic interest which makes it irreplaceable. It is all too easy to lose these qualities as a result of ill-considered repair or restoration." Bath City Council 1993

Shops comprise a complex mixture of architectural elements which vary depending on the age of the shopfront, the style of the parent building and the historical impact of local skills and fashions. The type of retail use will also have a direct bearing on the design of the shop and how it has subsequently been adapted.

Understanding how these small elements combine to create a shopfront helps a wider appreciation of shopfronts and their conservation. Even apparently minor elements such as a door handle or ventilator in a stallriser contribute to the aesthetic appearance and historic significance of a shopfront and should be retained where possible. This section outlines the different elements of shopfronts and interiors and provides details on the materials and their significance. The importance of how the different elements combine to create a certain style or type of shopfront cannot be overlooked and each element should therefore be considered both individually and as part of a whole.

Figure 130: Cast iron column St Andrews (facing page)

Figure 131: Traditional sun awning

Fig: 131

Figure 132a: Drawing showing a typical Victorian shopfront

1. Cornice: decorated with egg and dart detail
2. Fascia: narrow with surrounding decorative detail
3. Console bracket: elaborate, Classically inspired design
4. Pilaster: plain with plinth. Often decorative in Victorian shops
5. Fanlight: will usually have a hinged mechanism for opening
6. Double doors: partially glazed with panelling and gunstock stiles
7. Window: three horizontal panes
8. Stallriser: plain design but may have detail to match pilasters

Figure 132b: Drawing showing a typical 1930s shopfront

1. Cornice: usually minimal in design and plain
2. Fascia: an integral part of the shopfront with no decoration and usually deep
3. Blind box: integral to the design so lies flush with the shopfront
4. Clerestory: glazed panels with margin panes. Glass may also be opaque
5. Fanlight: will usually have a hinged mechanism for opening
6. Door: glazed with margin panes
7. Window screens: glass and timber screens situated to the rear of the window
8. Stallriser: plain design
9. Vent grille: often of bronze or chrome it allows air into the shop

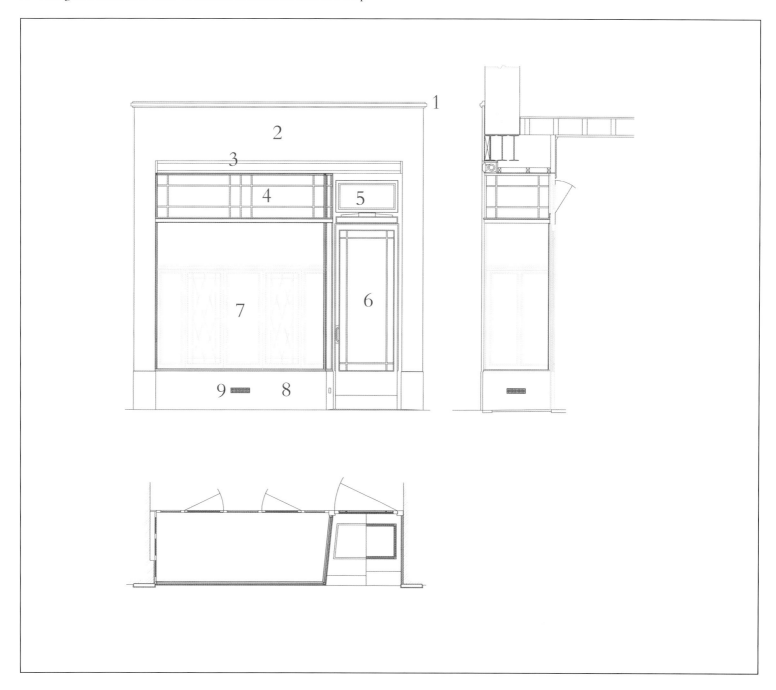

SHOP WINDOWS AND DOORS

As all shops comprise a window and an entrance, the style of shop windows and doors is a vital part of the overall design. Shops windows and doors were traditionally constructed of seasoned timber but technological developments introduced alternative materials, notably metals such as bronze and chrome, typically applied to a timber core. The types of timber used varied but certainly in the late nineteenth and early twentieth century exotic hardwoods like mahogany and walnut were favoured for their decorative qualities as well as oak which is a durable hardwood.

Shop window frames, known as sashes, are usually fixed rather than opening windows and the earlier shops, pre-1830, will have multiple small panes. From the 1840s onwards there was a move to larger panes, initially divided horizontally with either two or three panes depending on the height of the window before graduating to much larger expanses of glass.

Figure 133: Deuchars, South Street, Perth. Bow-fronted shops used multiple panes of Crown glass to create their curved windows

Figure 134: Astragal detail, Deuchars, South Street, Perth

It has been generally understood that shop windows, unlike domestic ones, are glazed from the inside with the astragal mouldings facing to the outside and this was certainly the case in Edinburgh.[189] Similarly in Bath it is suggested that "*in shopfront design, in contrast to domestic design, the moulded face of the glazing bar always faces outward as this presents the best appearance*".[190] Ellis writing in 1906 also confirms that shop fronts should "*always be fixed upon the inside*".[191] However, although this may be the case for shops in Bath and Edinburgh, shopfronts in other parts of Scotland suggest that this is not the case as in Perthshire for example, shops are glazed externally with the mouldings to the inside, contradicting the generally held belief that the moulding should be external.[192]

It is possible that early shops were glazed in the same way as houses because that was standard joinery practice and changing to different practices was a gradual process. The influences of London and Bath styles may have reached Edinburgh but were perhaps slower to extend to other areas. It is undoubtedly a more practical option to glaze externally as glazing internally may be difficult and perhaps this consideration over-rode any aesthetic influence. However, examples from the mid-Victorian period onwards suggest that having the decorative moulding to the exterior was becoming more common for shop premises.

Fig: 134

This highlights the particular importance of understanding that local fashions may differ from what is generally regarded as the norm. The fact that shops are glazed in a particular way in Edinburgh or Glasgow, for example, does not mean that this is the situation nationally and close attention should always be paid to small details.

Fig: 133

Georgian and earlier Victorian shops will often have a set of storm doors. These are typically a pair of outer doors which open inwards being 'shop hung' so that they fold back into the entrance and appear like panelling. Some may be a single door with a central hinge to allow it to fold neatly in half. These substantial doors may have flush panelling which is common in some districts and generally related to prevailing architectural fashions.

Inner shop doors usually retain a glazed panel so that customers can see into the shop, encouraging additional natural light and it permits visibility for people entering and leaving the shop. Referred to as *sash doors*, in order to maximise the area of glass, gun-stock or diminished stiles are used. Here the stile is narrower at the glazed section which means the glazing can be larger. As Allen describes:

"This is done both for effect, and to allow for more area of glass, which is secured within the framing by loose beads mitring round the panels and screwed to the framing after the glass is in." [193]

For inter-war shops, the glazing of the door increased in line with the general move to a greater transparency of the shop. The doors were therefore largely glass although sometimes made use of margin panes in keeping with the geometric theme of many 1930s shopfronts.

The availability of metal products offered considerable design options for shopfronts. During the twentieth century bronze was favoured for high class shopfronts and was used by shopfitters such as Frederick Sage for their quality shopfronts. Chrome was also used in the inter-war period for shopfront sashes with its highly reflective surface.

Fig:135   Fig:136

Georgian, Victorian and early twentieth century doors and windows will usually be constructed of a superior, slow-grown timber compared to the fast-grown softwood available today. They are also an integral part of the history and architecture of a shopfront and should be respected, particularly as they may form part of a wider architectural scheme for the building. Likewise, their associated ironmongery including door handles and lock fittings are often of high-quality brass and their design may be associated with a previous occupier or part of the overall design scheme for the shop and their retention is therefore of importance.

135 & 136: This early nineteenth century shop in Dunkeld has flush-panelled doors. These contrast with the more elaborate late Victorian panelled doors in Crieff.

Figure 137: Drawing showing glazed door with gunstock stiles

Figure 138: Bronze frames were fashionable in the inter-war period

Fig: 137   Fig:138

SIGNS, LETTERING AND ADVERTISING METHODS

The signage of shops is as important as the architecture and materials used in the shopfront. Shopkeepers need to advertise their business so that potential customers know what can be purchased on the premises and will also use it to gain advantage over rival businesses to attract customers. Signs may also be an indication of the calibre of the shop and the goods it sells. Associations with certain names, symbols or heraldry can reflect the perception of the quality or otherwise of the premises. Signs form an important part of the history of shops. Bartram states:

Figure 139: Cut and gilded signs like this Campbeltown shop were fashionable for late Victorian and Edwardian shopfronts © Argyll & Bute Council Library Service, McGrory Collection

> *"The appeal of old fascias is not always entirely due to their normally good form, their patina of age, their sympathetic material and colour. There is undeniable nostalgia about them, creating visions of the High Street before chain stores and supermarkets moved in."[194]*

Like other aspects of shopfront design, signage design is influenced by a number of inter-related factors including legislation, available materials, fashion and the personal preferences of shopkeepers and their architects. Their very purpose means that they are transient and only relevant while a particular occupier or business is in that shop.

Fascias and lettering

The majority of shops will have a fascia advertising the name of the proprietor and business. Perry notes the importance of designing the fascia as part of the overall shop scheme stating that "*it is essential that the fascia is designed and constructed to be in keeping with the remainder of the work irrespective of the materials used in its construction*".[195]

Like other aspects of shop architecture, lettering and fascia styles were subject to the various fashions

Fig: 139

Fig: 140

Fig: 141

Figure 140: Donaldson, Butcher, Earlston. The modest painted signage is perfect for this shopfront

Figure 141: Old shop signs are sometimes uncovered during building works. These form part of the history of a shop

prevalent at the time. New styles like Art Nouveau and Art Deco had a significant impact on fascia design. Certain styles of lettering also became strongly associated with certain brands or companies. For example, the Boot's logo is instantly recognisable, a style which has been used by the company for over 100 years.

There are several methods of introducing lettering to a fascia:

- **Paint**: The painting of the letters onto the fascia or stonework is usually carried out by a professional sign writer. In certain localities the particular influence of a local sign writer may be evident as each will have their own style and preferences. A popular lettering style for shopfronts was the English vernacular letter. This developed in the eighteenth and early nineteenth century it described as having *"boldness and clarity"* which has *"a handsome form with strong verticals and very slender horizontals"*.[196] The use of raising and shading produced a three dimensional effect to painted letters, enhancing the effect.

- **Glass-fronted signs**: Towards the end of the nineteenth century, the use of V-cut lettering became fashionable. Here the letters are cut into the wood panel and then gilded with gold leaf. The use of gold leaf provides a reflective quality which 'lifts' the lettering. A sheet of glass is usually placed over the top for protection and may have additional gilding to add depth to the letters.[197] Impressing V-section letters into metal sheets (copper) and using steel dyes before covering them with glass to create 'Brilliant' signs was a similar technique but a cheaper method.[198] These signs remained in use into the inter-war period although were much more traditional in appearance than the sleek, modern signs.

- **Applied lettering:** Stock letters were manufactured in a variety of materials and styles.

Wood, metal or porcelain were the usual options and these were painted, grained, marbled or gilded to allow sufficient variation for different retailers.

- **Illuminated signs:** The wide availability of electricity during the inter-war period added a new dimension to lettering as shop signs could be lit properly for the first time. The development of neon as a lighting material offered great possibilities and was very much in keeping with Moderne architecture. However, this was not always a welcome approach as Burford states: *"a well-armed Committee of Public Taste might make an abatement of the nuisance, but in so doing it would have to face the responsibility of interference with one of the most successful advertising methods which have yet been achieved"*.[199]

Fig: 142

Figure 142: Applied timber or metal letters are very effective

Figure 143: 'Road Maps' hanging sign, St Andrews

Figure 144: A Padlock is a traditional sign used for an ironmongers

Figure 145: The simplest of signs can still be effective at advertising the business

Figure 146: Examples of shop advertising (facing page)

Fig: 143

Fig: 144

Hanging signs

Although hanging signs had been used in the eighteenth and nineteenth century, they had been controlled by burgh authorities as they were potentially a nuisance in the street. In recent years there has been a revival in some areas of traditional style hanging signs. These are usually hung from a metal bracket and are either painted boards or three-dimensional signs. The can be particularly effective where a fascia sign is not appropriate or is very limited in size.

In the nineteenth century, three-dimensional signs were fashionable, their style reflecting the nature of the business such as a boot for a shoe retailer, a mortar and pestle for a pharmacy and three golden balls for a pawn broker. Other popular types include a red and white pole for a barber and a padlock or key for an ironmonger.

Other forms of advertising

Shop owners took every opportunity to advertise their wares and were increasingly inventive in how this was achieved.

Clerestory glazing: Lettering was incorporated into the display windows, often in the clerestory as special panels stating the products available for sale. These were popular in the 1920s and 1930s, especially for chemists and grocers.

Engraved brass stall plates: These were also used from the mid nineteenth century onwards. Bath shopfronts describes them as *"wide, splayed or curved stall plates were engraved with ornamental lettering, often with simulated returns in enamel"*.[200] These lent an air of elegance and importance to a shopfront although they may be vulnerable to removal where they no longer correspond to the current user.

Heraldic signs and crests: In some locations, notably in the Deeside towns of Braemar, Banchory and Ballater, royal crests are displayed on the shopfronts indicating that the business is 'by Royal Appointment'.

While these do not advertise the shop per se, they are a form of promotion, indicating that the shop has a certain standing and reputation and therefore is an important business in the area.

Lettering on doors and windows: An effective way of advertising was to place the name on the door or window of the shop. This could be etched or gilded and was usually associated with high-class retailers.

Entrance floors: These were used to promote the business either with the name of the proprietor or with the business type such as 'Chemist'. These could be in mosaic, marble or sometimes brass was used.

The transient nature of shop occupation impacts on shop signs. Surviving old signs should be regarded in the same way as other architectural elements of a shop. They are equally important in adding interest and variety to a streetscape. The use of modern, plastic fascias which are unsympathetic to the building can detract from the aesthetic value of a street and may also give an appearance of a lack of permanence. If old lettering is uncovered during work to a shopfront, the details should be recorded and every effort made to ensure that the original fascia does not suffer further unnecessary damage. In some cases they have been found to suit the modern shop such as the Meeting House, Whitehall Crescent, Dundee which is now occupied by Tayside Solicitors Property Centres. In others they may be overlaid in a reversible way like the sign for 'Stark, Chemist' in Gatehouse of Fleet which was retained beneath a modern retail sign.

Fig: 145

BLINDS AND AWNINGS

In the past, awnings were considered a practical necessity, particularly for south facing shops where strong sun could quickly cause goods to deteriorate and the shop to heat up. This is why butchers and other fresh food shops traditionally favoured the north-facing side of streets out of the glare of the sun.

Blinds were widely used from the mid nineteenth century and remained popular well into the twentieth century notably through the inter-war period and into the 1950s. These large sail cloth or canvas blinds had the added benefit of offering shoppers and traders protection from the weather. They sometimes had side aprons or wing blinds which hung at the side of the shopfront although these were widely disliked because they could interfere with the pedestrians walking past. Internal roller blinds were also used inside shop windows to protect goods from the sun.

Blinds provided an ideal opportunity to advertise and frequently had the name of the business or owner emblazoned on the canvas. Blind manufacturers and shopfitters also typically had their name badge on the front of the blind box.

There are two basic arrangements:

- Addition of a blind box, often above the fascia which is typically planted onto an existing shopfront;
- Integral blind box hidden behind the fascia which is incorporated into the shopfront design.

The commonly used mechanism involves a spring roller onto which a blind cloth is fixed and iron arms allow the blind to be pulled out into an open position along metal slides using a long-arm pole with a hook fixed on the end. When in use, steel storm chains help secure the blind in the event of adverse weather. The metal arms and slides then fold back into place when the blind is in the closed position. Where the shop had a particularly long frontage (over six metres) or was a complex shape, there would need to be more than one blind.

An alternative method is a concertina type arrangement where the blind is pulled out and creates a zig-zag detail. These were popular for inter-war shopfronts and when either open or closed they contribute to the design of the shopfront. Like the blind rail, these were

Figure 147: Where no integral blind box exists, one may be applied to the building façade

Fig: 147

Figure 148: Typical Arrangement for a Traditional Awning (after Perry, 1933)

1. Awning: traditionally made of canvas or sailcloth
2. Storm chain: to prevent excessive movement
3. Blind rail: Metal or timber facing which protects the blind when in the
   closed position
4. Arm: metal arms which fold back when blind is closed
5. Blind box: timber box, often metal-lined to prevent rot
6. Spring-roller mechanism: to allow the blind to be pulled out and then
   retracted

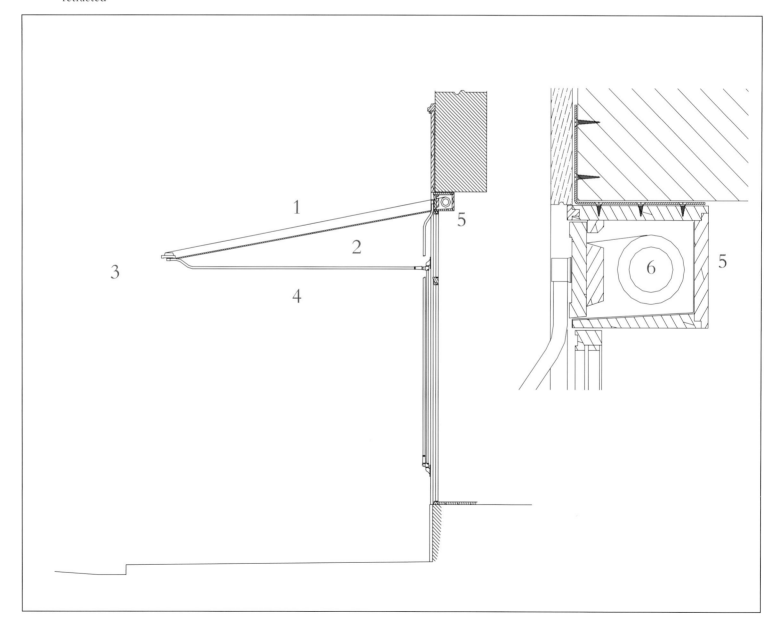

Fig: 149

Fig: 150

Figure 149: In corner positions several blinds may be required to protect the shop

Figure 150: Traditional awnings can be only partially pulled out where required

Figure 151: Wing blinds may be necessary at certain times of the day

Figure 152: Concertina arrangements are common in 1930s blinds

commonly made of chrome or bronze. The interior of the blind box was typically lined with sheet zinc so that when the blind was rolled away in a damp condition, it did not rot the timber of the box.[201]

Whilst many traditional blinds are no longer used, the blind mechanisms will often remain insitu and capable of being renovated for use again. Typical problems are that the mechanism may fail over time and need overhauled or the blind cloth may need to be replaced but this can be relatively easily achieved. Although originally blinds were of canvas, there may be suitable modern alternatives available; a woven fabric, whether linen, cotton or polypropylene, is preferable to a sheet of plastic. The blind box, particularly if retro-fitted, is vulnerable to rot because of its exposed

position on the shopfront. Decay can be rapid if the box is not fitted with an appropriate lead capping and it may be necessary to replace the box in new timber and to ensure that the lead is renewed.

Traditional awnings can have a long life and are more sensitive to the appearance of historic shopfronts than modern blinds. The considerable practical and aesthetic benefits of these have enjoyed appreciation in recent years and the renovation of blinds is becoming more widespread.

Fig: 151

Fig: 152

VENTILATION

For the comfort of staff and customers and for the protection of stock, it was crucial to have shop premises adequately ventilated by encouraging a flow of fresh air. Unlike domestic windows, shop windows are usually fixed (with the exception of lifting windows) so there have to be alternative systems for introducing cool air. In the nineteenth century, ventilation became an integral part of shopfront design, particularly important when gasoliers were in use because these created significant condensation. Writing on shopfront construction in 1933, Perry states:

"Ventilation as applied to shopfront construction is a highly important factor, …proper and efficient ventilation can be carried out to a great degree of perfection without the aid of mechanical appliances such as electric fans, which only circulate the air in their immediate vicinity."[202]

The main methods of ventilation include:
- Ventilators at the window heads;
- Grilles in stallrisers;
- Opening fanlights;
- Lifting windows.

Ventilators are narrow features at the window head which allow a flow of air through what is otherwise a fixed window. They can be plain or decorative and may be fixed or 'hit and miss' ventilators with a sliding mechanism which allows the flow of air to be controlled.

Ventilators tended to work in conjunction with vent grilles in the stallriser. As the air enters the shop it rises and warms and is then expelled through the ventilators at the window head, thus ensuring a flow of fresh air over the interior face of the glass.[203] For 1930s architecture these vents were not only practical but also became an important part of the aesthetic design of the shop.

The use of hopper opening fanlights above the entrance door proved popular particularly with fresh produce retailers like grocers and butchers. These allowed air into the premises, controlled by a ratchet system which permitted varying degrees of ventilation. These are a simple and practical way to introduce ventilation and many remain in use today.

Fig: 153

Fig: 154

Figure 153: Decorative 'hit and miss' ventilator

Figure 154: Small ventilation panels in the stallriser form part of the architecture of the shop

Fig: 155

Figure 155: Hopper opening fanlights located above the door allow in additional ventilation

Figure 157: Newmarket Street, Ayr. Lifting windows were popular with fishmongers through the 1930s

Fig:157

Lifting windows

Some trades such as butchers and fishmongers were late to move into permanent shops from their location on market stalls and, even then it seems, were reluctant to entirely give up the idea of trading from a stall. Initially their shops resembled market stalls[204] but even when shops became more enclosed some retained the idea of the market stall by having the front window of their shop capable of being opened. There is perhaps the idea of openness and inspection of goods associated with fresh produce, people getting the opportunity to look at what is for sale close up. It therefore seems that this association continued into the permanent shop with the 'lifting window'.[205]

A lifting window has a fixed upper section but the lower sash slides up behind, similar to a sash and case window. The upper fixed window could be decorated because it was not required for display, the goods being laid on the window slab as Ellis describes: *"most of these trades do not require the upper parts of the window for show, and the front may be broken up with bars, or otherwise ornamented in this part".*[206]

Not only favoured by butchers and fishmongers, grocers also took advantage of an opening window. Lipton's, for example, typically had a double-fronted shop with one side having an opening sash and the other fixed. The opening side displayed fresh dairy produce like butter whereas the closed side was for dry groceries or for ham.[207] For a double-fronted shop, this was not an uncommon arrangement as usually one single opening window was sufficient.

There are several practical reasons for the use of a lifting sash, notably for ventilation but it also had other advantages in that it allowed the window to be dressed and cleaned easily and it also gave the opportunity to sell through the window.

For fresh food shops the need for ventilation was paramount. Ellis states that for butchers, fishmongers and greengrocers, *"their stocks deteriorate quickly if confined"* and

Figure 156: Flow of ventilation in a shopfront (after Perry, 1933)

1. Vent grille in stallriser

2. Ventilation grille at window head: may be metal or timber. May have a 'hit and miss' arrangement to allow the flow of ventilation to be controlled

3. Cold air is drawn in through the vent and into the shop via a grille in the window board

4. Warm air flows out through the vent at the window head keeping a fresh flow of air

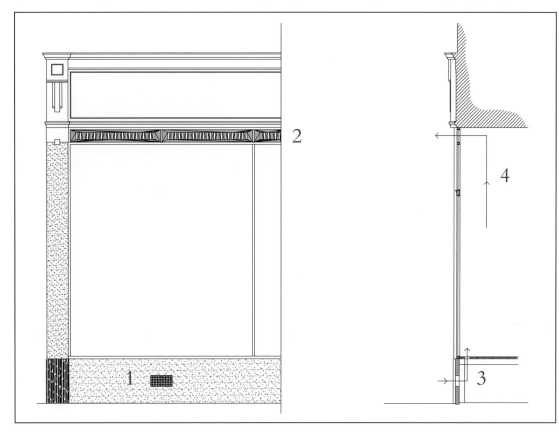

Fig: 158

this is achieved through an opening window.[208] The use of a marble or slate slab also helped to keep the foodstuffs cool, particularly when filled with ice, although during the 1930s a terrazzo slab was more commonly used. A pipe running with cold water down the window was also installed in some shops. As the food needed to be removed on a daily basis and the shop cleaned down, the lifting window allowed convenient access to clean the marble slab and usually a drain was included to allow water and ice to be easily removed.

Displaying of products in an attractive way was viewed as an important way of enticing customers to purchase goods. Displaying small goods like fish effectively is easier if there is ready access to the front of the window, especially if there is a deep marble slab located in the window. Graham, writing in the 1930s in *The Modern Grocer* states:

"The aim in new installations is to secure maximum visibility and balance, while giving at the same time the opportunity of dressing, at least, the provision window from the front by means of a lifting sash. This treatment is quite unnecessary for a grocery window, as the construction of the window bed and approach from the rear does not call for it."[209]

It is also the case that a fresh window needed to be laid out every day, whereas a dry groceries window, for example, would be changed much less frequently. Accessibility was therefore paramount for the fresh goods window and the lifting arrangement offered the maximum opportunity for ease of arranging goods.

The use of lifting windows continued well into the twentieth century with shops in the 1930s still being designed with lifting windows.[210] New shopfronts for fishmongers all had lifting windows and they clearly used them for display and selling purposes. In contrast, new shopfronts for butchers had abandoned this design

Fig: 159

although they continued to hang meat up at the door of the shop or sometimes poultry across the exterior of the front window.

In the post-war period stricter regulations were introduced in relation to food hygiene and new practices were made possible with the introduction of electric refrigeration and cooling and ventilation systems. These effectively made lifting windows redundant and were regarded by some as unhygienic. Although their use persisted, notably amongst fishmongers, in the post-war period their use gradually receded and the shops were often replaced with new, fixed windows leaving only a small legacy of surviving windows.

Figure 158: This pair of shops in Jedburgh both have lifting windows together with additional ventilation in the door panels

Figure 159: Cast iron fretwork in stallrisers allows in maximum ventilation, particularly for butchers and fishmongers

SHOP SECURITY

*Figure 160: Hinged
timber shutters in
Kircudbright are an
attractive option for this
domestic style shopfront*

The security of shops has always been of importance to retailers. This was not only to protect goods but also the valuable glass of the shopfront. The methods employed vary depending on the age of the shopfront and its design and a shop may incorporate a number of different methods.

The main methods of protecting shopfronts are:

> External removable shutters;
> Rising or lifting shutters;
> Roller shutters;
> Storm doors;
> Shop gates.

*Figure 161: Rising
shutters were installed
in Victorian shops
in Cockburn Street,
Edinburgh as depicted
in the drawing of 1863
by Peddie and Kinnear.
Many of these timber
shutters remain in
practical working use
today
© RCAHMS (Dick
Peddie & McKay
Collection). Licensor
www.rcahms.gov.uk*

External removable shutters

The traditional way to protect shop fronts was to use external timber shutters, made for both windows and doors. These were lifted from the front of the shop during the day where they were stored in a close or storeroom and then replaced at night. Constructed of timber they were particularly heavy although half height shutters were made to alleviate this problem. The tall shutters were also made in narrower widths to reduce their weight.[211]

Various methods were used for securing the shutters. There would usually be a shutter slot within the window into which the shutter fitted and could then be held in place by a horizontal iron bar. Additional bolts secured it into the frame of the shop. In Edinburgh New Town, holes

Fig: 160

in the frames allowed threaded bolts to be passed through from the inside and screwed into the shutter to hold it in place.[212] Alternatively, they may also be secured using studs fixed onto the sill plate.[213]

Very few shops now retain these shutters and even in 1893 Allen noted that external shutters for houses and shops are "*now almost obsolete*".[214] They are now very rare although examples still in working use can be seen in Market Square, Kelso. They are also still used in Edinburgh New Town, often on the glazed doors such as in William Street. Surviving external shutters remain an effective protective mechanism for shops and where they exist should always be retained.

Rising or lifting shutters

Rising shutters are timber panelled shutters which sit in a well behind the stallriser when the shop is open but are pulled upwards to cover the glazing when the shop is closed. The mechanism is similar to that of a sash window with a weighted pulley system which allows the shutters to be pulled into position easily. Where the window is tall, or where there is restricted space below the stallriser, there may be a system of two shutters.[215] To reduce water ingress, there is often a cover plate for the sill which is pulled across when the shutters are lowered.

These shutters will typically be found where there is sufficient space below the shop to accommodate them. A basement area is usually required for this. Working examples can be seen in Cockburn Street, Edinburgh which date to 1866, but further examples are known to exist in other Scottish towns such as Jedburgh. They remain a practical alternative to modern shutters and are extremely effective if maintained in good working order.

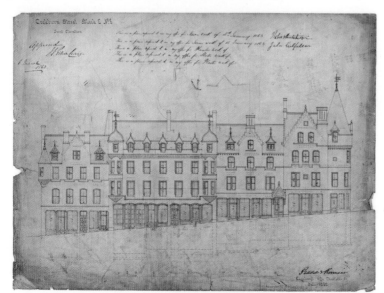

Fig: 161

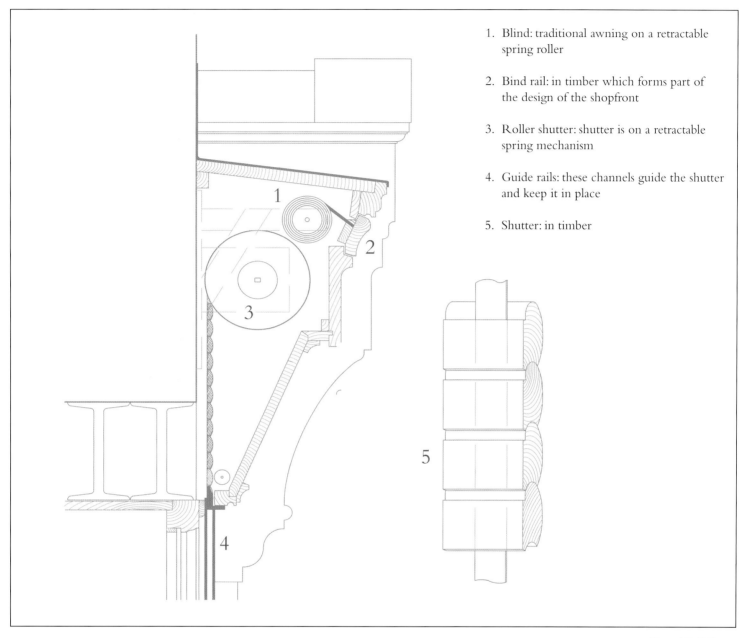

1. Blind: traditional awning on a retractable spring roller

2. Bind rail: in timber which forms part of the design of the shopfront

3. Roller shutter: shutter is on a retractable spring mechanism

4. Guide rails: these channels guide the shutter and keep it in place

5. Shutter: in timber

Figure 162: Roller shutter and blind combination (after Ellis, 1906)

Roller shutters

Roller shutters were available from the 1840s but were slow to be introduced. However, by the end of the nineteenth century they formed an integral element of the shop design, constructed of iron, steel or timber. Unlike the modern external roller shutters retro-fitted onto shopfronts, traditional arrangements were designed as an integral part of the shopfront. They therefore either fitted neatly within the window soffit, hidden behind the deeper and angled fascias fashionable in the latter nineteenth century or, for internal revolving shutters, could be fitted behind the stallriser and then lifted up into position.[216]

Storm doors

Some nineteenth century shops were fitted with storm doors which could be folded back into the lobby and then appear as timber panels in the entrance. These 'shop hung' doors have a hinging arrangement which allows the face of the door to lie flush against the door stop making them read as timber panelling. It also means that when open, they allow a clear access into the shop without impeding shoppers. The principle is similar to that which is used for timber window shutters in domestic properties. These are an effective protection for a shop entrance and many shops retain these in working use today.

Figure 163: Timber shop gates are a practical option for shops with entrance lobbies

Fig:163

Figure 164: Specially designed modern shutters installed as part of the Bo'ness Townscape Heritage Initiative

Shop gates

In the latter decades of the nineteenth century, shop entrances gradually became deeper and splayed. The panels to the sides of the entrance were now glazed where they had formerly been hidden by masonry and storm doors. This meant that the traditional door arrangement with storm doors was not possible and instead the lobbies were left open with the door recessed. However, this left the entrance vulnerable and encouraged people to loiter there when the shop was closed which was considered undesirable.

As a deterrent, shop gates were introduced. Constructed of timber or iron, these could be highly decorative and were sometimes an integral part of the overall shop design. The gates were usually fixed and therefore lifted off the fixings and taken into the shop during the day. Some however, could be discreetly folded back into the lobby area or were of a metal concertina type, typically favoured by butchers. Today, many shops still use their gates to prevent people from standing in the lobby when the shop is closed thereby offering some additional security.

Modern security systems

For modern retailers, problems with theft and vandalism combined with measures required for insurance cover have encouraged the use of particular modern systems, notably the proliferation of external roller shutters in certain localities. However, these are both aesthetically harmful to a shopfront and potentially destructive to historic fabric through the fixings to attach them to the shop. It is also known that these can actually be detrimental to an area by creating dead frontages and discouraging people from using the area after closing time. Lack of use of an area can encourage vandalism whereas a more open appearance to security is recognised as encouraging window shopping and makes people feel safer than where the shops are all hidden by security shutters.[217]

An alternative to externally mounted roller shutters is demountable wire mesh shutters. Although these allow visibility into the shop they can become rusted and damaged easily as well as being potentially cumbersome to remove and replace on a daily basis. As a result they are often left in the closed position, even during opening hours and they are therefore not necessarily an appropriate solution.

In some localities there has been a more creative approach to security through the use of bespoke wrought iron or other metal gates. If carefully designed and specified these can be very successful and are a more attractive option for historic shopfronts. If fitted correctly and maintained these have a potentially long life. Other retailers may seek measures such as behind-glass lattice shutters or laminated or toughened/armour-plated glass. Such measures will be appropriate for certain shops although not always for historic premises so appropriate advice should be sought.

Fig: 164

EXTERNAL FINISHES AND CLADDING

Shops typically exhibit a variety of external finishes and the type used will often depend on the age and style of the shopfront. The most commonly used material to delineate a shopfront is paint, although other finishes including ceramics and stone cladding are also used to face shopfronts. Glass products, notably Vitrolite, are dealt with in the following section.

Paint and varnish

Paint has been historically used on shops as a protective measure for timber, to make shops more visible and to delineate one shop from another. There is limited information on what colours were used although they would have been related to the fashions of the period and the available colours. It is likely that high class shops would have had sophisticated paint schemes and perhaps made use of specialist techniques such as gilding or with decorative patterns. For example, in the 1770s the shopfront of Elizabeth Bowies Gold Lace manufactory in Edinburgh was painted 'verdegrease' green with mahogany coloured doors and interior shelving with gilded edges.[218]

The Georgian and Regency periods had a restricted palette of colours although a painting by George Scharf of The Strand in London in 1824 shows that the shops were painted in many different colours. While some were a sombre green, others were brightly painted blues and reds suggesting that shops made a lively contribution to early nineteenth century streetscapes.

During the Victorian period there was a vogue for paint effects to imitate materials such as marble and for gilding. Marbling of shopfronts was applied to columns and pilasters to raise the status of the shop making it appear more exclusive. There is also evidence in some historical photos of quite intricate and detailed paintwork

Fig:165

to shopfronts. Photographic examples from Perth of shops occupied by painter and decorator firms indicate that different colours and patterns were used to decorate the pilasters.[219] Black and white photos do not permit the identification of the actual colours showing only tonal differences and patterns. It is no surprise perhaps that painters and decorators used their shopfronts as a way of advertising their particular skills. Jennings advocates this approach stating that the "*actual framing of the shop front should be good, something out of the common, a creditable specimen of decorative work*" although suggests that it should not "*show eccentricity*" but instead should show "*an original and attractive conception, an unmistakably handsome, appropriate setting for his display*".[220]

Graining and marbling fell out of favour, partly due to John Ruskin's suggestions that it was an architectural deceit. However, Jennings contends that this is an ancient method of decoration which although expensive and time-consuming, is extremely durable.[221] It is a finish that is now rarely seen and if undertaken must be executed with considerable skill in order to be of a good appearance.

In the Edwardian period a stained or varnished finish became fashionable, particularly as it contrasted well with other high-quality materials such as brass. However, these finishes were applied to superior, exotic hardwoods such as mahogany or teak and were therefore an appropriate finish which showed off the wood.

Although varnish remained in use during the inter-war and post-war period, paint continued to be the most commonly used finish for timber. In the inter-war period contrasting colours like black and white, echoing Art deco styles were favoured and elaborate paint schemes were no longer fashionable as they did not fit with the minimalist ideals of Moderne shopfronts.

Fig: 166

Figure 165: James McNicoll's shop in Perth was typical of the late nineteenth century with its marbled pilasters and fascia © Courtesy of Perth Museum and Art Gallery, Perth & Kinross Council

Figure 166: This Edwardian entrance shows the high quality timber with its varnished finish

Figure 167: The use of render and paint is common throughout Scotland like this example in Haddington

Figure 168: Green marble was a popular material for cladding shopfronts in the 1930s

Maintenance of paint finishes for any property is an important part of general property care. As these finishes protect the wood from rot it is essential that they are properly maintained and regularly redone. Varnished finishes can be particularly prone to damage by sunlight where the shop is south facing. Stallrisers and pilaster plinths are also extremely vulnerable because of the water and dirt which is washed across them so may need repainting more often. For listed buildings and conservation areas relevant permissions may be required for the alteration of a paint colour on a shopfront and the appropriate advice should be sought prior to undertaking work.

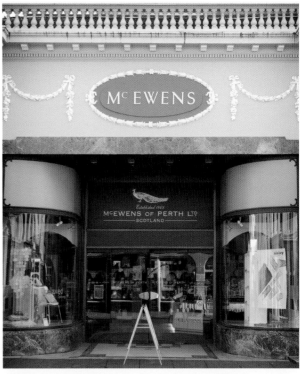

Fig: 168

Fig: 167

Render

A render applied to stone or brickwork is used in some locations to delineate the shopfront. This may be smooth or lined-out and will often be painted. In towns like Haddington, the painted render of the different shopfronts is part of the character of the town. While many of these finishes are cementitious, traditionally a lime wash or harl would have been used.

Stone cladding

There are various stone products which are used to face shopfronts particularly marble and polished granite. These became available in the twentieth century and proved to be particularly fashionable in the inter-war and post-war periods. The sections of stone allowed the shop to be re-faced to provide a totally new and contemporary shopfront. Stone cladding is particularly effective for the stallriser as this is an area of the shopfront which is affected by dirt, water and salt from the pavement and road. It may also suffer from impacts and stone is therefore both practical and aesthetically pleasing.

The variety of stone used is considerable although there are particular colours and types that are favoured. Green marble was especially fashionable in the inter-war period as well as polished black granite. White travertine marble is occasionally used but has a slightly coarser finish than some other products.

Terrazzo is a manufactured product using chips of marble in a cementitious mortar. Available in different colours and textures it could be manufactured as panels or laid insitu. Panels were applied to shopfronts to create smooth finishes, typically in white or cream colours. Popular in the 1920s and 1930s it is a material associated with food shops and also Italian cafes. It was also popular for lobby and shop floors and was sometimes cast into specialist forms such as for fish slabs.

These stone cladding products are generally extremely durable and easy to maintain. Where a section has become cracked or lost it will often be possible to obtain a new piece to match.

Glazed Ceramics

Ceramic materials became popular from around 1840 although it was the last two decades of the nineteenth century when tile manufacture and use was at its height. A very versatile material, it was used for floors and for interior and exterior walls including hospitals, town halls, churches and shops. For retail premises it was favoured by fresh produce shops notably dairies, butchers and fishmongers.

Fig:169

Tiles are aesthetically very pleasing and durable and offer the possibility of individual schemes reflecting the nature or name of the business.

Tiles are a fired clay which is then decorated with a glaze to produce an aesthetic finish which is easy to clean. Originally tiles were laid in lime mortar, but from 1870 Portland cements was the product widely used for the fixing and grouting of ceramic tiles which makes them much more difficult to remove.[222]

Ceramics are available in many different design styles and methods of decorating including hand-painted, tube-lined and relief moulded.[223] Shopkeepers could choose tiles from catalogues, similar to those used by iron foundries, to promote their products. Many chose to have individually designed murals which related to their particular location or business.

Encaustic or geometric tiles were popularised in the late nineteenth century. These small tiles could be used to create elaborate patterns using the different shapes and colours. The inlaid or encaustic tiles with their delicate clay patterns were now available on a mass-produced basis so were affordable to shopkeepers. By the Edwardian period mosaic tiles became fashionable. These were rarely used for shop walls but were popular for entrance lobbies particularly when they incorporated the name of the owner.

Fig: 170

Scotland's greatest tile firm was James Duncan Ltd of Glasgow who operated as a tile-fitting firm from around 1865 to 1965. They specialised in tube-lined tiles which had a raised surface giving depth the image. They are well known not only for having created the Buttercup Dairy Company tile scheme which was once seen across Scotland but for impressive murals in many other shops, particularly butchers and fishmongers. They also carried out work for co-operative societies and one of their best surviving schemes exists in the former Paisley Provident Co-operative building at Causeyside Street, Paisley.[224]

Terracotta is an architectural ceramic particularly used in the late nineteenth and early twentieth centuries to construct and clad buildings. When it has a polished glaze, often white or green, it is known as faience.[225] It was particularly popular in the inter-war period for its sleek and smooth lines and was popular with chain stores including Burton's and Woolworths for their purpose-built retail premises.

Although tiles are hard and generally well-fixed to the substrate, they can become damaged through impact, drilling of fixings or by inappropriate cleaning. Damage is often evident in butchers shops where meat carcasses were traditionally hung up from metal hooks and the meat cut which caused the tiles to be damaged and the surface pitted. At floor level, tiles may be cracked in vulnerable corner positions where there has been impact from fixtures or equipment.

Where tiles have been damaged, it is not uncommon for shop owners to paint them to give them a better appearance. Painting of tiles does not necessarily cause damage but subsequent inappropriate removal of the paint can. Tube-lined tiles with their raised decoration may be especially vulnerable if care is not taken when cleaning and use of sharp cleaning objects can easily remove the delicate glazed surface.

Where a tile has been lost it is usually possible to commission a suitable replacement. Care should be taken not to use modern tiles to fit into a historic tile scheme as the colour, size and depth of the tile will rarely be a satisfactory match.

Terracotta and faience may also deteriorate. As this may be used in a structural way rather than just an aesthetic cladding like ceramic tiles this is a potentially more significant repair and specialist advice will be required.

Overall, ceramics are a highly durable and enduring material and historic tile schemes represent an important part of the history of a shop.

Figure 169: Tiles proved to be particularly popular for stallrisers and had the added advantage of being an advertising medium

Figure 170: The former Burton's store in Dumbarton is constructed of white faience and still trains the sign 'Montague Burton, The Tailor of Taste'

GLAZING AND GLASS PRODUCTS

Figure 171: Technology was sometimes pushed to extremes such as this almost circular showcase of curved glass in Stonehaven

Glass is the material which has had the most profound impact on shopfront design. Its development from small panes in the Georgian period to huge expanses of plate glass at affordable prices has meant that shops have always followed quickly in the wake of technological developments in the glass industry.

Crown and plate glass

In the eighteenth century, crown glass was preferred in Britain compared to the broad glass manufactured on the Continent. The Glass Tax had been doubled in 1777 and was applied by weight so thinner and therefore lighter glass attracted a lower duty. For Georgian small-paned shop windows, crown glass was used which had a lustrous finish and could be made thinner which helped to keep the excise duty lower.

The Chance Brothers took out a patent in 1838 for polished plate glass and in 1845 the Glass Tax was finally repealed which halved the cost of plate glass making it significantly more affordable and therefore in demand. For shopfronts the technological improvements, the affordability and the fact that plate glass was fashionable made it the ideal material for shopfronts. Techniques through the nineteenth and into the twentieth century continued to improve making larger and larger sheets not only available but within the budget of shopkeepers.

Other products such as curved glass could also be made in significant sized sheets and again affordable for at least the wealthier retailers such as drapers and department stores. Curved glass therefore became associated with quality shopfronts and the retailers within.

Figure 172: 'Bullseye' glass in door of late eighteenth century shop, Perth

Fig: 171

Stained and painted glass

Stained or painted glass was popular from the late nineteenth century onwards and especially during the Edwardian era through to the inter-war years. These glass products provided a decorative finish to a shopfront and were usually applied to the clerestory of the window where they also had a practical element by hiding lamp fixings in the shop window. Stained glass was also used for the upper fixed section of lifting windows.

These coloured glasses were fitted within leaded frames and featured patterns of the period such as Art Nouveau designs. This Movement encouraged the use of *"ordinary commercial glasses for decorative purposes and to evolve a type of design suitable to the medium"*.[226] By the inter-war period the patterns tended to be either plain geometric glazing or specific motifs such as the sunrise design favoured in the 1930s.

Fig: 172

Fig: 173

Translucent glass

Translucent glass products were also available which are defined as "*those which transmit light with varying degrees of diffusion so that vision is not clear*".[227] Etched and sandblasted glass products were developed to allow designs to be applied to glass after manufacture for various purposes. Acid etching or embossing used hydrofluoric acid to create a pattern. For shopfronts this was an effective way of introducing a design to a large expanse of plate glass or for reinforcing an advertisement through the incorporation of products or the proprietors name. Opaque glasses were also used for window screens to increase privacy in the shop but to still allow in daylight, such as in a barber's shop.

Prismatic glass

Other glass products include prismatic glass in stallrisers which Frost defines as "*a translucent rolled glass, one surface of which consists of parallel prisms made in three angles giving nominal angles of refraction to a beam of light through the glass*".[228] It was produced for shops from the 1890s. Manufactured in the UK by the British Luxfer Prism Company, it was effectively a solution to the problem of dark, hard-to-light spaces within commercial properties.

Encouraging light into buildings in a predictable way it helped to light the back of shops and basement areas in the period prior to the mass introduction of electricity. However, the subsequent development of electricity meant the demise of this product and it only rarely survives in stallrisers, pavement lights and occasionally the clerestory of shopfronts.

Hollow glass blocks were occasionally used decoratively for modern shopfronts such as in the stallrisers of Casey's sweet shop in St Mary's Street, Edinburgh which dates to the 1950s. This product remained popular in the post-war period and has enjoyed something of a revival in recent years.

Vitrolite

The glass product we most commonly associate with inter-war shopfronts is Vitrolite, a rolled opal glass. Pigmented structural glass was first available around 1900 and it had several trade names including Cararra, Sani Onyx and most widely known in the UK, Vitrolite which was manufactured by Libby-Owens-Ford in America and then under licence in Britain. In 1932 Pilkington's set up the British Vitrolite Company at their Ravenshead and Doncaster Works and one of the first major commissions was for the Mersey Tunnel in 1934.[229] During the inter-war period this sleek glass product became synonymous with the streamline age and with Art Deco architecture. It has many appealing properties making it suitable for a variety of uses it being impervious to many acids and stains and is described as having a "*hard, brilliant, fire-finished surface*".[230]

Vitrolite has a highly-polished surface and was available in many different colours including green,

Figure 173: Stained glass was popular in the Edwardian period

Figure 174: Chevrons and other geometric designs were commonly etched or sandblasted on glass for 1930s shopfronts.

Figure 175: Black Vitrolite was the most popular colour for shopfronts and was widely used although engraving the material with drawings like this cockerel is rarer

Fig: 174

Fig: 175

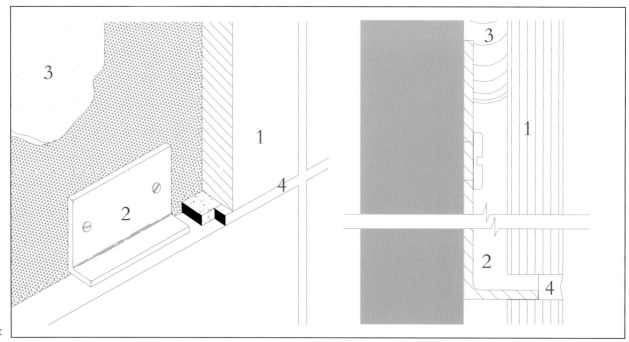

Figure 176: Drawing showing fixing of Vitrolite

1. Vitrolite panel

2. Supporting bracket

3. Mastic

4. Cementitious grout

white, black, yellow and pink. The most popular colour for shopfronts was black which was used in combination with chrome sashes. Available in standard sizes up to 144 inches by 62 inches and usually ¼ inch thick, it could be accurately cut to size.[231] The material was also extremely versatile as it could be bent into different shapes or carved and the surface could be decorated by being inlaid, sand-blasted and even factory painted with gold and silver.[232]

The sheets were available in 1-1/32 inch or 7/16 inch in thickness which were then applied to timber lath or panelling and secured in place with brass or steel shelf angles. A hot asphalt-based mastic was used to attach the sheets of glass onto the prepared substrate and a cement mortar used to finish the joints between the sheets.[233] Various fixing methods were used for the Vitrolite and these seem to have varied from place to place with some adopting a timber framing base.[234]

The glass was vulnerable to thermal expansion so needed suitable expansion joints to prevent cracking. It was understood that black Vitrolite was particularly vulnerable to thermal expansion and should therefore not be used for external cladding although in the case of shopfronts black proved to be the most popular colour so this advice was not followed.[235] Loss of mortar and deterioration of mastic also occurs and over time the cementitious mortar fails allowing water ingress behind the panels. This can cause the panels to become loose and may affect the integrity of any timber panelling and cause rusting of any additional fixings.

As a glass product, although extremely hard, it can be damaged through impact causing cracks either at corners

or wavy cracks across the tiles. Where signs or other shop fittings have been fixed the Vitrolite may become damaged and Vitrolite stallrisers and pilaster plinths are also extremely vulnerable to impact.

Finding an appropriate solution for Vitrolite repairs is problematic. Silicone sealants have been used for some joints although it is not always considered to be satisfactory, particularly in terms of colour and in effecting a good appearance for the very fine joints.[236] As Vitrolite has not been manufactured since 1968, obtaining a suitable replacement for lost panels is difficult. Salvage sources are one option although it may be difficult to source a suitable match and in sufficient quantity. It may therefore be necessary to move some panels from less noticable to more prominent positions although removal without causing damage to remaining panels should not be undertaken without a full understanding of the material and its fixings.

There are alternative glass products available although none have the brilliance and depth of colour of Vitrolite. Alternatives include spandrel glass, where a colour is applied to the back of the glass and Armour-clad by Pilkington's. In some shops various alternatives have been used including use of painted plywood, slate and formica to replace the original material. These replacement materials are rarely successful.

Vitrolite shopfronts form a striking element within the townscape. They are becoming increasingly rare and in spite of the problems with their conservation every attempt should be made to retain them.

SHOP INTERIORS

The interior of a shop will be closely related to past or current uses and they therefore present a strong link with the social history of the premises. Interior fittings had to be chosen to suit particular retail uses and could include:

- Specialist showcases such as for jewellers and tobacconists;
- Counters and shelving;
- Tile schemes for food shops;
- Decorative plasterwork to ceilings;
- Match boarding finish for walls;
- Window screens located to the rear of the window display area;
- Unusual items such as a wall safe.

Both the retailer type and the quality of the retail use will have a direct bearing on the interior fittings. Match boarding is a more functional material associated with many typical shop interiors but higher class shops may have used exotic woods such as walnut or ebonised mahogany. Decorative plasterwork may also feature in some interiors and where a row of shops has been built, each shop may have a similar or matching plaster ceiling.

Window screens are located to the rear of the shop window display area. Of glass and timber these sometimes use opaque glass to prevent viewing into the shop but still allow light through. These form a barrier between the display area and the shop, focusing attention on the goods for sale. Screens may be full or half height and will be hinged in places to allow access into the window.

Figure 177: Glazed window screens form a barrier between the shop and the window display but still allow in natural light

Fig: 177

Fig:178

Figure 178: High quality joinery with glass name plates is typical of Victorian and Edwardian pharmacies

Chemists may also retain the large glass carbides and other bottles which were originally used for chemicals but are now generally filled with coloured water for display purposes.

Grocers and confectioners

Food stores usually had long timber counters with either storage space or sets of drawers below. Food preparation counters were typically marble-topped for cleanliness and to keep foodstuffs cool. Floors were usually tiled with geometric or mosaic tiles. Walls had specialist shelving, sometimes quite decorative which were sized appropriate to the use; confectioners would be designed to accommodate sweet jars, for example.

The quality of fittings would have been related to the type of retailer with some being of a particularly high standard, such as those for the Scottish confectioner, Birrell. Like the chemists and tobacconists, these fittings are usually of a high quality and are a valuable asset to a shop.

Tobacconists, chemists and jewellers

Shops which sold small and sometimes high value items required specialist showcases and glass-fronted shelving which could accommodate these items. Chemists also typically have drawer units with applied glass name plates indicating the nature of the drugs or items to be stored there. Some shopfitting firms, such as Pollards of London, specialised in jewellers fittings, meeting the particular requirements of this trade for quality and specific sizes and style of showcases. These fittings were often produced in mahogany or other polished hardwoods and are now quite rare so should always be retained wherever possible.

Butchers, fishmongers and dairies

Fittings in a fresh produce shop will usually include a tile scheme on both the floor and walls. Floor tiles will often be encaustic or geometric tiles and are available in a variety of patterns. Wall tiles will vary depending on the age of the shop and whether it is a bespoke scheme

Figure 179: Specially commissioned murals were a feature of butcher and fishmonger shops

Fig: 179

or has been specially commissioned. Shop owners could buy picture panels from the large tile manufacturers such as Maw & Co, Minton Hollins, Pilkington and Minton. Their catalogues provided a choice of pictorial panels, border tiles and plain tiles so that a suitable scheme could be devised.

Where funds permitted, shop owners could commission their own mural which was individual to their shop. James Duncan Ltd of Glasgow specialised in providing shop owners with these murals which were then displayed around the walls of the shop. Many of these tile schemes depicted idyllic rural scenes of farm animals or of sailing boats and mermaids for fishmongers but they were often related to the local area. For example, a former Co-operative butcher in Camelon, Falkirk depicts the nearby Forth and Clyde Canal and a former butcher in Gourock has images of Clyde steamers. Likewise, the butcher at 165 High Street, Linlithgow has panels showing the Avon Viaduct and Linlithgow Palace as well as more generic images of cows and sheep more related to the business.[237] Others proved to be of personal importance. In Canongate, Edinburgh, the former Croan's fish shop has an image of a fishing boat depicted on tiles of the curved wall inside the shop. This boat, the 'Mary Croan' was part of the Newhaven fishing fleet.

Butchers and fishmongers made use of marble to display goods and to keep them cold. Marble slabs were fixed into the windows and also to counters. Terrazzo slabs were also popular in the 1930s as their smooth surfaces were easy to clean.

Some fresh produce shops may also retain a small timber and glass office or booth to the rear of the shop which were used by a cashier. The sales staff would weigh the goods for the customer and it would then be paid for at the booth to prevent the staff from having to handle money and foodstuffs together. It is rare to find such an arrangement in a shop today.

Drapers, shoe shops and department stores

Often the most affluent retailers were the drapers and so they installed superior fittings to reflect their customer base. Special shelving to accommodate the clothes and materials were required and tweed merchants, for example, will have shelving designed to fit the exact size of the bales of tweed cloth. Similarly, shoe shops required shelving designed specially to suit the length of shoe boxes. Long timber counters were used in the shop, needed for cutting and displaying the lengths of cloth and fabric.

Fig: 180

Department stores in particular may be very well appointed, particularly regarding stairways, lifts, open atria, and themed tearooms. They may also be equipped with compressed air tubes for the delivery of cash to a central cashier's office.

Surviving interiors

Where a business has had a long association with a shop there may be a good survival of interior fittings, partly because the shop is still serving its original purpose. However, where a shop has changed hands regularly, successions of new occupiers may have been reluctant to adapt their retail requirements to a historic layout. However, there have been cases where fittings for one purpose have proved well suited to another retail or commercial use.

Where a building is listed the interior and exterior is protected. If any alterations are planned the need for appropriate consents must therefore be established prior to undertaking any work. The local authority will determine whether the special interest of the building will be so affected as to require listed building consent.

Figure 180: Henderson Street, Bridge of Allan: this butcher's shop retains its timber cash booth but these are rarely in practical use

Figure 181: Interior fittings for the Hose and Glove Department, J & R Allan Ltd, Edinburgh by shopfitters E Pollard & Co Ltd © RCAHMS (Dunn and Findlay Collection). Licensor www.rcahms.gov.uk

Fig: 181

Section 2:
Conserving Scotland's Shops

Survey of Extant Historic Shops in Scotland

The High Street can be seen as a palimpsest of social change undergoing transformations from year to year and day to day. In this process much evidence of bygone enterprise is obliterated, yet by scratching beneath the surface of today's array of shops and stores we can uncover substantial fragments of the past. Morrison, 2004, p1

The contribution made by historic retail buildings

In Scotland, the great variety of townscapes derived from their location, local architecture and craft traditions means that no two towns are the same. The character of a place is a combination of features and qualities which make a building or group of buildings of significance. Closely associated with the use of local materials and traditional construction techniques, these features contribute to a region's distinctiveness. Character is of importance to the people who live there because it gives a feeling of familiarity and recognition and therefore a sense of belonging and identity. It helps to encourage local pride and may bring additional benefits such as tourism.

Within these townscapes, retail buildings make a significant contribution both to the economy and to the visual appearance and aesthetic quality of a place. They contribute to the character of a place but also form part of the social and cultural fabric of a town reflecting the people that live and work there. Retaining and conserving traditional shopfronts is undoubtedly a sustainable approach. Many traditional shops can be repaired and their existing fabric carefully restored at less cost that the wholesale replacement that is often undertaken. The removal of historic cast iron and timber shopfronts is unnecessary and unsustainable. Similarly, the systematic stripping out of traditional interiors is inappropriate as many of these high-quality fittings can be used for modern retail use.

However, in some ways shops are so numerous in our towns and cities and their use so transient that historically there has been little regard paid to their conservation and protection. A lack of understanding of the significance of some types of shops, particularly those of more recent architectural periods, has contributed to their removal. As a result, in some locations the survival of traditional shops is poor, characterised by the replacement of traditional designs with bland, modern materials. In recent years, the steady expansion of national chain stores and supermarkets together with the progressive use of materials like aluminium, plastic fascias and PVCu means that our retail centres have, to some extent become homogenised. Regular re-fronting of shops has taken place and in some locations little historic fabric survives. This has been particularly the case for Scotland's cities and larger towns although smaller towns have also fallen victim to this pattern. Such changes in retail buildings can seriously detract from the character of a place, concerns which have been raised in newspaper articles and were highlighted notably in the *Clone Town Britain Report.*[1]

The Scottish Government acknowledges the importance of retail buildings and the contribution they make to the Scottish economy. SPP 8 Town Centres and Retailing[2] sets out the Governments aims to "*promote distinct, competitive places and encourage regeneration*" as well as improving the physical quality and sustainability of town centres. The launch of the Town Centres and High Streets Learning Network in 2009 confirms the need for professionals in the various fields to work together in order to improve town centres and make them work effectively.

Survey of extant historic shopfronts and regional identity

A survey of retail buildings in Scotland was undertaken between 2006 and 2009 covering the majority of Scotland's towns and cities. Funded by Technical Conservation Group, Historic Scotland, the aim of the project was to identify surviving examples of shopfronts which were good representatives of their period of construction. This was the first time that any comprehensive and Scotland-wide survey of retail buildings had been undertaken. Shops of all periods were examined including post-war shops to around 1960. This gave an opportunity to compare and contrast areas and to discern patterns of architectural development on a local and wider basis.

The survey involved visiting each town and undertaking a photographic survey of retail buildings, background research and discussions in each locality with planners, conservation officers and retailers. Given the

Figure 182: John G Irvine's shop, Lerwick © Shetland Museum and Archives (facing page)

extensive geographical area covered and the vast number of shops which exist, it is not possible for such a survey to be detailed, but instead it gives a broad overview of the extant historic shops, highlighting where more in-depth investigations may be appropriate. The information gathered from the survey has fed into this publication and informed the research findings.

Scotland has a diverse geography and geology with its Lowlands, Highlands and Islands and these have all influenced the types of retail architecture to be found. The architecture reflects both wider architectural fashions and also local circumstances such as the design preferences of local architects, the traditions of tradesmen and the type and quality of the retailers. All of these inter-related factors have left behind a complex legacy of local variation within a wider architectural context.

The survey of retail buildings has identified that there were distinct periods of retail expansion in many Scottish towns. Reflecting peaks of wider economic prosperity, large numbers of new shops were constructed and existing ones re-fronted in the latest architectural fashion. The notable periods of expansion are the 1880s and 1890s together with the early years of the twentieth century which were a time of improving prosperity. In contrast, periods of economic decline or uncertainty will often mean a halt to work and sometimes almost a fossilisation of what is there because of the lack of funds available to carry out any alterations. The exception to this theory is the 1930s, a period of economic depression, but one which also witnessed considerable re-fronting of shops, particularly in Glasgow.

The type of retailers present in a town also has a significant impact on the architecture. Some retailers prefer particular styles or materials and in a wider sense,

Figure 183: This 1935 shopfront for Martin's drycleaners at 310 Sauchiehall Street, Glasgow was typical of the bravery of design executed in the city in the 1930s © Glasgow City Archives and Special Collections, Mitchell Library

there have also been attempts over time to influence the types of retailers in particular locations. The occupiers of the earliest shopping booths were controlled by the burgh authorities who sought to influence the types of trades who could locate in particular parts of the burghs so that less desirable trades such as butchers and tanners were not in a central location. In more recent years, there have been deliberate attempts to influence town identity by encouraging particular types of retailers for example the creation of Scotland's Booktown, Wigtown in Dumfries where the town is dominated by bookshops and hosts its own book festival every year. Other towns have followed this example including Castle Douglas which is 'Food Town' and Kirkcudbright as 'Artist's Town'. The Argyle Arcade in Glasgow also trades very successfully within a specialist market with almost all of the shops there occupied by jewellers.

Overview of survey findings

Within most towns there will be at least some surviving traditional shopfronts. This may be a fascia with Victorian console brackets or it may be a more intact shop, complete with interior fittings. The pattern of survival is varied and uneven although certain localities have a greater number of surviving shops than others, and there may be distinct architectural periods evident, depending on the economic history of the town.

Examples from across Scotland are included in the gazetteer of shops in this volume. These are not in any way comprehensive but instead are good examples of their type which may be regarded as the cream of surviving shopfronts. However, the exclusion of other shops is not to suggest that they are of lesser value, all traditional shops contribute to the historic environment.

Scotland's largest cities of Edinburgh, Glasgow, Dundee and Aberdeen dominate the retail sector within their area. However, the occupation of premises by national chains together with a frequent turnover of occupiers means that the numbers of traditional shops which survive is poorer than smaller towns. There is, for example, little evidence of Glasgow's Art Deco heyday and sadly the vast majority of its striking Vitrolite shopfronts have been swept away. Edinburgh, however, does retain some interesting examples, particularly in its neighbourhood shopping districts away from the main centres of Princes Street and the Royal Mile. The focus for many years of conservation bodies within Edinburgh and its status as a World Heritage site means that many good examples of shopfronts have been conserved in the city and Edinburgh World Heritage and its predecessors have often been at the forefront of shopfront conservation. Aberdeen with its granite architecture is similar to Glasgow in the style

Fig: 183

of the shopfronts along Union Street, the main shopping thoroughfare. Here the vast caverns of the ground floor shops are now largely replaced by modern shopfronts. In Dundee, there has been considerable conservation work in the city, notably on reinstatement of cast iron shopfronts and work in Reform Street to rediscover the original vision for this planned street. Dundee also has a number of good examples of inter-war faience buildings.

Although the main shopping streets of these cities have tended to lose much of their earlier shop architecture, it is also fair to say that they often exhibit the best examples of modern retail architecture and so reflect recent and emerging styles and tastes.

In the hierarchy of population centres within Scotland, the next tier of centres including Paisley, Stirling, Inverness, Perth, Ayr, Dunfermline and Dumfries, these towns have a mixed survival of shopfronts. Often competing with larger centres and attempts to ensure their place in the retail hierarchy has meant that they have sacrificed historic fabric to keep up in the race for customers. Most have large indoor shopping centres which attract the important High Street chain stores leaving the traditional areas for independent and speciality shops. Perth is unusual within this category as having a significant number of surviving traditional shops. However, in the other towns, often in the lesser streets there are examples of traditional shopfronts.

It is in the smaller towns that there tends to be a good survival of traditional retail buildings. Towns such as Kelso, Forfar, Dunbar, Crieff, Castle Douglas, Girvan, St Andrews, Stonehaven, Tain and Thurso are examples where the towns have both good survival and often a variety from Victorian, Edwardian and the inter-war periods. These are generally the best places to see traditional shops and often interiors. However, some towns, like Kilmarnock and Fort William have seen significant redevelopment so the numbers of surviving examples may consequently be reduced.

For the very small towns and villages the picture is mixed and will depend on their economic fortunes both past and present. Some, like Comrie in Perthshire have many surviving examples as do some in the Borders such as Earlston and Duns. However, in some areas, the pressure for residential development has meant that shops have been converted to domestic use and these conversions have sometimes resulted in the total loss of the shopfronts.

The islands have different economic responses, being more isolated, and this is reflected in their architecture. The pattern of survival is therefore not necessarily the same as on mainland Scotland. The gable-end buildings found in Orkney and Shetland give a particular style of

retail building and their conservation is also important as part of their wider architectural styles. Rothesay also has an architectural heritage related to its former popularity as a seaside resort in the 1930s and it therefore retains many good examples from this period indicating the different types of influence which will be found.

Figure 184: Gable-end buildings with ground floor shops are part of the architecture of Lerwick

This section gives a flavour of the shops which exist in Scotland and highlights the considerable variety which is a feature of Scottish towns and villages. Some of these features may, at first consideration, seem quite minor, but in the wider context of the townscape and of the history of the town these elements are important. Although the examples given here are ones where there are similarities of design between shops, it is often the sheer variety of ages of shopfronts and materials used which gives a place character and identity. These examples tend to come from small to medium-sized towns. The cities of Edinburgh and Glasgow do have particular local styles but these are spread over a larger area and the impact may therefore be more diluted than in a smaller place.

Although the survey has highlighted patterns and similar architecture across the country, there are also examples of individual identity where a local tradesman has made his mark. These are potentially significant within the wider context because of the sense of local identity which they can bring to a place. Towns are not all the same and that is partly because of the immense contribution made by traditional shopfronts.

It is evident from previous sections and from what follows that the state of the economy is a defining factor in the architecture of shops. It is sensitive to the affluence of retailers at any time and the wider economic situation has a direct bearing on what happens to shops, whether they remain stagnant and preserved in time or whether they are replaced in a thrust to modernise and renew. Retail buildings have never stood still and have always been subject to the vagaries of fashion and affluence. This is part of their history and is embedded in their elements.

Retailers are also driven by practicality and the need for the shop to do its job. This means that often it is not the architect or the shopfitter but the client, ie, the shopkeeper, who dictates what is required. This will be defined by his business, how it operates and how it may operate in the future.

Recognition needs to be given to the role of the independent shopkeeper. For many of these people, running a shop has been a way of life and there remain in Scotland, albeit in reducing numbers, family businesses which have operated for several generations. Many of these businesses are at the root of independent retailing and the fact that these firms have continued to operate

has also meant that traditional retail architecture has often survived. Where a shop has been purpose-built for a specific retail trade, unless there are dramatic changes in the business, the shop will often still meet those requirements and may therefore have required little alteration over the years.

Although many of these shops are listed and located in conservation areas, not all will have statutory protection. It is therefore crucial to appreciate the contribution which they make to the townscape so that historic fabric is not destroyed. A defining characteristic of the shops in the pages that follow is that certain architectural features may be prevalent in particular towns. This does not mean that shops that do not share these features elsewhere, or that shops without these elements may not have other character-defining aspects. Apart from Kingussie, all of these towns have conservation areas that cover at least part of the retail core.

Figure 185: A Glasgow shopkeeper of the 1790s © Culture and Sport Glasgow (Museums)

Fig: 185

SURVEY CASE STUDY 1: COMRIE, PERTH AND KINROSS LOCAL CHARACTERISTIC: LATE NINETEENTH CENTURY SHOPFRONTS WITH CONSOLE BRACKETS

The Perthshire village of Comrie is located on the edge of the Highlands and was relatively isolated until the opening of the Crieff to Comrie railway in 1893. This allowed what had been a small weaving village to expand rapidly. Although the New Statistical Account of 1838 notes that there are three butchers, three bakers and more than twelve grocers, by the end of the century shop numbers would have doubled. This level was then probably maintained with little alteration to the shops in the town. However, the area has enjoyed relative prosperity in recent years as a commuter and retirement location which has also seen the village expand with new housing developments.

Today, Comrie has an unusually high number of retail premises at around thirty all located on the main street through the village. The shops almost all date from the 1890s to the turn of the twentieth century. There is also a rare surviving example of a Charles Rennie Mackintosh building with ground floor shop and surviving interior dating to 1905. This shop is externally quite plain but others in the village are decorative, using cast iron columns and tiled stallrisers, materials typical of the period.

The most notable feature of the townscape is the extensive use of console brackets and, in particular so-called 'Bookend' consoles. These were fashionable in the late nineteenth century when fascias became deeper and angled to accommodate integral roller blinds. They are larger than normal console brackets and often have a decorated outer face or other embellishment. They pay little regard to their classical roots and instead incorporate decorative flower patterns or use human figures or animals in their design.

There are four shops with bookend console brackets intact and other shops in the town have different styles of console bracket in keeping with their Victorian architecture. Although they all date from this period, there therefore is considerable variety in the designs and styles of these shopfronts.

Significance and rarity: Bookend consoles are no longer common and therefore surviving examples are of significance. They are an attractive architectural detail which reflects the age of retail expansion in the village

Fig: 186

and are therefore closely connected with the architectural history and development of Comrie. The number of shops here which retain their original late Victorian features is of significance and this village is therefore of importance.

The majority of the shops are listed and Comrie is a conservation area offering important protection to these shopfronts.

Figure 186: Shop in Comrie with bookend consoles

Figure 187: The deep profile of bookend console brackets makes them a prominent feature

Figure 188: Bookend consoles are very decorative

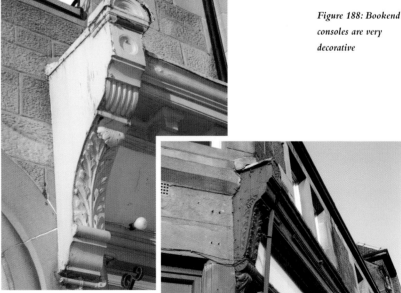

Fig: 187

Fig: 188

SURVEY CASE STUDY 2: KELSO, SCOTTISH BORDERS
LOCAL CHARACTERISTIC: PILASTERED SHOPFRONTS

Scotland's Border towns have a strong sense of identity and history connected with their Common Riding, rugby and historic buildings. Kelso is an ancient town with a medieval abbey and has the largest town square in Scotland, an impressive centre-piece surrounded by Georgian and Victorian town houses. The town suffered serious fires in 1645 and 1742 which destroyed substantial parts of the centre so most buildings date from the mid eighteenth century onwards; the former Tolbooth, in the Market Square was rebuilt in 1816. The railway came to Kelso around 1850 and this, like Comrie, offered opportunity for expansion. Railways brought goods, materials and also visitors.

The most notable retail architecture in Kelso is the large number of pilastered shops, possibly mid nineteenth century reflecting the railway expansion, but some are later nineteenth century. Pilasters were used from the late eighteenth century but became particularly fashionable for 'polite' shopfronts from the 1820s. From the 1850s onwards they were extensively used in shopfront design and although early examples are quite plain in design, they became much more elaborate later in the nineteenth century in keeping with Victorian favour for decoration and embellishment.

Kelso probably has the greatest concentration of pilastered shopfronts in Scotland with approximately twenty-five shops in the town centre. There are rows of shops with neatly designed and matching shopfronts and it is these long runs of pilasters which offer the streetscape its distinctiveness. These give a sense of just how fashionable pilasters were and their enduring appeal since their first construction.

The materials used include timber, stone or cast iron and some of the cast iron elements are of particular interest because they were made locally. Like many other Scottish towns, Kelso had its own foundry and surviving examples in Bridge Street have 'Kelso Foundry' stamped on the plinth.[3]

The rows of shops in Bridge Street are of particular interest. A bridge at Kelso was first built in 1754 although the existing bridge dates to 1800 following floods in 1797. In the late nineteenth century the entrance to the town from the bridge, past the abbey and through Bridge Street to the Market Square was improved. A curved entrance at the Abbey end was designed to create a grand entrance to the town. On one side of the street, numbers 21-31, the pilasters are of cast iron with a timber balustrade above but on the other at number 46 they are stone. However, the architectural detail matches on both sides of the street, in spite of being executed in different materials. These shops date to 1872 and 1873. This mirror arrangement but executed in different materials is particularly unusual. The Statutory List for numbers 21-25 states that they are listed at Category B *"for their remarkable cast-iron shopfronts"*.[4] Number 46 is listed Category C(S).

Retail architecture has therefore been part of a wider scheme to improve Kelso and to present its entrance in a grand way. This recognises the importance of shopfronts and how their architecture is of significance when considering the wider townscape.

Significance and rarity

Pilastered shopfronts are found throughout Scotland and there is therefore nothing unique in Kelso having shops with this detail. However, it is the large numbers surviving together with the way they are used which enhances the townscape here. They date to a time of economic expansion and therefore reflect the fortunes of the town. Bridge Street is particularly notable because the shops here have been designed to complement each other as part of a larger scheme to enhance the entrance to the town. However, many of the others are simple pilastered shops which offer regularity and formality to the townscape.

Kelso town centre is a conservation area and many of the shops are listed and therefore offered statutory protection.

Figure 189: Blair Jeweller's shop, The Square, Kelso with its plain, mid nineteenth century pilasters

Fig: 189

Fig: 190

Fig: 191

Figure 190: Bridge Street, Kelso, a grand entrance to the town with rows of pilastered shopfronts in stone and cast iron

Figure 191: Pilasters, Bridge Street, Kelso

SURVEY CASE STUDY 3: ROTHESAY, ISLE OF BUTE, ARGYLL AND BUTE
LOCAL CHARACTERISTIC: MOSAIC TILED STALLRISERS

Rothesay is the main town on the Isle of Bute, located off the Ayrshire coast. The town became a thriving tourist attraction for Victorian day trippers who travelled there on the Clyde steamers. It remained a popular seaside resort until the 1950s although, like many similar British resorts, subsequently declined with the vogue for foreign travel. It has many buildings associated with its former popularity as a seaside resort together with a rich heritage of ornamental ironwork including lamp standards, bandstands and other features, many of which were produced at Macfarlane's Saracen Foundry. Walter MacFarlane had a strong connection with the island.

The striking feature of some of the shops in the town is the use of mosaic on the stallrisers which also match the entrance lobby. Use of tiles for shopfronts and their interiors has been popular since the end of the nineteenth century. They are clean and easy to wipe down and so were widely used. They seem to have been particularly popular in seaside locations where perhaps they were regarded as more robust against the sea air than other materials such as timber.

Mosaic comprises a pattern of small tiles (tesserae) which can be combined to create elaborate decorative patterns. During the late nineteenth century, tile manufacturers attempted to create imitation mosaic because it was such a time-consuming and costly material to lay. Maw & Co had a patent for their imitation called 'patent mosaic' which they developed in the 1860s. Rival company, Craven Dunnill also produced a similar product. These imitation mosaic tiles still had the decorative advantages of mosaic but were cheaper to lay.[5]

In Rothesay, around six shops have mosaic tiled stallrisers generally with matching lobby entrance floors. The designs with Art Nouveau influences using flowers and stylised plant forms suggest an Edwardian date.

Significance and rarity

The use of these mosaic stallrisers matching the lobby floor has only been found in Rothesay during a survey of Scotland. It may be, however, that they existed elsewhere but have not survived. It is also possible that they were more extensively used in Rothesay but have been either covered over or replaced with a different material. Their use over a number of shops suggests that they were the work of a local tile contractor who favoured this style and may also relate to a period of modernisation and upgrading in connection with improved economic circumstances in the town.

In terms of condition, some have been painted over and others have lost tiles and are therefore in poor condition. A number of the shops are not listed and are potentially vulnerable but would benefit from conservation work to restore them to their original appearance.

Figure 192: 39 Victoria Street, Rothesay has a mosaic floor in an Art Nouveau style with matching stallrisers

Fig: 192

Figure 193: This pair of shops in Tower Street have matching stallrisers and lobby floors. The stallrisers were painted over but have recently been restored

Fig:193

Figure 194: Mosaic is hard-wearing but cracks may appear through building settlement

Fig: 194

SURVEY CASE STUDY 4: DUNBAR, EAST LOTHIAN LOCAL CHARACTERISTIC: TILED SHOPFRONTS

The historic East Lothian town of Dunbar is a Royal Burgh. Adjacent to the sea it has an impressive natural harbour although the wide High Street with around 100 shops running north to south is protected from the coast. The prominent Tolbooth in the centre of the High Street has been recently renovated as part of the Heritage Lottery Fund Townscape Heritage Initiative, a project which included wider regeneration and conservation projects including a shopfront enhancement scheme. The town is notable as the birth place of nineteenth century environmentalist, John Muir and a museum in the town celebrates his life.

Figure 195: Numerous shops in Dunbar have brick-shaped ceramic tiles, mostly used on the stallriser. Many are an ox-blood colour

Figure 196: Tiled panel depicting cows in lobby entrance, West Port partially hidden by paint

Like the seaside town of Rothesay, the main feature of the shopfronts here is the use of tiles particularly on the shop stallrisers. The tiles in Dunbar are largely a brick-shape with a glazed finish of a burgundy or ox-blood colour although other colours, such as green also exist. Although spread throughout the town, there is a concentration of tiled shop frontages in West Port. One of the shops here has a small lobby mural of cows (recently been painted over) which was presumably once a butcher's shop.

Some of the tiled shops are individual whilst others are pairs or rows of shops. The row of shops at 27-35 High Street dates to the turn of the twentieth century and have a slightly projecting ground floor. These shops have green tiled stallrisers and attractive encaustic tiled entrances. All these shops were designed to match, both in terms of the detail such as the balustrade, the doors and the tiled entrance floors as well as the stallrisers. This combination of matching features still allows the shops to have their own identity, but links them together making for a more powerful townscape element.

Significance and rarity

Although tiled shopfronts are not rare, the numbers of good examples which do survive is not extensive. Like, Rothesay, it may be that this has been the work of a local tiler who has used the same style of tiles on several shopfronts. Although these may be regarded as a small feature, their impact is greater because so many of the shops have these creating a link through the town.

Over time, tiles, particularly on stallrisers, can become chipped and damaged. Some owners may have resorted to painting over them to improve their appearance although this can be carefully removed with appropriate materials and the tiles restored.[6]

A number of these buildings are listed and Dunbar is designated as a conservation area.

Fig: 195

Fig: 196

Figure 197: Tiled stallrisers are sometimes painted over

Fig: 197

SURVEY CASE STUDY 5: ST ANDREWS, FIFE
LOCAL CHARACTERISTIC: CAST IRON SHOPFRONTS

Figure 198: Butler &
Company, Church
Street, St Andrews
is typical of the
shopfronts in the town
with a pair of heavy
columns

St Andrews is East Fife's main town and a popular holiday resort because of its recognition as the home of golf, its historic buildings and beach. The town was the seat of a medieval cathedral situated on the sea front which is now ruined. It also has numerous buildings connected with its status as a university town. St Andrews serves the wider rural area and has a large number of shops spread over two main streets with linking streets based on a grid pattern. It has many specialist shops reflecting the tourist and university trade.

The notable feature of St Andrews is the significant number of cast iron shopfronts totalling around twenty-eight. This does not include those known to have existed and now removed which totals a further eight shops.[7] Scotland was famous for its iron founding and was the home to many of the most important names in the industry including Walter MacFarlane's Saracen Foundry, The Sun Foundry and the Lion Foundry. In addition to these substantial firms, there was a small, local foundry in St Andrews itself.

The town had several prominent architects who had an interest in shop architecture and took advantage of the availability of the cast-iron features available. The designs of local architects, John Milne (1823-1904), David Henry (1835-1914) and James Gillespie (1854-1914) are evident throughout St Andrews town centre.[8] They date largely to the 1880s and 1890s when the town's retail sector was expanding rapidly and there was considerable demand for re-fronting of shops in the latest style.

There is a great variety of shopfront styles and while some are extremely decorative with ornate Corinthian columns others are quite plain and functional in design. Some designs are repeated over different shops, as the architects favoured certain column styles for their shops. There are also others which mimic the cast iron shopfronts but which are executed in polished granite giving an interesting variation in the streetscape.

In order to advertise and promote their business, the iron foundries generally left a stamp with their name visible on the cast iron. However, there are few discernible marks on the shops in St Andrews, the exception being 131 South Street which has the foundry mark of George Smith of The Sun Foundry. Others, such as 9 Church Street have also been attributed to George Smith from the design of the columns.[9] However, a work book for architect David Henry notes the payment of £12.17.6d to '*Macfarlane for Iron Columns*' for a now lost shopfront at 59 Market Street and this is presumably a reference to Macfarlane's Saracen foundry.[10]

Significance and rarity

Cast iron shopfronts are found throughout Scotland and examples created by foundries large and small exist in High Streets everywhere but generally only occasional examples survive. What is special about the shops in St Andrews is that the town has probably the greatest concentration of cast iron shops in Scotland, and an additional detail of interest is that they were designed by architects local to the town. There is therefore a historical link with the iron industry and its contribution to shop architecture and also at a local level to the architects who designed many of the late nineteenth century buildings in St Andrews.

A significant number of these shops are listed and therefore have the benefit of statutory protection.

Fig: 198

Figure 199: Although some shops have plain columns many are decorative, similar themes being found in shops throughout the town

Fig: 199

Figure 200: Decorative cast iron columns, Church Street

Fig: 200

SURVEY CASE STUDY 6: KINGUSSIE, HIGHLAND
LOCAL CHARACTERISTIC: CURVED GLASS ENTRANCES

The Highland village of Kingussie was a planned village of the Duke of Gordon dating to 1792. The railway was brought to the town in 1863 and it was subsequently made a Police Burgh in 1866. The village, set in a beautiful natural landscape, is a tourist destination in summer for walkers and families and in the winter for skiers. The High Street is the main route through the village although a by-pass completed in 1980 takes the non-local traffic along the A9 trunk route.

What is particular about the shops here is the large number which have curved glass entrances. Of around thirty shops in the centre, eight have curved glass entrances. This type of glass became fashionable and affordable in the Edwardian period and remained popular into the 1930s as a way to create an elegant and inviting shop entrance.

The style of shops in Kingussie varies with some single-fronted and others double-fronted. Unusually, they generally lack any tiled entrance floors, most having plain concrete. One of the particularly interesting examples is 18-20 High Street which has an unusual showcase arrangement and a slightly awkward entrance to number 18. This shop also retains its coloured glass in the small-paned clerestory although the glass at number 20 is plain.

Photographic evidence suggests that these shopfronts did not exist at the turn of the century although some may have existed before the outbreak of World War I and some certainly date to the inter-war period, such as 18-20 High Street.[11] The similarity in many of the designs suggest the influence of local tradesmen and architects who favoured this design.

Significance and rarity

It is common to see curved glass in both Edwardian and inter-war shopfronts and a particularly good example of its use is at 12-16 Market Street, Stonehaven. It may also be used in rows of shops forming an elegant set of entrances. However, it is rare to find its use so extensive and consistent across a retail centre in such a variety of shops. In this way Kingussie is special in the shopfronts that exist there.

Very few of the shopfronts here are listed and there is therefore a potential vulnerability for these shops. Curved glass is also vulnerable to breakage because it may be harder to incorporate protective measures such as a shop gate due to the configuration of the shopfront. It is also potentially expensive to replace a large sheet of curved glass.

Figure 201: The curved central entrance with recessed door is typical of many of the shops in Kingussie

Fig: 201

Figure 202: Curved glass gives shops an elegant entrance

Figure 203: This larger shop has a much deeper entrance but retains the curved glass

Figure 204: This unusual pair of shopfronts incorporates a showcase with curved glass and utilises coloured glass in the clerestory

Fig: 202

Fig: 203

Fig:204

CASE STUDY 7: DUNFERMLINE, FIFE
LOCAL CHARACTERISTIC: TWO-STOREY SHOPFRONTS

The Fife town of Dunfermline is the home to the great Dunfermline Abbey and its historical connections with Scotland's monarchy. It is a substantial town which is a main retail, business and leisure centre for the surrounding area. The town centre has a pedestrianised High Street with several other shopping streets radiating from this. A modern shopping centre is located to the rear of the High Street. Like other towns of a similar size in Scotland such as Dumfries and Stirling, Dunfermline has lost many of its historic shopfronts with the dominance of national retailers and frequent turnover of occupiers.

Nonetheless, the town retains a number of two-storey shopfronts which are of particular interest. Two storey shopfronts became fashionable from the mid nineteenth century. This design was made possible through the availability of plate glass and cast iron which were combined to create entire façades for the first time. These allowed transparency into the building increasing natural light to the upper floor and offering improved display opportunities. Reputedly, the attractive window displays were used as a way of attracting the attention of people who were passing on the upper decks of trams. Two-storey shops remained fashionable into the twentieth century, largely for drapers and clothiers who had larger premises and sought improved façade design for their premises. Examples are usually found in city centres and larger towns like Dunfermline.

In Dunfermline, several shops have arched upper floors using cast iron which date to the turn of the twentieth century. Like many other fashions, they indicate a period of prosperity in retailing and also perhaps the preferences of particular local architects. The property at 25 High Street is a single shop with cast iron arcading to the upper floor. Constructed in 1901 within an earlier building, there are also later alterations to the ground floor shop dating to 1921.[12] The pair of shops at 16-18 Douglas Street have very similar fascias with dentilled cornice which incorporates

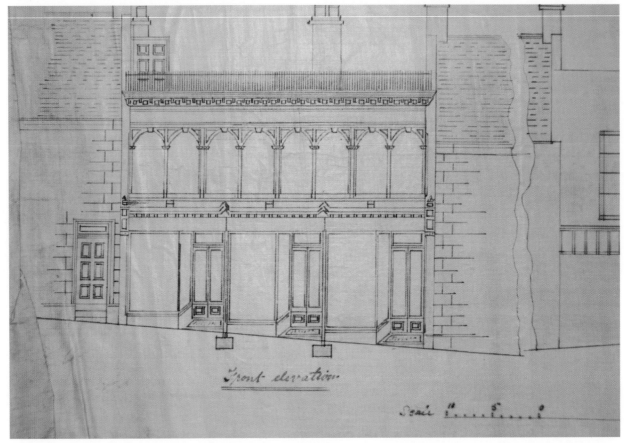

Figure 205: Dean of Guild Court drawing for 16-18 Douglas Street, Dunfermline, 1901
Image courtesy of Fife Council Archives

Fig: 205

small pediments. The upper arcaded floor of cast iron is also of a similar design and dates to 1901 with late ground floor alterations.[13] The double shopfront at 49 Queen Anne Street is slightly earlier, dating to 1897 and created by Dunfermline architect Thomas Hyslop Ure (1863-1913). Designed with a single ground floor shop and first floor saloon, it was converted in 1908 to create two ground floor shops although it later reverted to a single shop and remains that today.

Significance and rarity

Two-storey shops were once extremely fashionable but fell out of favour in the post-war period. Where examples still remain the second floors are rarely used for display purposes. Not many examples survive and the concentration of these in Dunfermline is therefore of interest. Unfortunately there is some loss of historic detail on their ground floors with the upper floors remaining largely intact.

Figure 206: Dean of Guild Court drawing for 49 Queen Street reproduced courtesy of Fife Council Archives

Figure 207: The arched cast iron upper floor of 25 High Street, Dunfermline

Figure 208: 49 Queen Anne Street retains small panes of coloured glass in the clerestory of the upper windows

Fig: 206

Fig: 207

Fig: 208

The Conservation of Shops

By studying the building itself, together with old drawings, photographs and such remnants as can be found by searching the ground for rubbish, the design can usually be recovered. Earl, 1997, p 67, on replacement of architectural features

Legislative framework

In order to conserve shopfronts it is vital to understand their architecture, their history and their materials, within the context of the framework of legislation that aims to protect historic buildings of all types. This section considers how conservation might be achieved and includes case studies of good conservation practice.

Historic buildings require planning permission for certain types of alteration as any other, but they may be offered additional protection if they are listed or are located in a conservation area. In Scotland, the primary legislation is the Planning (Listed Buildings and Conservation Areas) (Scotland) Act 1997. Presently in Scotland, there are over 47,000 buildings listed by the Scottish Ministers and 631 Conservation Areas designated by local planning authorities. Local authorities determine the need for consent and decide applications for changes to them.

Under Section 1 of the 1997 Act, the Scottish Ministers have responsibility for compiling or approving lists of buildings of special architectural or historic interest and this is undertaken by Historic Scotland which is an executive agency of the Scottish Government. The criteria for listing are related to several factors including the age and rarity of the building, its features of architectural interest and any close historical association, such as with a particular architect. These buildings are afforded statutory protection making it an offence to alter them without permission.[14]

The buildings are categorised according to their importance. There are three categories of listed building in Scotland: Category A, buildings of national importance; Category B, buildings of regional importance; and Category C (S), buildings of local importance. This category replaces the former non-statutory C. Historic Scotland provides additional guidance on the care of the historic environment through the Memorandum of Guidance which is currently being replaced by Good Practice Guidance.

Under Section 61 of the 1997 Act, planning authorities must determine areas of "special architectural or historic interest, the character or appearance of which it is desirable to preserve or enhance" known as conservation areas. Designation as a conservation area means that the local planning authority and the Scottish Ministers have a statutory duty to protect the character of the area and to pay particular attention to planning proposals.

There are various types of government guidance to supplement the planning legislation and ensure a consistent approach by the appropriate authorities. These include Circulars, Scottish Planning Policies (SPP) and Planning Advice Notes (PAN). National Planning Policy Guidelines (NPPG) are now being replaced by Scottish Planning Policy documents. These will run alongside existing NPPGs until all are replaced. *SPP1: The Planning System* replaces NPPG 1 and gives an overview of the planning system, and now all SPP are proposed to be rolled into a single draft Scottish Planning Policy. Other relevant documents include *NPPG 8: Town Centres and Retailing* and *SPP23: Planning and the Historic Environment*. Planning Advice Notes cover particular issues in planning and give advice on good practice. They cover such aspects as small towns, retailing or telecommunications.

Local planning authorities may also produce design guidance for shopfronts and for advertising which explain policies and offer additional advice specific to their area.

There are therefore several protection mechanisms in place which offer protection for historic retail buildings and where a building is listed, any alterations to it, including to a shop and its interior, will require listed building consent. However, their protection may prove challenging because although a shop may be of individual merit, the surrounding parent building may not be of sufficient architectural quality to take it above the level for listing.

Conservation philosophy

In terms of conservation philosophy, the conservation of shops should follow the principles which apply to all historic buildings. The principles for conservation are set out in Historic Scotland's Scottish Historic Environment Policy. This incorporates aspects of *The Stirling Charter: Conserving Scotland's Built Heritage* published in 2000. The six articles reflect issues such as recording of buildings, education, repairs and statutory provisions.

Figure 209: Maggie Gullane's sweet shop, North Berwick, 1930 © East Lothian Museums Service. Licensor www.scran.ac.uk. (facing page)

The general philosophical approach to be adopted should follow the ethics set out in various International Charters including the Burra Charter and Venice Charter:

- Minimal intervention;
- Minimal loss of fabric;
- Reversibility;
- Legibility;
- Sustainability.

A correct philosophical approach to repairs can only come from a thorough understanding of the building and the nature and cause of any defects. Repairs must be honest and not disguised or artificially aged in any way. At the same time they should be sympathetic in appearance to the building. Buildings inevitably suffer damage and loss of architectural detail over their lives. Whether these features should be reinstated is a difficult philosophical issue as a replaced item can never be the same as the original as Fawcett explains:

"..An original element, even if damaged, is of infinitely greater value than a replica, however carefully copied from the original that replica might be. Nevertheless, if the life of a building can be appreciably lengthened by strengthening, or even replacement, of structurally defective fabric, due consideration must be given to this possibility."[15]

Earl agrees with this commenting:

"Where the principal interest of a building resides in its architectural design, it can rarely be wrong to replace missing elements, provided it can be done with absolute certainty and without loss of authentic fabric."[16]

The issue of replacement of lost features is of particular significance in relation to shopfronts because so often there are features which have been lost or deliberately removed such as console brackets, tiles and cast iron brattishing. Where architectural detailing has been lost it is important to approach this sensitively so that the integrity of the shopfront is maintained. As Earl states, *"where reinstatement is the right course, there must be careful attention to every detail of architectural and craft vocabulary, however, small"*.[17]

In many cases, having an established maintenance regime can help to prevent unnecessary repairs. Earl states that *"with proper maintenance the life of most kinds of buildings can be extended almost indefinitely"*.[18] At a time when there is a greater awareness of the importance of conserving buildings from the point of view of a sustainable approach, proper maintenance is essential to ensure the future of a building.

It also needs to be remembered that shops are not museum objects, they are places of work which must meet the needs of the retailer or they will become obsolete. However, even where there is a traditional shopfront or historic interior fittings, with a creative approach historic fabric can usually be accommodated and will often be an asset to a business. It is therefore crucial to respect the surviving features, to understand them and to establish if they can be enhanced and conserved.

Grant-aided schemes

In certain districts there may be grants available for the conservation and enhancement of shopfronts. These may be locally specific schemes such as the Perth Central Area Façade Enhancement Scheme or may be related to a centrally funded conservation-led regeneration scheme. Townscape Heritage Initiatives funded by the Heritage Lottery Fund and Conservation Area Regeneration Schemes supported by Historic Scotland are two types of scheme which may include shops as eligible for funding. Grants will usually have a maximum amount payable, to ensure value for money, as well as exemplary standards in the work which can be funded.

These schemes not only conserve shopfronts but also contribute to economic regeneration in an area by bringing buildings back into use and by encouraging investment and improvement.

Investigating traditional shopfronts

Before undertaking any works it is clearly necessary to carry out a proper survey of a building to establish its architecture, materials and any periods of alteration. This will help to identify its construction, any defects and the condition of the building as well as its intrinsic character and historical development. While a physical investigation will provide information on the building fabric, if any alterations are to be carried out it is essential that the history of the building is fully understood and background investigations may therefore be required. Shops may appear to be outwardly simple in structure, but there may be many hidden layers of influence and alteration over a long period of time. This may include earlier signage, hidden columns and pillars and interiors masked by later fittings. An investigation into the history can help to prevent any unexpected details coming to light during the works.

There are numerous sources of information available for research into historic shops. The usefulness of these will depend on the location of the shop, its retail history and its age. These sources will be held in a variety of locations such as local archives, museums, libraries and private collections. Large retail organisations such as Boots and the Co-operative Society hold substantial records relating specifically to their firms and often have their own dedicated library of archives. Some firms may have deposited their records with a local museum, library or a national archive. With the increasing digitisation of records, many sources are now easily accessible through the Internet.

The various sources of information are:

Dean of Guild Court plans and other architects plans: The Dean of Guild Court has a long history within Scottish burgh society. Their role arose out of dealing with neighbourhood disputes and plans were submitted to the Court for consideration where alterations were to be undertaken or a new building to be developed. These generally include elevation and plan drawings and although early examples may be less detailed, from the late nineteenth century many of them are beautifully drawn and carry specifications of materials. These therefore help to identify the age of the shop, its architect and its original design. They are an invaluable record although their survival is patchy with only certain burghs of Scotland still possessing them in their local authority archives.[19] Other architects plans are held in national collections such as the Royal Commission on Ancient and Historical Monuments of Scotland (RCAHMS).

Maps: These can be useful to complement other sources helping to identify when buildings were erected. GOAD plans and fire plans are specific on floor structures and uses within buildings and their occupiers so may be particularly useful for retail research.[20]

Images: One of the most useful sources of information for retail buildings is photographs. There are numerous collections dating from the mid nineteenth century which feature town centres and therefore, by default, shops. Postcard collections such as Valentines will often have general street views but other photographic collections may be specifically focused on the architecture, such as the Magnus Jackson Collection held in Perth Museum and Art Gallery or photographs in the Mitchell Library Collections, Glasgow. The RCAHMS also hold a substantial collection of architectural photographs, prints and drawings. Other public and private art collections may also contain images of street scenes and retail buildings which can help in understanding particularly earlier shops.

Newspapers, trade journals, catalogues and directories: Literature relating to newspapers, magazines and Post Office directories can be useful for adverts for businesses and for associated trades such as shopfitters. This type of information can supplement other details uncovered. Some adverts include images of shops, either drawings or photographs, which were used to assist customers to identify the premises. Some manufacturers such as iron foundries and tile firms produced their own catalogues to advertise their products. These can be used to identify particular elements such as a tile scheme or cast iron frontage and this may also help to date a shopfront.

Valuation Rolls: These are available from April 1855 and are annual returns which detail owners and occupiers of properties together with the rental value of the building.[21]

Business records: The majority of retail businesses will have held records relating to their activities. If they operated as a limited company they will have been registered and their records may be available from Companies House or in the National Archives of Scotland. These can help provide invaluable information about the proprietors of a business, their purpose and where and how they operated.

Promotional and advertising literature: Shop owners sought to advertise their business with promotional leaflets, trade cards and postcards. Surviving examples of these can provide additional information about a retail building and its history. These are particularly useful where they include images of shopfronts.

Researching the history of a shop can offer a fascinating insight into the architect who designed the building, the materials used and the businesses that operated there. This information is invaluable in any conservation project. It is also particularly useful for helping to date shopfronts which can be challenging. For some shops, the style and date may be immediately obvious, such as an Art Deco inspired Vitrolite shopfront which clearly dates to the 1930s. A Victorian shopfront may also be obvious although Edwardian shops may use similar designs and those at the end of the nineteenth century and early twentieth century are often very similar in style. It can therefore be difficult to fit shops into an exact style, particularly where there have been changes and alterations; a shop may have a Victorian frame of pilasters and a cornice but the sashes and stallrisers may be of a later period. This is where thorough investigations are required to ensure that all of the periods of development are fully understood.

CASE STUDIES IN THE CONSERVATION OF HISTORIC SHOPS

The nature of retail buildings with their transient occupation and need to meet retailers specific requirements means that conservation is not always viewed as a priority. Instead, there is often a 'quick-fix' approach taken and a desire for shops to be of a modern appearance in order to satisfy retail needs. Where a shop is part of a wider chain of shops, either regionally or nationally, there is focus on the branding of the premises and in some cases this may over-ride the needs of the building. The use of standard fascias, illumination and corporate colour schemes can detract from historic townscapes where they are undertaken without sensitivity to the buildings and their setting.

However, there are cases where a considered approach has been taken to a shopfront and the result is often extremely successful and reflects the care given to the property. These projects are exemplars thanks to close attention to detail, borne from a sound understanding of the property itself. They generally involve conservation professionals, particularly where they are part of a grant-aided scheme although it is often the shop owner who initiates an interest in conserving the premises and may undertake the necessary background research.

This small sample of case studies demonstrates good practice and ways improvements to traditional shopfronts can be successfully achieved.

Figure 210: The mosaic floor of a former butcher's shop is ideal for its current use selling flowers

Figure 211: 107 South Street, St Andrews, 1928 by Frank Pride

Fig: 211

CONSERVATION CASE STUDY 1: CONSERVATION OF A HISTORICALLY SIGNIFICANT SHOPFRONT IN A CATEGORY A LISTED BUILDING

Background

The bow-fronted shop at 515 Lawnmarket, Edinburgh is in the ground floor of Mylnes Court, Lawnmarket, Edinburgh. Dating to 1690, this Category A listed building incorporates earlier fabric. The shop is of considerable significance because it is the only surviving example of a Georgian shop type once prevalent in Edinburgh.

This single-fronted shop has an entrance door with fanlight on the left and a high bow-fronted window to the right, the bow being shallow and in a five and three arrangement totalling fifteen small panes. Slender pilasters either side of the door are connected by a narrow fascia, just sufficiently deep for a name to be inscribed. Below the window is a door which formerly led to the basement, now hidden by a display case. An interesting aspect of the shop is that although the bow window is five panes wide, the two left hand columns of panes are effectively limited in their use because of a large internal masonry pier. The bow front therefore raises the status of the shop but actually in practical terms the effectiveness of the bow is limited in its ability to permit natural light and display. This is particularly interesting in the development of shop architecture.[22]

Restoration project

The work required proved to be quite extensive and involved repairs and renewal of various architectural elements of the shop. Some modern interventions such as the entrance door and tiled steps required to be altered together with more fundamental repairs to the timberwork and stonework.

The owner was keen to improve the appearance of his shopfront because he felt that the condition of his shopfront was detrimental to his business. The potential of a grant from the Old Town Renewal Trust encouraged him to undertake improvements to his shop. Architect Ian Riddell was appointed for the project and carried out extensive background research using photographs held by the Royal Commission on Ancient and Historic Monuments of Scotland (RCAHMS). These helped to

Figure 212: Before the conservation work was undertaken the shopfront was in poor repair and had a number of modern alterations which detracted from its appearance © Ian Riddell

Figure 213: After restoration

Fig: 212

Fig: 213

identify missing elements although the shop owner had retained pieces of the shopfront that had been broken including a pilaster. Comparisons were also made with shops elsewhere in Edinburgh, particularly for the door, such as shops in Dundas Street.

The restoration work involved carefully identifying the timber that needed to be replaced and piecing in new work. There was also extensive replacement of stonework as this had deteriorated, partly because of the design of the shopfront which was allowing rainwater to accumulate on the lintel.

As a shop within a Category A listed building and one of a type no longer existing in Edinburgh, this shop is of national significance. Its location in the Royal Mile also means that its appearance is a potential tourist attraction in itself, an aspect recognised by the shopkeeper. The significance of the building and the availability of a grant from Edinburgh Old Town Renewal Trust resulted in a conservation-led approach with a philosophy of minimal intervention and replacement was only where necessary, with suitably matched materials. Investigative research was undertaken prior to work being started in order to establish the details of original features such as the door.

A recommendation made by the architect was that it would have been better to adopt a two stage approach to this type of conservation. The first stage should be for investigating the work required in a thorough manner

Figure 214: Some of the joinery was replaced including although as much original material as possible was retained

Fig:214

and to allow necessary archival and research investigations to be undertaken. The second stage should then be for supervision of the work itself. Dividing the work in this way allows for a full investigation to be undertaken making for a more realistic costing and programme in the end. With commercial properties such as a shop, the shopkeeper seeks minimal disruption to his business and being fully informed about the extent of the work is therefore of considerable importance in allowing him to accommodate the works.[23]

It is evident that an apparently small property like this is potentially extremely complex and requires a highly detailed investigation. The work required in undertaking such research should not be underestimated but is essential if the intervention works are to undertaken on a fully informed basis.

Figure 215: Stonework repairs were required including the partial replacement of the lintel above the basement door

Fig: 215

CONSERVATION CASE STUDY 2: HISTORIC PAINT SCHEMES

Figure 216: The gilding of the shop at 9 Church Street, St Andrews makes for a striking statement in the street

Figure 217: Example of paint analysis undertaken at William Street, Edinburgh © Edinburgh World Heritage

Fig: 217

Background

The use of paint colours for shops varied over time depending on what was available and what was fashionable. The Victorians, for example, enjoyed brightly painted and gilded shops or the use of marbling and graining techniques whereas inter-war shops tended to be painted in contrasting colours such as black and white. Some colours may also have been chosen by particular types of retailer; for example, black is often favoured by antique dealers and jewellers. The importance of certain colours for retail branding in the twentieth century is also recognised. However, the significant cost of elaborate paint techniques and the fact there are less people skilled in these crafts, means that these are rarely part of modern shopfront design.

In some locations or for certain buildings there may be a desire to recreate a scheme which existed in the past. The introduction of historic paint schemes in any property can be challenging and requires accurate analysis of the paint and a careful understanding of the history of the building. Often, when a feature is undisturbed it will retain all the successive layers of paint from its introduction to the building. Successive schemes can be read from paint samples under a microscope. Even so, for shopfronts, changes of occupiers or use over time and varying ages of shopfronts within a street or townscape can make it difficult to recommended particular paint colours. However, in some locations historic paint schemes have been successful and three examples follow.

St Andrews

As has been highlighted earlier in this section, St Andrews has a significant number of cast iron shopfronts. The St Andrews' Preservation Trust was founded in the 1930s to help conserve the towns important historic buildings. Recognising the significance of the cast iron shopfronts, the Trust undertook a survey of both extant and lost shopfronts and carried out background research into the architects who designed them.[24] In 2008 the Trust initiated a scheme to repaint some of the cast iron shopfronts in their original colours.

This involved undertaking paint analysis of the shopfronts to establish the original colours. The first to be investigated was 9 Church Street, Listed Category C(S) and designed by local architect James Gillespie in 1892.

This shop had originally been owned by a painter, glazier and decorator and when paint analysis was undertaken by conservator, William Kay it was discovered that the shop had once been beautifully gilded.[25]

The shop with its pair of Corinthian capped columns was repainted in a dark green with the detail on the columns highlighted using gold leaf. The end result is extremely striking and the shop owner, Elspeth Methven, has been delighted with the result. The Trust plans to assist further work on other shopfronts in the town if owners are willing to take part in the grant-funded scheme.

Fig: 216

William Street, Edinburgh

William Street in Edinburgh New Town was erected in 1820s and has ground floor shops accessed via platts. Numbers 33-41B incorporate a row of Listed Category B houses and shops dating to 1824-25 which were restored in 2006-07 with a grant from Edinburgh World Heritage Trust. The works directed by architect Richard Shorter included reinstatement of iron railings, external shutters, fanlights and doors, all informed by the original features and details surviving on some of the shopfronts. External hanging shop signs were included as part of the scheme to complement subtle fascia signage.[26]

Paint analysis was undertaken to establish the colours used in these early shops. Like the cast iron shops in St Andrews, the fact that this row of shops could be dated accurately was helpful to understanding the paint layers. Following the investigations, discussions took place with building owners and an authentic palette of colours for this street was agreed.

42–44 Market Street, Haddington

This seventeenth century tenement in the centre of Haddington incorporates medieval fabric and from later periods. Listed Category B, it was restored in 1997-98 with Simpson and Brown as the architects who designed four flats and three shops. The exterior of the building was lime harled and lime washed in ochre and the windows painted 'nursery green' using evidence from the existing paintwork.[27]

It was also decided to grain the doors of the shops in a traditional fashion. Graining was a fashionable way of altering the appearance of timber to appear like another, usually more expensive, type of wood. Like marbling it was regarded by John Ruskin as an 'architectural deceit' and fell out of fashion in the late nineteenth century.

Although there was not specific evidence for the use of a graining paint scheme in the past for these shops, it was felt to be an appropriate finish for this historic building.[28] The work was undertaken by conservator William Kay who also worked on the St Andrews shopfronts.

This is a significant and prominent historic building within the burgh of Haddington which was sensitively restored. The use of a traditional graining paint scheme here was part of the wider consideration for the building.

Adoption of historic paint schemes

In all the cases discussed, the reinstatement of a historic paint scheme was done with expertise and on the basis of sound historical research and understanding of the building. However, this type of scheme may not always be

Fig:218

as successful unless there is similar background research and expertise is available. It is also essential to include the building owner or owners in the discussions when trying to implement such a scheme as without their co-operation the project is unlikely to be successful.

In particular, it may need to be borne in mind how the scheme will accommodate particular retail branding. Most chain stores have colour schemes associated with their brand image, some of which may be very bright colours which may be felt not to be appropriate. It is therefore necessary to have early discussions with organisations to ensure that the scheme will be successful. However, it should be remembered that there are examples of where corporate branding has been altered to accommodate a local colour scheme. A good example is Inverary where the buildings are largely whitewashed with black margins. This uniformity is adopted in many planned estate villages and can be seen elsewhere in Scotland, such as at Kenmore. This general scheme therefore forms part of the overall townscape and alterations can significantly disrupt the visual appearance of the buildings. In Inverary, even chain stores, such as R S McColls have a black and white painted frontage in keeping with the other buildings in the town.

For many shops a good modern paint scheme may be more appropriate and these can be creative such as the Linthouse Urban Village (LUV) shopfront scheme in Glasgow where art students designed new shopfront paint schemes to liven up the streetscape. Similar initiatives have been undertaken in the Merchant City where art students have painted interior schemes.

It should also be borne in mind that altering paint colours, even to what may be viewed as a more appropriate colour, may require appropriate permissions, such as Listed Building Consent.

Figure 218: R S MColl's shop, Inverary

Figure 219: Sign designed for a shop in Linthouse Urban Village using bright paint and ceramics

Fig: 219

CONSERVATION CASE STUDY 3:
RESTORATION OF INTER-WAR TILE SCHEME IN A
CATEGORY C(S) LISTED BUILDING

Figure 220: The lobby tiles had been badly damaged

Figure 221: The tiles were carefully matched by Craven Dunnill to ensure a suitable match in terms of size, design and colour

Fig: 221

Background

The building at 136-138 High Street, Dunbar is a mid eighteenth century three storey tenement which is listed Category C(S). The shop at number 138 is a former Buttercup Dairy Company shop probably dating to the early 1920s. This firm once owned dairy shops throughout Scotland but it is believed that less than twenty-five shops now survive.[29] This shop is a particularly good example retaining many original features including the entrance tiles, door, console brackets and tiled stallriser. This is the first Buttercup Dairy Company shop to be conserved and the work was partly grant-funded through Dunbar Townscape Heritage Initiative (THI).

Andrew Ewing started the Buttercup Dairy Company in Leith in 1908 and the business quickly expanded with a particular stronghold in the east of the country. Architect James Davidson Cairns (1866-1947) of Edinburgh was employed to carry out some drawings for the company and they had a distinctive design which included a tiled lobby panel featuring a girl holding out a buttercup to a brown cow and a mosaic tiled entrance lobby floor. In addition to the tile scheme, the shops all had common architectural features including a glazed door and fluted console brackets.

The tiles were designed by James Duncan Ltd of Glasgow who won the contract for all of the Buttercup Dairy shops. Duncans were the largest tile firm in Scotland and operated from 1860s until 1965, specialising in tube-lined tiles. Many of their murals are signed 'James Duncan Ltd' or 'JD Ltd' and frequently used green and white as the main colour arrangement.

Tile Conservation

Ceramic tiles are a very durable and hard-wearing material. They are secured in position by a hard cementitious mortar and grout. However, they can become chipped or cracked particularly through the use of inappropriate fixings and drilling of holes for screws. Tube-lined tiles which are the type used here, have a delicate raised decoration and are therefore particularly susceptible. The pattern of tiles for the Buttercup Dairy scheme also includes a plinth with a projecting, profiled rail tile which is vulnerable to damage.

The lobby panel tiles at this shop had been covered over with a timber board by a previous occupier and the tiles were damaged as a result. New owners, Richard and Lynda Amos were keen to restore the tiles to their former condition. Lynda Amos investigated the background to the tiles and the Buttercup Dairy and painstakingly sourced suitable matching tiles from Craven Dunnill at Jackfield, Ironbridge who specialise in this type of work. Dunbar THI were operating a shopfront improvement scheme and partly funded the cost of the restoration work.

An experienced tiler removed the damaged tiles and replaced them. Tiles which had only minor damage were left insitu so that the maximum amount of original material was retained. The work was completed in September 2008 and the result is that the distinctive tiles have now been fully restored enhancing the shopfront and making it an attractive feature in the townscape.

In this case the enthusiasm for restoring the tiles came from the shop owner who, despite operating a business unconnected with a dairy or the tiles, saw the merit in them as an attractive shopfront and one which is an asset to the business. Grant assistance was available from the Dunbar THI to offer additional financial support, but much of the research work was undertaken by the shop owner, who also bore partial costs for the restoration.

Fig: 220

Figure 222: The damaged tiles were carefully removed and replaced with the new matching tiles

Fig: 222

Figure 223: The completed panel following restoration works
All images © Lynda Amos

Fig: 223

Fig: 223

CONSERVATION CASE STUDY 4:
EXTENSION OF A SHOP IN A CATEGORY C(S) LISTED BUILDING

Figure 224: Irvine's shop prior to alterations

Figure 225: The interior prior to alterations

Background

Blairgowrie is located north of Perth and, as the largest town in the district, has a substantial number of shops. HW Irvine's, Pork Butcher, is located on the outskirts of the town at 17-19 Perth Street. Henry William Irvine set up here in 1922 and expanded the business in 1923, renovating the shop with a new tile scheme. The business grew and the upper floor was added in 1959. Primarily pork butchers, the premises had its own slaughter-house until 1990.[30]

The existing premises comprised a small, rectangular shop entered by an angled, recessed doorway. The frontage had a tiled stallriser, fascia with console brackets and a stained glass clerestory with the words 'Pork Butcher and Bacon Curer'. The entrance lobby had a mosaic tiled floor and lobby panel featuring a rural scene with pigs. These tiles are essentially a green and white scheme with tube-lined tiles to the mural. The name 'H. W. Irvine, Bacon Curer, Butcher' also featured in tiles in the window.

The shop was fully tiled inside, including the ceiling, in white tiles with a pictorial panel of pigs in the window similar to the one in the lobby. The floor was of black and white geometric tiles. Located at the rear of the shop was a small office with a preparation area beyond.

While many tiled butchers do survive, this shop is significant both because of the long family association with the premises and for its intact tile scheme and use of stained glass in the clerestory. Overall it is a very good example of an inter-war butchers shop.

Alterations and extension

The business was sold to Lawrie & Symington Ltd and the shop extended and upgraded to include what had formerly been part of the house. Walker Interiors, Dundee were appointed as the designers and grant assistance of £7500 was provided by Perth & Kinross Heritage Trust who operated a façade improvement scheme in Blairgowrie.

The alterations involved knocking through into the house to enlarge the shop. The new shop was matched as close as possible to the existing premises including matching the existing tiles. The floor in the new section

Fig:224

Fig: 225

utilised the same black and white geometric floor tiles and on the walls, white tiles with the green border. The façade style was extended with new stained glass clerestory to match the existing and the fascia, pilasters and consoles were also copied to give a matching extension.

It can be difficult to decide how to approach an extension for a historic property and whether it should mimic the existing style or should completely depart from it and therefore be recognised as being new and different. In this case, the shop mirrored the style of the original shop although the new and extended premises are undoubtedly very different from the shop which existed before. It was formerly small and dark and this shop with the additional windows and doors is lighter and feels modern. However, it is a sympathetic alteration designed to meet current hygiene standards whilst maintaining much of the original tile scheme.

Fig: 226

Fig: 227

Fig: 228

Figure 226: The shopfront following the extension

Figure 227: The interior following the extension

Figure 228: The new joinery work was carefully matched with existing features

CONSERVATION CASE STUDY 5:
RENOVATION OF A SHOPFRONT AND REINSTATEMENT OF ORIGINAL PROPORTIONS AND DETAILS IN A CATEGORY B LISTED BUILDING

Figure 231: Following works, the original window height was reinstated and historic features uncovered (facing page)

Background

Later Victorian and Edwardian shops were typically very tall with large expanses of plate glass. In late nineteenth and early twentieth century Glasgow, many tenements were constructed with these exceptionally tall shopfronts maximising the opportunity for natural light. In recent years there has been a tendency to lower the height of these fascias and to introduce internal suspended ceilings. This drastically alters the appearance of the shop and the wider tenement. The external application of other features such as roller shutter doors, alarm system boxes and exterior lighting can also be detrimental to both underlying historic fabric and to the aesthetic appearance of the building.

The tenement at 133-155 Stockwell Street, Glasgow was designed by A B McDonald, Minister for Public Works in 1905 in a French Baroque style. Listed Category B, this substantial red ashlar tenement is three stories high with ground floor shops.[31] The shop at 139 Stockwell Street was vacant and in a poor state of repair. It had suffered from a number of inappropriate modern interventions over the years including a dropped fascia, exterior ventilation fan and externally mounted roller shutter doors. Although these features considerably detracted from the overall appearance of the shopfront, much of the original fabric remained hidden behind these later interventions, including the fascia and framing of the window, the ventilator at the window head and a decorative pilaster to the left-hand side of the door.

Conservation

A new firm of architects, Do Architecture wishing to set up in Glasgow acquired the premises. They unpicked the property removing all the external shutters and the lowered fascia to reinstate the window height to its original position. The traditional fascia level was then used for the name, following the original design intention of the tenement.

A feature of the renovation was to retain bare brick walls for the interior of the shop. This look suits the use of this shop by the architects' firm and is in keeping with their modern architectural image.

The work to this shopfront was aided with grant assistance form the Merchant City Townscape Heritage Initiative who have funded a number of shopfront restoration projects in the area. These projects have helped to rejuvenate this part of Glasgow and to encourage a variety of retail businesses into the area including cafes and designer clothing companies as well as small, independent retailers. [32]

This project demonstrates how the simple reinstatement of the original proportions of a shop and the removal of inappropriate alterations can dramatically enhance a shopfront and transform it into desirable retail premises.

Figure 229: Prior to the restoration works the shopfront had a number of inappropriate interventions including a roller shutter door and lowered fascia

Figure 230: 139 Stockwell Street at night

Fig: 229

Fig: 230

162

CONSERVATION CASE STUDY 6: RETENTION OF TRADITIONAL SHOP INTERIOR IN A CATEGORY C(S) LISTED SHOP

Background

The property at 60-62 Barclay Street, Stonehaven is a former shoe shop. The building dates to 1890s and comprises a typical flat arrangement above a ground floor shop. The shop has an offset door with encaustic tiled entrance and two pane window. The original storm door remains, being of a half-fold style rather than two separate doors because of the glazing to the right side of the entrance. The shopfront is in its original late Victorian style, the original owner having been George Alexander a boot and shoe maker. In 1928 the property was purchased by a chiropodist, Mr Anderson, and this family remained there until 2005.[33]

The shop interior is fully-fitted out with shelving for a shoe shop with timber shelving to three sides of the front shop. The shop retains its timber and glass window screens and there is a large fixed, multi-paned window in the back shop. There is also a fire-surround in the front shop where an open fire would once have been located.

Figure 232: The shopfront at 60–62 Barclay Street, Stonehaven

Fig: 232

The shop was leased two years ago to a hairdresser on condition that the interior and exterior of the shop remained unchanged.

Alterations

Occupying a shop with a fully-fitted traditional timber shelving interior is challenging for a use such as a hairdresser which has very specific requirements in order to be able to carry out its trade.

In this case, the front shop was left untouched and mirrors are hung across the shelves for customers when they are having their hair cut. The shelving system has proved useful for holding equipment such as towels and for display of hair products for sale. The original sales desk with its roll top is used as the business counter.

The window screens proved useful as these allow in some light but also provide privacy for customers. The screens can be opened partially or fully to allow in additional light.

The tenant had left the fascia a plain green paint and instead used window transfers to advertise the business although it was felt that these were too subtle. Use of the original external bracket was therefore being considered for a hanging sign.

Two sinks for washing customers' hair were successfully accommodated in the back shop so that the front shop would not be altered.

This unusual occupation of a traditional shop demonstrates how a use such as hairdressing with its particular requirements can be sensitively met and accommodated within the original furniture and shelving of a former shoe shop. It also demonstrates how it is often the long ownership within a family which protects a shop interior like this. In this case it is also that the family have continued ownership of the shop and, aware of its significance, have been keen that any new occupation would not detract from the history associated with this building and its interior.

Fig: 233

Fig: 234

Fig: 235

Figure 234: The interior of the front shop now used as a hairdressers

Figure 235: The basins accommodated in the back shop

LICENSED TO SELL **TOBACCO** AND **PATENT MEDICINES.**

The Legacy of Historic Retail Buildings in Scotland

"Just as important as the shops were the shopkeepers. To these people running the shop meant so much more than a business. Somehow it felt as if they'd turned the premises into living entities; and they themselves were cherished and long standing members of the community. And how proud they were to still be serving it!" J. Londei[34]

The rich heritage of historic shops is woven into the fabric of the Scottish townscape. Their history is complex, reflecting a myriad of influences; burgh regulations, retailer aspiration, local craft skills and the wider impact of architectural fashions and the economy. These elements have combined to create a timeline of retail history with some towns reflecting particular styles, materials and ages of development in a more pronounced way than others. St Andrews with its cast iron, Glasgow with its embracing of the Art Deco Movement and Inverary with its black and white shops. These give a distinctiveness to town centres, sometimes in a subtle way or hidden by later alterations, but they are significant in ensuring a place has its own identity at a time when the use of mass produced plastic fascias and the increase in the dominance of national chains have been criticised for creating homogenised town centres.

So what is the legacy of historic retail buildings in Scotland? In the twenty-first century, modern retailing with its vast supermarkets and out-of-town shopping centres could not be further from its origins in the piazzas, booths and bow-fronted shops. Modern retail premises aim to meet every need of the customer and the vendor. The architecture of retail buildings has had to endlessly change and adapt, sometimes forgetting its true architectural roots in the process. Yet, shops are essentially still designed for the same purpose: for security of the goods, for adequate display to encourage sales and to provide a degree of comfort for both shopper and shopkeeper.

The legacy of surviving shops across Scotland is patchy and erratic. Whilst some districts such as Scottish Borders and East Lothian have a diverse range of traditional shops, other towns have fared less well. There appears to be a direct correlation between the size of a town and the survival of historic fabric with larger towns typically having a poorer survival of traditional shopfronts than smaller centres. The Border towns with their strong identity and perhaps

more isolated locations in some cases, has encouraged the retention of independent shops and often long-standing businesses with their associated shop premises.

However, even in these settings, the desire for a modern image has been at the forefront of shop owners minds and renewal of shopfronts is therefore part of the inherent history of retail buildings. The most striking example is probably Glasgow which embraced the inter-war Moderne designs but almost as quickly replaced them with the new materials of the post-war era sweeping away the Vitrolite and chrome as though it had never existed. Shopkeepers can rarely afford to be sentimental about their shops and where there is a turnover of occupiers this is even less relevant. Nonetheless, where there is a long family association with a property this will often engender a sense of loyalty in customers and pride in the owners at the longevity of their occupation.

The focus recently on the importance of town centres to communities, supported by local and national grant-aided projects, has resulted in a greater emphasis on the importance of retail buildings. Many of these projects have encouraged shopfront improvements and conservation. Such examples of good conservation practice are vital to demonstrate what can be achieved and how with understanding and an appropriate conservation response, that shopfronts can be successfully restored. Such work has potential economic benefits to retailers by making premises more attractive and thereby encouraging customers. The contribution made by shops to towns in terms of their economics and their aesthetics cannot be underestimated. Shops are a vital part of any vibrant community and retaining and enhancing historic retail buildings is central to the improvement of any town centre.

The survey of Scottish shops demonstrated the vast numbers which do survive, often in excellent condition. Their owners are extremely proud of their premises and

Figure 236: Linklater & Co's shop, Scalloway, Shetland c1890s © Shetland Museum and Archives (facing page)

167

*Figure 237: West Coast
Fisheries shop, Ayr*

*Figure 238: Pharmacy
window, Edinburgh
(facing page)*

the history associated with these buildings. It has also been shown that there are many examples where individual identity is evident contradicting the suggestion that town centres all look the same.

The quote at the head of this section suggests that shops are about more than their architecture; they are about the people who are associated with the premises and their place in the community. While no-one would suggest that a nostalgic, museum-like state is suitable for retail premises and certainly pastiche, 'stage-set' shopfronts are almost always inappropriate, there is no doubt that original shopfronts and interiors with their patina of age, their inherent historical layers of shopkeepers, customers and retail practices have a genuine atmosphere that cannot be recreated. Such original shopfronts whether 1850s or 1950s are a precious and increasingly rare element of our historic environment. The good examples, whether Georgian, Victorian or twentieth century deserve to be

retained and perhaps, retail practices should adjust to accommodate the architecture rather than the other way around. The result of carefully considered conservation is a shop that customers want to shop in and premises that shopkeepers can be proud of.

The uncovering of earlier historic fabric, a sign, tiles or shelving add interest to a shop and can be accommodated in the majority of retail premises. Without retaining and conserving shops from all periods, the legacy of retail buildings in Scotland will be distorted and lack conviction. Historic retail buildings add interest and variety and form an integral part of the social fabric of any town. Their removal can only diminish town centres but conserving them ensures that the historic record of retailing in Scotland remains as a visible presence in our High Streets, a daily reminder of the legacy of several hundred years of Scottish trade.

Fig: 237

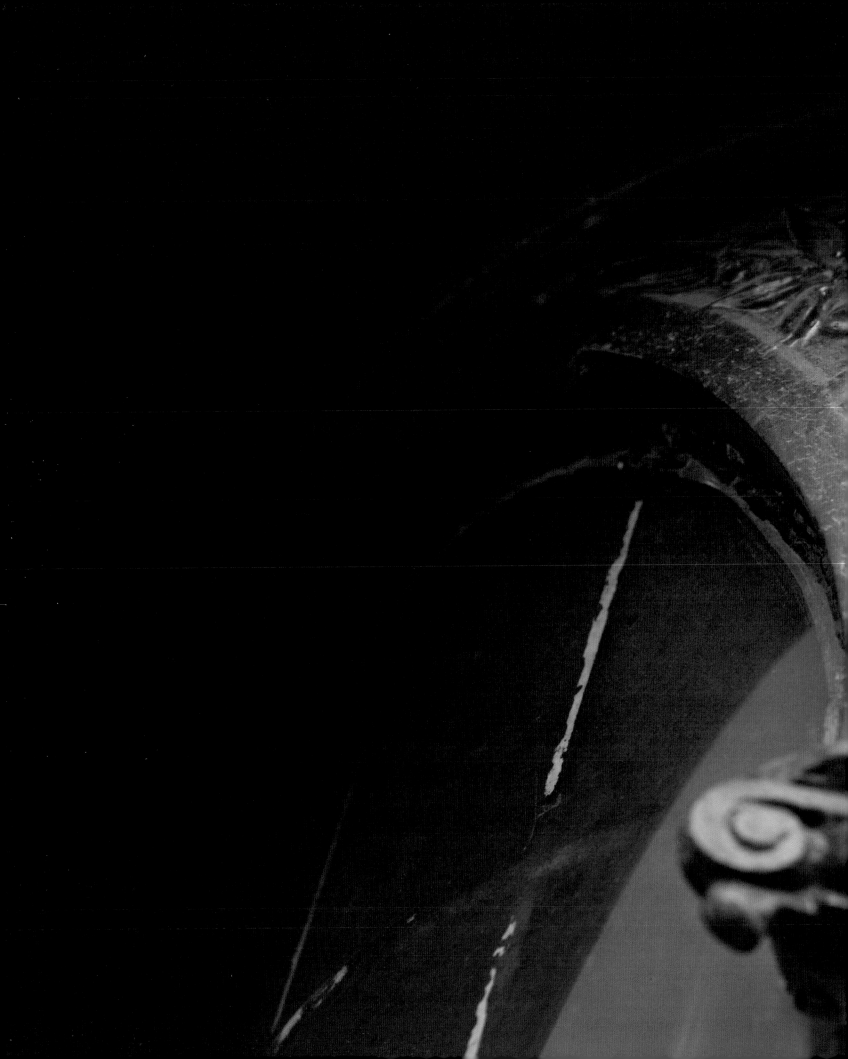

Section 3: Gazetteer,
Glossary and References

GAZETTEER OF HISTORIC SHOPS

Throughout Scotland there are good examples of historic shopfronts and their interiors from the Georgian period through to the post-war. This gazetteer aims to highlight where particularly fine examples can be seen and these demonstrate rarity, use of particular materials or styles associated with particular architectural periods. It does not aim to be a complete or exhaustive list but instead is a sample of some of the best examples. Throughout Scotland many other quality shops can be found.

The shops are arranged by period and within those by town alphabetically. Although a significant number are Listed Buildings, others are not although they may be located within Conservation Areas.

Seventeenth and Early Eighteenth Century

Edinburgh

Gladstone's Land, 477b Lawnmarket, High Street

Restored seventeenth century piazza with ground floor booth. An impressive five storeys and attic high with arched ground floor. Owned by National Trust for Scotland and open as a visitor attraction.

Listed Category A.

Elgin

42-46 High Street

Dated 1688. Piazza with arched ground floor. Renovated 1980 and now with modern shops.

Listed Category A.

Elgin

Braco's Banking House

Dated 1694, house with piazza ground floor consisting of three round-headed arches. Restored 1976.

Listed Category A.

Georgian and Regency

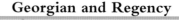

Dunkeld

2-6 High Street

Circa 1809 three storey tenement with two early ground floor shops. Both shops are double-fronted with central doors with fanlights above.

Listed Category B

Edinburgh

515 Lawnmarket

Early nineteenth century high bow-fronted shop with door below leading to basement. A rare survivor of a type once common in Edinburgh.

Listed Category A.

Edinburgh

William Street

Row of pilastered shopfronts with platt accesses dating to 1825. Many other good examples can be seen in St Stephen Street, Scotland Street and other parts of the Edinburgh New Town.

Listed Category B.

Georgian and Regency

Glasgow

Argyle Arcade

Dated 1827 by John Baird I. It is Scotland's first purpose-built arcade and has a cast iron hammerbeam roof. Populated largely by jewellers shops.

Listed Category A.

Kelso

1-5 Woodmarket

Grand building of mid-eighteenth century date fronting the impressive town square. Pair of simple pilastered shopfronts probably 1830s-1840s. Original wooden shutters retained and which are still in working use.

Listed Category B.

Perth

12 South Street

Late eighteenth century bow-fronted shop. Fascia for name incorporated into design. Gothic fanlight above door. Occupied by Deuchar family since 1912.

Listed Category B.

Sanquhar

High Street

Post Office which is the oldest continuously working Post Office in the world dating to 1712. Bow-fronted window with no fascia which has had some later alterations to the window frames.

Listed Category B.

Victorian

Aberfeldy

Bank Street

P & J Haggarts, Tweed Merchants, 1899 purpose-built premises. Three storey Scots Baronial style with curved glass entrance and good surviving interior. The interior of the shop features decorative plasterwork, window screens, fitting rooms and barley-twist cast iron columns.

Listed Category B.

Beauly

Campbell & Co, Tweed merchants have been in the Highland town since 1858. Their shop premises are a late nineteenth century building with two storey, c1900 extension. Retains some interior fixtures and shelving.

Listed Category C(S).

Bridge of Allan

64-68 Henderson Street

Row of late nineteenth century bungalow shops. Number 66 is a butcher's with fully tiled interior with tiles by either Minton's or Pilkington's depicting sheep and game birds in diamond shaped panels. Rare survival of a timber cash booth to rear of shop.

Not listed.

Comrie

Drummond Street

Double-fronted shop with delicately-carved carved 'Bookend' console brackets. Barley-twist ironwork to downpipes. Interior of matchboarding and timber shelving survives.

Listed Category B.

Victorian

Comrie

38 Drummond Street

Double-fronted late Victorian shop with unusual elliptical fascia.

Listed Category C(S).

Crieff

60 & 62 King Street

Former butcher shop located in corner position erected in 1889 for Irvine butchers. Granite columns and extensive use of cast iron particularly for fretwork to stallrisers and to side entrance door. Interior has magnificent mosaic tiled floor and fully tiled walls with white tile scheme with diamond shaped panels with farm animals in a sepia colour.

Listed Category B.

Cromarty

2 High Street

Striking late nineteenth century cast iron shopfront by Macfarlane's Saracen foundry. Heraldic type cresting above cornice. Mosaic floor inlaid with name 'D Junor' although mosaic is damaged in places.

Listed Category B.

Cumnock

38-42 Ayr Road

Impressive row of three bungalow shops with Gothic detailing dated 1897 by D Menzies. Geometric tiled lobby entrance floors and some surviving interior joinery.

Listed Category B.

Edinburgh

North Bridge Arcade

Small shopping arcade by architects James Dunn and James Finlay 1899-1902. Mosaic ceiling and central cupola with stained glass. Curved glass to shopfronts. Restored by Edinburgh World Heritage.

Listed Category A.

Edinburgh

Jenner's, 47-52 Princes Street

Iconic department store which dates to 1893-5 by W Hamilton Beattie with further extension in 1903 by A R Scott. Fireproof construction and was one of the largest department stores in Britain when reconstructed. Impressive top-lit saloon.

Listed Category A.

Forres

79 High Street

Building 1830-40 with late nineteenth/ turn of twentieth century ironmongers. Sign on façade of building stating 'Pat MacKenzie, Ironmonger' with cut and gilded sign with plate glass covering. Alterations to shop windows but pilasters and console brackets survive.

Listed Category C(S).

Glasgow

Gardner's Warehouse, Jamaica Street

Four storey, cast iron façade dated 1855-56. One of a series of cast iron warehouses built in Glasgow in the mid nineteenth century. Now a public house.

Listed Category A.

Victorian

Glasgow

126 Nithsdale Road

Late nineteenth century former fishmongers with fully tiled interior depicting mermaids and sailing ships by Glasgow tile firm, James Duncan Ltd. Lobby panel was removed to People's Palace Museum due to vandalism. Shopfront retains a lifting window.

Listed Category B.

Helensburgh

48 Princes Street West

Late nineteenth/ turn of twentieth century pharmacy with high quality fitted interior including curved glass cabinets. Carbides and other glass bottles also retained. Modern shopfront.

Listed Category B.

Inverness

Queensgate Arcade

Shops within arcade built 1897 by Duncan Cameron. Tall shopfronts have polished granite with treacly-brown faience by Doulton of Lambeth. Some alterations to glazing. Whole arcade is Listed Category B.

Listed Category B.

Kelso

46 and 23-29 Bridge Street

Shops either side of curved entrance to Bridge Street dating to 1872-73. Number 46 is constructed of sandstone and numbers 25-31 have cast iron pilasters with timber balustrade.

Number 46 is Listed Category C(S) and 23-29 Listed Category B.

Musselburgh

25 High Street

Double-fronted shop with elaborate detailing including egg and dart and Ionic style colonettes. Fanlight over recessed entrance door.

Listed Category B.

Perth

33 St John Street

1898 by James Smart for MacKendrick butchers. Fully tiled interior by Maw and Co and marble slabs to windows. Carved animal heads to window and door openings. Some later renovations to shopfront.

Listed Category B.

St Andrews

Bell Street, Church Street, Market Street, South Street

Almost 30 cast iron shops spread throughout the town. Of varying designs and by different foundries.

Many are Listed.

Strathpeffer

Spa Pharmacy

Late nineteenth century pharmacy which retains some of its original interior fittings, bottles and jars.

Listed Category B.

Early Twentieth Century

Banff

53 Low Street

Early twentieth century shopfront in parent building of 1801. Long shopfront of delicate cast iron with mosaic entrance tiles. Pilasters with stylised consoles and fluting.

Listed Category B.

Callander

33 Main Street

Corner position with Art Nouveau stained glass to clerestory of shop and to adjacent single-fronted shop. Retains traditional awnings.

Not Listed.

Camelon, Falkirk

The Hedges

Former Co-operative Society butchers with fully tiled walls and frieze depicting detailed scenes of the Forth and Clyde canal. Tile scheme by James Duncan Ltd of Glasgow. Modern shopfront. Now used as an office.

Not listed.

Coldstream

59 High Street

Edwardian butchers shop with blue and white tiled interior including large mural depicting sheep in a mountain setting. Shopfront has two lifting windows with high stallriser below. Mosaic entrance floor has the name 'Tillico' inset into the floor.

Listed Category B.

Coldstream

61 High Street

A former veterinary pharmacy which was started in 1830 by George Wilson. This is where sheep dip was first made and Wilson's Sheep Dip was sold from here for many years. The shopfront is grand with six polished pink granite columns. The interior retains its original timber shelving and counters similar to a normal pharmacy including the glass name plates on the drawers.

Listed Category B.

Comrie

Mackintosh building

Dated 1904 for Brough and MacPherson drapers by Charles Rennie Mackintosh. Plain, unassuming exterior but retains beautiful interior joinery of original shelving and counters with typical Mackintosh detailing.

Listed Category A.

Dunbar

101 High Street

Tall, early twentieth century tenement with ground floor shop. Cast iron columns by Macfarlane's Saracen Foundry. The shop was originally a butcher's and has a mosaic tiled floor and fully tiled walls. Some original butcher's hooks and fitting as well as a small wall safe also survive.

Listed Category C(S).

Early Twentieth Century

Forfar

26 Castle Street

Purpose-built premises by TR Souter 1909. David Irons & Son, ironmongers. Property retains an early hydraulic lift of 1896 which is an older section of the building. Shopfront has mosaic lobby floor, high quality joinery, glass block stallrisers and curved glass to building corners. Good traditional signage.

Listed Category C(S).

Gatehouse of Fleet

Stark Chemist, High Street

Pharmacy dating to 1908 which has a double-fronted shop with cast iron colonnettes. Sign is v-cut and gilded lettering 'Stark, Chemist'. Interior retains some of the original pharmacy shelving. The premises were used in the making of the cult film, 'The Wicker Man'.

Listed Category C(S).

Girvan

34-40 Dalrymple Street

Row of three shops each with curved glass entrances with showcases. Ventilation grilles to window heads. Encaustic tiled entrances and matching doors.

Listed Category C(S).

Gourock

25 Kempock Street

Former butchers shop with tiled interior including mural depicting scenes of the River Clyde with steamers by James Duncan Ltd of Glasgow.

Not listed.

Jedburgh

11 Exchange Street

Former Co-operative store designed by J P Allison, architect. Two openings at first floor level with substantial panes of plate glass to maximise natural light and display. Later alterations to ground floor.

Listed Category A.

Kilsyth

55-63 Main Street

1904-5 tenement with shops by architect George Hay. Art Nouveau influences in architecture and one shop retains traditional chemists interior.

Listed Category B.

Linlithgow

165 High Street

Butchers shop dating to 1912 with fully tiled interior by James Duncan Ltd including murals depicting Avon Viaduct and Linlithgow Palace.

Listed Category B.

Milnathort

Heaven Scent Café, 19 South Street

Double-fronted Edwardian shopfront with good example of stained glass.

Not listed.

Early Twentieth Century

Newburgh

Sun Gallery, 154 High Street

Early twentieth century double-fronted shop with elliptical fascia with sun motif.

Listed C(S).

Paisley

25-29 Causeyside

By Robert B Miller 1907-8 for Paisley Provident Co-operative Society. Shopfronts largely altered to ground floor but retains impressive tiled entrance to building above by James Duncan Ltd. Depicts nautical and heraldic scenes and also roses reminiscent of Glasgow style.

Listed Category B.

Perth

15 High Street

Unusual two storey shopfront designed in 1905 by Adam Currie, shopfitters and joiners for Woods the bakers. Ground floor altered but upper floor still retains oriel window and stained glass.

Listed Category B.

St Andrews

131 South Street

Dated 1906 by architect James Scott. Entrance with mosaic tiled floor. Delicate glasswork to clerestory with Mackintosh style rose.

Listed Category B.

Inter-war

Arbroath

16 Keptie St

Former Lipton's grocers, early twentieth century with original tiled interior possibly by James Duncan Ltd. Tiles have shamrocks, thistles and 'L' for Lipton and black and white chequered floor tiles. Shopfront has some alterations but retains original doors.

Listed Category B.

Ayr

West Coast Fisheries, 6 Newmarket Street

Vitrolite shopfront for fishmongers on prominent corner site dating to 1935. Black Vitrolite with decorative medallion depicting a cockerel and good lettering. Corner position with two lifting windows. Impressive terrazzo slab in the interior.

Listed Category C(S).

Blairgowrie

19 Perth Street

Irvine's Butchers dating to 1922 with tiled interior. Recently extended and modernised in a sympathetic style.

Listed Category C(S).

Inter-war

Blairgowrie

The Dome Café, 14–20 Leslie Street

Interior and dome by W J Brewster Grant & Henderson, Blairgowrie for the Visocchi family in 1925. The café has a terrazzo frontage giving it an unassuming style. The interior retains many of the original café fittings including the horseshoe counter and carved bench seating. The rear saloon has an impressive dome to introduce natural light.

Listed Category B.

Castle Douglas

179 King Street

Former Maypole Dairy/Lipton's shop. Double-fronted with central doorway. Green and white tiled floor usual for Maypole Dairy but frontage is typical of 1930s Lipton's shop. The companies both formed part of Allied Stores. One of a small number of former Lipton's and Maypole shops surviving in Scotland.

Not listed.

Bo'Ness

East Parting

By Matthew Steele, 1926. A striking, cube-like Modernist white block with large expanses of plate glass which was originally Weevling's drapery. Some later alterations to fenestration.

Not listed.

Dumbarton

89–93 High Street

Former Burton's store in white faience dated 1937-38. Upper floor retains the original sign which says 'Montague Burton, the Tailor of Taste'. Ground floors largely altered.

Not listed.

Bo'ness

Anderson buildings, 24–32 South Street

A row of purpose-built bungalow shops dating to 1934 and constructed under an Anderson bequest. Matching joinery detailing.

Listed Category C(S).

Dundee

Draffen's Department Store, 36 Nethergate

Built 1935 by architects Thoms & Wilkie following a fire at this site. Three storey and attic, tall and narrow department store. Bronze shopfronts by Frederick Sage and Co, shopfitters. High quality department store of its period but now vacant.

Listed Category B.

Inter-war

Dundee

45 Murraygate

Impressive Art Deco department store for Marks and Spencer. 1936 by James Munro and Sons with Robert Lutyens. Painted render façade with tall, metal windows. Modern shopfront to ground floor.

Listed Category B.

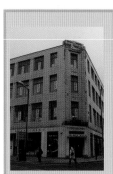

Dundee

Willison House, Robertson's furniture store, 56 Barrack Street

Four storey faience commercial retail building dated 1934 by Findlay, Stewart and Robbie. Faience in poor repair in places.

Listed Category B.

Dunfermline

Former Gas showroom, 6 Canmore Street

Inter-war showroom by architect Robert Henderson Motion dated 1937. Originally had a lecture theatre on first floor.

Listed Category C(S).

Edinburgh

Bread Street

Former St Cuthbert's Co-operative Society store and headquarters. First curtain wall design in Scotland in 1936 by T Waller Marwick. Now Point Hotel.

Listed Category A.

Elgin

122/ 122A High Street

Burton's store with bronze shop window frames in geometric design dating to 1936. Black polished granite frontage. Rare survivor of one of this store's shopfronts as most have been altered.

Listed Category C(S).

Galashiels

17 and 21 High Street

Pair of shops and number 17 is a former Maypole Dairy Company shop of which only a handful now survive. Single-fronted shop with 'Maypole' inset into mosaic lobby floor. Original ironmongery survives. Interior retains green and white floor tiles and wall tiling may exist behind later alterations. Butchers shop at number 21 has original meat hooks and butchers fittings.

Listed Category C(S).

Gatehouse of Fleet

John R Fergusson's shop, 5 High Street

Former draper's shop which still retains its 'Brilliant' sign made by the Brilliant Sign Company of London. A rare survivor. Tiled entrance floor and showcase to lobby.

Listed Category B.

Glasgow

95 Buchanan Street

1926 by George Arthur Boswell, bronze and marble shopfront in French style for Ciro pearls. High quality shopfront but subsequently altered and more recently bronze-work has been painted.

Listed Category B.

Inter-war

Glasgow

Rogano, Exchange Square

By Weddell and Inglis 1935-36 and later alterations 1985. Cream Vitrolite and chrome shopfront with a lobster depicted on the facade.

Listed Category B.

Peebles

Eastwark House, 10 Eastgate

By James Davidson Cairns, 1931. Two storey shopfront providing an almost full wall of glass for maximum display and natural light. Art Deco detailing.

Not listed.

Hawick

27 and 29 High Street

Pair of 1930s shopfronts. Butchers and fishmongers in white Vitrolite with chrome detailing. Cream tiles to fishmongers and good interior terrazzo slab. Particularly good chrome signage and concertina blinds. Lobby tiles to fishmongers state 'Fish for Health'.

Listed Category C(S).

Peebles

57 High Street

1930's black Vitrolite shopfront with bronze window frames. Formerly a Co-operative Society shop.

Not listed.

Innerleithen

94 High Street

Former Buttercup Dairy shop unusually retaining two panels with the Buttercup Dairy image of the girl with the cow. Double-fronted shop. A glass-fronted sign for 'McKay, Provisions, Groceries' has also been uncovered beneath later signage.

Not Listed.

Rothesay

47 Victoria Street

Jewellers shop dating to 1936 in impressive black Vitrolite with some surviving interior shelving.

Listed Category B.

North Berwick

Station Hill

Attractive row of bungalow shops on sloping site. Small paned windows to clerestory and matching entrance doors. Stone balustrade to lower section.

Not Listed.

Sanquhar

15 High Street

Shop paired with adjoining bakers. Interior has tile scheme by James Duncan Ltd depicting Highland scenes of lochs and mountains around three walls of the shop. Tiled butchers counter.

Not listed.

Inter-war

Sanqhuar

W Forsyth & Son, 40 High Street

Single-fronted butchers with timber fascia. Tiled lobby and fully tiled interior with panels by Pilkington's.

Listed Category C(S).

Selkirk

40-44 High Street

Unusual surviving example of a pair of shops originally a Buttercup Dairy and an adjoining butchers, JA Waters. Retains original tile schemes in lobby entrances by James Duncan Ltd.

Listed Category B.

St Andrews

107 South Street

1928 by Frank Pride. Prominent corner building designed in a traditional style in timber to fit in with the historic townscape of St Andrews. Decorative joinery and traditional awnings.

Listed Category C(S).

Stirling

Friars Street

Row of 1930's bungalow shops with curved glass entrances and traditional awnings. Attractive low-rise row.

Not Listed.

Stonehaven

26-32 Evan Street

Art Deco row of shopfronts for Co-operative Society possibly by Tawse and Hall, 1936. Part of the stunning Carron Tearooms which front onto Cameron Street. Shopfronts executed in granite and bronze.

Listed Category C(S).

Stonehaven

60-62 Barclay Street

Former shoe shop dating to 1928 with good surviving fitted interior shelving. Single-fronted shop with traditional awning and original storm doors.

Listed Category C(S).

Stonehaven

12-16 Market Square

Former Ramsey Drapers in corner position to Market Square. Two storey shopfront to Market Square with sign stating 'Millinery, Outfitting, Costumes'. A particularly good and unusual example of a showcase island executed in curved glass. Mosaic entrance floors and decorative double doors.

Listed Category B.

Stromness

Victoria Street

Former Italian café with terrazzo floor with name 'Fugaccia' inset into the entrance. There are mosaic fascias above the openings advertising products including 'Soda Fountain', and 'Coffee Saloon'.

Post-war

Aberlour

Walkers, High Street

Circa 1960 bronze and travertine marble shopfront with angled window and showcase. High quality and one of the best post-war shops of its type in Scotland.

Not listed.

Edinburgh

44 George Street

Trotters Opticians by Simpson & Brown, 1984–5 in Classical style using Ionic capitals to reflect the optician's occupation of the shop.

Listed Category B.

Edinburgh

Festival Fringe Society, 180 High Street

Quirky modern shop reflecting the famous occupier of these premises. By Edinburgh architects Benjamin Tindall with caricature figures gracing the shopfront.

Listed Category B.

Edinburgh

64 Princes Street

British Home Stores (BHS) department store, 1965, the first of the Princes Street Panel buildings to be erected. By Kenneth Graham of Robert Matthew, Johnson-Marshall & Partners.

Listed Category A.

Glasgow

Tinderbox, Ingram Street

Cafe designed by Graven Images in modern extension to Victorian Warehouse. Simple shopfront with modern cafe interior.

Not Listed

SHOPS: GLOSSARY OF TERMS

Arcaded entrance: A deep entrance into a shop popular in the 1920s and particularly 1930s. The entrance may be complex in shape with zig-zags, in-and-out detailing and elaborate plans. Simpler versions may be T-shaped or straight. May incorporate a showcase island, a free-standing island in the centre of the entrance. Popular with drapers and shoe retailers but fell out of favour in the post-war period when the front of a shop was regarded as valuable retail space and now a rarely seen feature.

Arcaded frontage: A series of arches forming the shop façade. May be columns, colonnettes, piers or pilasters.

Blinds: Originally canvas blinds on metal framing used to protect goods on display in windows from sunlight, possibly as early as the late eighteenth century. Also offered pedestrians and shoppers some protection from the weather although could also be considered to be a nuisance, particularly where side valances or wings were used. (See also *Dutch blinds*)

Blind box: A box which incorporates the blind. May be integral to the design of the shop (from mid-nineteenth century) or may be an addition usually above the cornice which has been retro-fitted.

Blind rail: The timber or metal panel which fronts a blind box and hides the awning and mechanisms when the blind is in a closed position. It is fitted with an eyelet to allow the blind to be pulled out into position.

Brattishing: Cast iron cresting of a decorative nature which is set on top of a parapet or cornice. Usually found on late nineteenth century shopfronts and sometimes associated with ironmongers shops.

Bronze: A metal alloy popular in the early twentieth century until inter-war period. It comprises tin and copper and was widely used for sashes to complement other materials like mahogany and marble.

Chrome: Chrome plating involves electroplating a thin layer of chromium onto a metal surface to provide a shiny, silver surface. The trade name 'Staybrite' may be used.

Clerestory: Upper part of a shop window which may be decorated with stained or painted glass or opaque glass. May also be used for display of names or products.

Column: Columns are vertical, structural elements which are usually circular in plan. They typically carry an entablature (fascia) or lintel and may be plain or decorated.[1]

Colonnette: A slender column often found at the corner of a shop lobby as a supporting column, usually in timber or cast iron but also in brass. Can be plain or decorated.

Console bracket: Used to mark the termination of one shop and beginning of another. Have their origins as classical brackets or corbels using an ogee curve which terminates in a volute at top and bottom.[2] They are located usually at the end of the fascia but may be placed *"either under the architrave to give visual support and interest in lieu of a capital, or under the cornice to form a definite end to the entablature"*.[3]

May be highly decorative and may be classical in inspiration but many are stylised in design and do not follow classical principles. Bookend consoles developed at the end of the nineteenth century are deep, highly decorative and much larger than normal consoles.

A shop may appear to be 'unbalanced' where one or more consoles have been removed and where the original intention was for a symmetrical appearance.

Cornice: In classical architectural terms this is the uppermost division of the entablature. For shops it is generally the top section of the fascia and marks a division between the shop and the building above. It may be decorated or plain. Usually of timber or stone, it may have a protective layer of lead for weather-proofing.

Dentil: A small block which is part of a horizontal series situated below the cornice often in late nineteenth century shopfronts. May also be used to decorate other features such as door pediments.

Department store: A larger shop, sometimes purpose-built, sometimes converted buildings. Has several different departments within one building, often originating as a drapers but then extending into other lines notably women's wear and children's wear.

Double-fronted: Shop with a central or off-centre doorway with two windows flanking.

Dutch blind: (Continental blind). Of curved design these are fixed to the shopfront and tend to obscure architectural detailing. Often of modern plastic materials and may be used to advertise through lettering on the front of the blind.

Encaustic tiles: These are Victorian tiles which are inlaid with clay to produce a decorative pattern. The idea was used in medieval times for religious buildings and Royal palaces but they were revived from the 1840s by Minton & Co and became a fashionable flooring for many Victorian buildings.[4]

Faience: A type of terracotta which has a glazed finish. A variety of glazes and sizes available. It may be structural or used as cladding. Sometimes used in the construction of shopfronts and popular as a facing for buildings in the 1930s particularly with Burton's tailors.

Fanlight: A glazed light situated above a door, often square or rectangular in shape. Glass may be plain or decorative and may have glazing bars of varying designs. Late eighteenth century shops tend to have narrow rectangular fanlights with classical detailing. Fanlights became larger during the later nineteenth century as shops became taller. In some shops, particularly late nineteenth and early twentieth century, it may be of a hopper type which is bottom-hinged and opens inwards to allow ventilation to the shop, especially in provision stores.

Fascia: This originated as the classical 'frieze' but was simplified for shopfront use, originally being narrow but during the nineteenth century deepened with the increasing use of it for lettering.[5] The board is usually of timber but in recent years plastic products have been introduced. Lettering may be painted on or three dimensional and attached to the board.

Lifting sash: See also 'Sash'. Found in shops which may have been a butchers or fishmongers in the past. The sash window slides upwards behind the fixed upper sash to allow the display to be arranged, for ice to be removed and for sales to be made to the street. Upper window may be decorated with stained glass and the window may be quite wide. Popular until 1930s but now rarely found.

Lobby: Small recessed area at front of shop leading to shop door sometimes referred to as a porch. May be square or curved in plan. Became increasingly deep during Edwardian period, often with curved entrances. Sometimes protected by a shop gate of timber or metal construction. May have a decorative floor of tiles, often encaustic or mosaic. The walls may be panelled, tiled or incorporate a showcase. The ceiling may be panelled, plastered or mirrored. Edwardian entrances can be particularly elaborate.

Luckenbooth: (Luckenbuith). Small timber medieval lock-up shop. In Edinburgh they were located adjacent to St Giles in the High Street.

Mosaic: Decorative ceramic made up of small tiles (tesserae) which combine to form a pattern. Patent or simulated mosaics were created to reduce the high costs of laying mosaic but still achieved a similar appearance.[6] Popular particularly in Edwardian shopfronts for the lobby floor.

Pent/Pentice: This is a small, sloping roof similar to a lean-to which forms a canopy over a door or opening. May subsequently become enclosed to form a more permanent structure.[7] Used from medieval times on the fronts of timber buildings.

Piazza: Inspired by continental architecture, the ground floor of buildings were arched with an open area which sometimes incorporated shop stalls or booths, eg, Gladstone's Land, Edinburgh.

Pilaster: A column, shaft and base which projects slightly from the wall but is generally not structural in nature.[8] Used for shopfront design particularly from the 1850s onwards. May be decorated or plain, often with fluting or reeding. May support entablature or not.

Prismatic glass: Glass blocks with horizontal, triangular ribbed detail which refract light so that it is directed into a room in a predictable way. Developed by the Luxfer Prism Company it was used in buildings before the wide availability of electricity.

Return frontage: Where a shop is in a corner position and there is generally a window facing onto another, perhaps secondary street. Often regarded as beneficial in retailing terms given the extra display window.

Saloon: Large high room, which introduces natural light through a glass roof or cupola. Found at the rear of larger stores like drapers and department stores. Associated with high-class shops.

Sash: The frame of the shop window which accommodates the glazing. May be timber, bronze or chrome. Metals typically have a timber core.

Screens (Window): There may be timber and glass screens situated to the rear of the window area creating a division between shop and display area. Found in Victorian, Edwardian and inter-war shops. Changes in fashion mean that these often do not survive.

Shopfitter: A specialised type of tradesman, sometimes having originally been a joiner, who fits both shop frontages and shop interiors. Popular in the early twentieth century onwards and especially in the inter-war period. Tended to favour modern designs and abandoned classical features in favour of more daring designs. Famous firms included Pollards of London, Harris and Sheldon, Birmingham and Archibald McEwan of Glasgow.

Shutters: A security feature for the protection of goods and of valuable glass. Wooden boards were available from the mid eighteenth century. They were lifted in and out of the shop and placed into special grooves or slots in the windows and fixed with an iron shutter bar. Roller shutters were introduced early nineteenth century but wooden lifting shutters remained popular into the early twentieth century. Metal roller shutters are now popular with shopkeepers as these may be perceived as offering a higher degree of security but can be visually intrusive, particularly for traditional shopfronts.

Single-fronted: A shop with a single display window and door to one side, either with a plain lobby panel or may incorporate a showcase.

Signage: General terms for the signs for a shop. May be as a lettering on a fascia board or as a hanging sign from the building. Hanging signs may also be in the form of symbols such as a mortar and pestle for a chemist, boot for a boot or shoemaker and three golden balls for a pawnbroker.

Stall plate: (Sill plate) An area on the sill of the display window which is curved or wide enough to take lettering, usually of the shop owner or their products. Often engraved in brass and popular with certain types of retailer such as chemists.

Stallriser: The vertical area between the sill and ground level. May be decorated or plain. Often in timber but may be stone, brick or ironwork and may have a ceramic tiled finish.

Terrazzo: A cementitious material which incorporates marble chips and a smooth surface is achieved using a grinder. Designed to imitate marble but considerably cheaper but is hardwearing and suitable for areas with heavy foot traffic.

Two-storey shopfront: A shop which has a display window at first floor level above the ground floor shop level. Sometimes constructed in cast iron. Popular from mid nineteenth century to early twentieth century but now rarely used for display. Particularly popular for tearooms above bakers.

Under-sill railings: Vertical iron railings which were situated below the sill plate instead of a solid stallriser. Allowed ventilation and light to the basement but now a rare feature.

Ventilator: A horizontal band at the window head which is used to allow ventilation into a shop. May be of cast iron and decorative or plain. May also be 'hit and miss' and can be slid across to vary the level of ventilation. Particularly necessary for fresh food shops and also because of the use of gas lamps which create condensation.

Vitrolite: A type of rolled opal structural glass popular in the 1930s as a facing for buildings and particularly shopfronts to give a sleek, shiny finish. Found in many different colours including black, cream, yellow and pink. No longer manufactured.

NOTES

Section 1

1 McWilliam, 1975, p24
2 Colville, 1822
3 Topham, 1774
4 Defoe, 1726
5 Shambles were the open meat markets and the term 'Shambles' is a medieval word Shamel meaning booth or bench. Flesshamel relates to the butchers of flesh-merchants who used these booths.
6 Sinclair, 1976, Account for Glasgow
7 The *Perthshire Courier*, 13 August 1829, p3
8 Adams, 1978, p99
9 Chapman 1970, p232
10 We know from burgh records that shops or booths existed in the 15th century, for example, a record dating to 11th February 1435 notes the sale of half of three shops or booths and two lofts at High Street, Glasgow by John de Rosse, burgess of Glasgow to Mr Robert de Moffat, treasurer of Glasgow (Glasgow University Archives, GB 0248 GUA 12403 (BL 51).
11 Clark, 2000
12 MacLaren, 1874, p74
13 Wood 1950
14 Wood 1940, entry for June 1662
15 Wood 1940, entry for 14th April 1643
16 Wood and Armet, 1954, entry for June 1682
17 Beatts, 1873
18 MacLaren, 1874
19 The *Perthshire Courier*, 13 August 1829, p3
20 Howard, 1995, p148
21 Wood, 1950 entry for 5 May 1675
22 Howard, 1995, p150
23 MacMillan, 1992, p15
24 Defoe, 1726
25 MacGibbon and Ross, 1887
26 Chapman, 1970, p21, p232
27 Renwick, 1912, entry for February 1758
28 Renwick, 1912, entry for 1793
29 Renwick, 1912, entry for 1799
30 Glasgow Police Act 1800
31 MacGibbon & Ross, 1887
32 In Miller Street, Glasgow, 'piazzas' were re-created by setting back the commercial frontages but this did not prove popular and was felt to encourage litter and vagrancy. In 2008-09 the frontages were in-filled to the original building line. (Information provided by Liz Davidson, Merchant City Townscape Heritage Initiative)
33 Henry Grey Graham, 1906, p140
34 Sinclair, 1976, Account for Edinburgh
35 Renwick, 1912, entry for 1758, August 1793
36 Shairp, 1981
37 Topham, 1774
38 Sinclair, 1976, Account for Kirkwall, Volume 7, p541
39 Taylor, J, 1996
40 The Shop Tax 1785, National Archives of Scotland, E326/4
41 Heal, 1988
42 Topham in Graham, 1906
43 Heal, 1988
44 SCRAN Andrew Gardner's shop, Edinburgh
45 From RCAHMS advert for Mrs Hamilton's Nursery Shop (B41598). Original held in Edinburgh Room of Edinburgh Central Library.
46 Heal, 1988
47 Graham, 1906, p141
48 *The Scotsman*, Saturday 19 October 1839, Page 1 (www.archive.scotsman.com). "Instructions, Rules, Regulations, Orders and By-laws, made by the General Commissioners of Police for the City of Edinburgh and Adjoining Districts"
49 Glasgow Post Office Directory, 1853-54, p199
50 Dumfries and Galloway Libraries, Information and Archives, reference RB2/5/30A, 3 January 1797
51 Morrison, 2004, p42
52 See Lennie 'Scotland's Bow-fronted Shops' in *Architectural Heritage* Journal, 2009 for a detailed consideration of the architecture of bow-fronted shops.
53 Morrison, 2004
54 Renwick, 1913, p526, entry for 14th August 1793, Memorial for the Magistrates and Town Council of Glasgow
55 See drawing of a barrel bow window in John Woodforde, 1985. A barrel shaped bow window survives in Ludlow, Shropshire.
56 Thomas Hamilton's 1831 drawing of West Bow, Edinburgh suggests a similar arrangement for numerous shops and an 1853 drawing of Canongate by James Grant clearly shows the high bow window above a cellar door. Similarly, a Dean of Guild Court drawing for a warrant dated 13 May 1829 shows alterations to a shop of a very similar style at 439 Lawnmarket.
57 Beatts 1873, p141
58 This shopfront was rescued when the building was demolished and is now held in the collection of Perth Museum and Art Gallery.
59 Sanquhar Post Office is proven to be the oldest continually operated Post Office in the world and is in the Guinness Book of World Records.
60 McWilliam, 1975, p120
61 Information provided by Liz Davidson. At the time of writing the building is in an extremely precarious condition and due for demolition.
62 The ground floor was altered as a bank in the late nineteenth century but the ground floor shops were more recently reinstated to the original design. Conservation work completed 1996 for EDI Group by Gray, Marshall & Associates
63 This particularly fine shop featured as an advertisement in *The Glasgow Advertiser* (forerunner to the *Glasgow Herald*) in January 1793.
64 Statutory List HB num 20400
65 Glendinning & MacKechnie 2004, p123
66 David Dean, 1970
67 Powers, 1989, p18
68 See Lennie 2009 'Scotland's Bow-fronted Shops' in *Architectural Heritage*
69 Dean, 1970
70 Youngson, 1988, p230
71 Stratten & Stratten publishers, 1891, p70
72 Powers, 1989

73 Eldridge, 1958

74 Frew, 1981, p127

75 George Scharf depicted a shop being constructed with pierced cast iron columns at 20 The Strand, London in 1834. See Jackson, 1987.

76 Frew, 1991, refers to manuscripts by Milne held in St Andrews University Muniments Collection MS 37447

77 Mitchell, 1866

78 High Street, Lerwick and 101 High Street, Dunbar have very similar designs by MacFarlane

79 Gomme & Walker, 1987, p114

80 Moss & Turton, 1989, 367

81 The company was acquired by Fraser's in 1957 and linked with McDonalds next door and the store was later renamed House of Fraser

82 Gomme & Walker, 1987, p115

83 The Ca' d'Oro suffered a major fire in 1987 when the interior and the 1925 mansard roof were destroyed and it was subsequently extended by two bays in 1988-89.

84 *The Illustrated London News*, March 15 1856, pp281-282

85 Powers, 1989, p6

86 Neumann, 1995

87 Newland's (1990:191) reprint of a nineteenth century carpentry manual, describes the use of prismatic glass in basements as a cast-iron frame with prismatic glass.

88 (www.luxcrete.co.uk, 14/03/06)

89 Bath City Council, 1993

90 Banister Fletcher, 1928, p864

91 Powers, 1989

92 Moss & Turton, 1989, p68

93 Jefferys, 1954, p326

94 Anderson's Royal Polytechnic Ltd was bought over by Lewis's in 1929 and the original Argyle Street store was rebuilt.

95 The history of this auspicious company has been well documented and has been published by Moss & Turton, 1987

96 Jefferys, 1954

97 Moss & Turton, 1989, p57

98 Morrison, 2004, p174

99 Morrison, 2004, p140

100 Cash Railway website (www.ids.u-net.com)

101 Schmiechen and Carls, 1999 p105

102 Adams, 1978

103 Schmiechen & Carls, 1999, p27

104 Schmiechen & Carls, 1999, p29

105 Corporation of the City of Glasgow, 1914, p140

106 Schmiechen and Carls, 1999, p29

107 It closed as a fish market in 1977 and has had various retail and leisure uses since.

108 J M McBain, 1887

109 Schmiechen & Carls, 1994, p41

110 Fellows, 1995, p72

111 Grundy, 1982, p41

112 Pevsner, 1968

113 Moon, 1993

114 Ellis, 1906, p234

115 Jefferys, 1954, p131

116 Fellows, 1995, p59

117 Adburgham, 1981, p276

118 Kenna, 1987, p57

119 McKean, 1987, pp10-12

120 McKean, 1987

121 Powell, 1996, p102

122 Jefferys, 1954, p41

123 Jefferys, 1954, p42

124 Grundy, 1982

125 Jefferys, 1954, p95

126 Beeching, undated, p62

127 Grundy, 1982

128 Burford, 1922

129 Dictionary of Scottish Architects (www.scottisharchitects.org.uk) 95-97 Buchanan Street

130 Bayer, 2003, p37

131 L-P Sezille, 1927

132 See Robertson and Yerbury, 1928, for images of shops by these and other French architects

133 Kenna, 1985, p4

134 Emberton was influenced by the Paris exhibition and adopted these ideas for his shops which utilised French ideas from the glass artist René Lalique. See 'The Modern Shop: The Influence of the 1925 Paris Exhibition' available online at http://www.architecture.com/WhatsOn/Exhibitions/AtTheVictoriaAndAlbertMuseum/Room128a/2006/ModernShop/TheInfluenceOfThe1925ParisExhibiti/LotusAndDeltaEdinburgh.aspx

135 Powers, 1989, p104

136 Stamp, 1982, the shop did not survive the bombing of London during World War II.

137 Grundy, 1982; Powers, 1989 p30

138 McKean, 1987, p94

139 The US National Park Preservation Brief 12 has a detailed account of Vitrolite and its history and uses. See http://www.nps.gov/history/hps/tps/briefs/brief12.htm

140 Presentation given by Katriona Byrne on Vitrolite shopfronts at 'Conserving Scotland's Retail Buildings' Seminar, Glasgow, 22 September 2008.

141 Grundy, 1982, p43

142 Grundy, 1982, p42

143 Abel, 1960

144 Powers, 1989, p31

145 McGrath, 1961, p572

146 Grundy, 1982, p42

147 *The Glasgow Herald*, 21 March 1921, p5

148 DSA website (www.scottisharchitects.org.uk); Historic Scotland statutory list HBNUM 33032

149 Burford, 1922, p18

150 Grundy, 1982

151 Bayer, 2003, p128. Photographic archives from Glasgow demonstrate that shopfronts of all sizes, types and locations were being re-fronted at this time.

152 Kenna, 1987

153 Robertson and Yerbury, 1928

154 Powers, 1989, p33

155 Powers, 1989, p32

156 Powers, 1989, p32

157 See Historic Scotland List descriptions, Historic Buildings Numbers 51249 and 43322

158 Powers, 1989, p32

159 Perry, 1933, p3

160 Robinson, 1983

161 Wordsall, 1979

162 Wordsall, 1979, p28

163 Gardiner, 1983

164 Jefferys, 1954, p285

165 North View of Edinburgh from the upper gallery of the Scott Monument, engraving by Joseph Ebworth 1848 (http://www.capitalcollections.org.uk Item 11118)

166 Dictionary of Scottish Architects website entry for 38-42 Ayr Road, Cumnock (www.scottisharchitects.org.uk) and also Historic Scotland List of Buildings HBNUM 24122

167 MacKeith, 1986

168 This building became the City Chambers in 1811

169 MacKeith, 1986, p15

170 MacKeith, 1986

171 See sales particulars "The Stirling Arcade" by solicitors, Fleming & Buchanan and auctioneers, Speedie Brothers Ltd held in Stirling Central Library S914.136STI

172 MacKeith, 1986; MacKeith, 1985

173 Jefferys, 1954, p465

174 Mathias, 1967 p96, 100

175 Mathias, 1967, p44

176 Mathias, 1967, p65

177 Jefferys, 1954, p260

178 Davis, 1966, p278

179 Murray, 1911,

180 Bonnar, 1961, p49

181 Birchall, 1994

182 Shaw and Wild, 1979, pp278-291

183 Mullay,1996

184 Information from Stonehaven Heritage website www.stonehaven-heritage. org The building was fully restored in 1999-2000 and is occupied as an Art Deco restaurant.

185 Dictionary of Scottish Architects www. scottish-architects.org.uk

186 See Historic Scotland listings for Carron Tearoom (HBNUM 41605), Listed Category B and 26-34 Evan Street (HBNUM 50257), Listed Category C(S)

187 See Historic Scotland List of Buildings HBNUM 35522 and Dictionary of Scottish Architects website entry for 11 Exchange Street, Jedburgh (www. scottisharchitects.org.uk). The ground floor has been altered but the upper floors retain the original design.

188 See Lennie, 2009, 'The Tiled Shops of James Duncan Ltd' in Tile and Architectural Ceramics Society Journal, Volume 15, pp3-13

189 Davey et al, 1995, p261

190 Bath City Council, 1993

191 Ellis, 1906, p239

192 See Lennie 2009 'Scotland's Bow Fronted Shops' in Architectural Heritage Journal

193 Allen, 1893,

194 Bartram, 1978

195 Perry, 1933, p47

196 Bath City Council, 1993, p57

197 Jennings, undated, p200 notes that such signs must be well ventilated or moisture gathers on the back of the glass and destroys the gilding. The fascia frame must therefore be ventilated and have sufficient drainage holes.

198 Morrison, 2004

199 Burford, 1922

200 Bath City Council, 1993, p55

201 Perry, 1933

202 Perry, 1933, p55

203 Perry, 1933, p54

204 Morrison, 2004, p86

205 Jackson, 1987. George Scharf's drawings of London in the 1820s show fish shops with a lifting window and shopkeepers clearly visible as if ready to sell through the window.

206 Ellis, 1906

207 See image in Morrison, 2004, p84

208 Ellis, 1906, p 235

209 Beeching, undated

210 Images of new shopfronts in the Mitchell Library Collection dating to the 1930s depict new fishmongers with lifting windows.

211 Ellis, 1906

212 Davey et al, 1995, p261

213 See Ellis, 1906 for descriptions of these methods

214 Allen, 1893

215 See Ellis, 1906

216 See Ellis, 1906

217 Hoey, Context 43

218 Daybook of A Deas, housepainter, 1774-78, SRO GD 1/548/1 quoted in Elizabeth C Sanderson, 1996, Women and Work in 18th century Edinburgh, Basingstoke: MacMillan Press Ltd.

219 Late nineteenth century images held in Perth Museum & Art Gallery in the Magnus Jackson Collection show shops in St John Street and St Johns Place with marbling. See also Lennie, The Historic Shopfronts of Perth.

220 Jennings. Undated.

221 Jennings. Undated.

222 Durbin. 2005. p989-1005

223 See Tony Herbert, 'The use of Tiles in Shops'. Proceedings from 'Conserving Scotland's Retail Buildings Seminar', 2008 at www.historic-scotland.gov.uk See also Herbert, 1996 The Manufacture and Design of Victorian Tiles in Relation to their Conservation in Architectural Ceramics, their history, manufacture and conservation. London: James & James (Science Publishers) Ltd.

224 See Lennie 2009 'The Tiled Shops of James Duncan Ltd' in Tile and Architectural Ceramics Society Journal.

225 MJ Stratton, 1993

226 Frost and McGrath, 1961, p311

227 Frost and McGrath, 1961, p620

228 Frost and McGrath, 1961, p622

229 Barker, 1977

230 Frost and McGrath, 1961, p341

231 Frost and McGrath, 1961

232 Jester (ed.) 1995

233 National Park Preservation Brief No 12, See http://www.nps.gov/history/ hps/tps/briefs/brief12.htm

234 Katriona Byrne-paper delivered at 'Conserving Scotland's Retail Buildings Seminar', Sept 2008. Also, unpublished dissertation 2007, A Material Modernity-a Study of Vitrolite and Vitrolite Shop Fronts in Ireland.

235 Hudd, 2008

236 Byrne, Hudd as previously quoted. Also see Timothy Dunns website www. vitrolitespecialist.com

237 See Lennie 'The Tiled Shops of James Duncan Ltd' 2009

Section 2

1 Simms et al, 2005

2 SPP8 Town Centres and Retailing, Aug 2006 http://www.scotland.gov.uk/ Resource/Doc/137867/0034251.pdf

3 Information provided by John Bolton, Scottish Ironwork Foundation

4 Historic Scotland, Statutory List of Buildings HBNUM 35720

5 Pearson, 2004, pp 477-478

6 See the Tile and Architectural Ceramics Society website for further information. www.tilesoc.org

7 See Catalogue of St Andrews Shopfronts by John Frew and Rachel Cheer, 2007. Held by St Andrews Preservation Trust, 4 Queens Gardens, St Andrews.

8 See papers by John Frew on St Andrews.

9 Information provided by John Bolton

of Scottish Ironwork Foundation

10   Catalogue of St Andrews Shopfronts by John Frew and Rachel Cheer, 2007

11   See publications on Kingussie by Uiga and John Robertson.

12   Listed Category B, Historic Scotland Statutory List of Buildings HBNUM 26001

13   Listed Category C(S) Historic Scotland Statutory List of Buildings HBNUM 26071

14   See "*Guide to the Protection of Scotland's Listed Buildings: What Listing Means to Owners and Occupiers*", 2006, Historic Scotland for further information on listing.

15   Fawcett, 1992, p10

16   Earl, 1997, p66

17   Earl, 1997, p67

18   Earl, 1997, p11

19   See Gray, 1994, *A Guide to Dean of Guild Court Records* for information on where the plans are held.

20   The National Map Library of Scotland holds extensive collections of maps from across Scotland. Some of these are available on their website at http://www.nls.uk/maps/index.html

21   These historic records are part of an ongoing digitisation project by the National Archives of Scotland. See the National Archives of Scotland website http://www.nas.gov.uk

22   See Lennie, 2009 'Scotland's Bow-fronted Shops'

23   Ian Riddell, 2008 'The Shop in the Lawnmarket and other Edinburgh Shop Frontages', paper given at Conserving Scotland's Retail Buildings Seminar, September 2008. See www.historic-scotland.gov.uk for edited transcripts of the talk.

24   See Catalogue of St Andrews Shopfronts by John Frew and Rachel Cheer, 2007, and papers by John Frew.

25   John di Folco, March 2009

26   EWH News, 2006/7 www.ewht.org.uk

27   http://www.simpsonandbrown.co.uk/projects/market.html

28   Information provided by Fiona MacDonald, Edinburgh World Heritage, Edinburgh.

29   See Lennie, 2009 'The Tiled Shops of James Duncan Ltd' for a more detailed description of the tiles and their history.

30   Laing, 2005

31   Historic Scotland Statutory List of Buildings HBNUM 32767

32   Details of this and further projects done by Merchant City THI can be found in a paper delivered by Liz Davidson at the Conserving Scotland's Retail Buildings Seminar, September 2008. See www.historic-scotland.gov.uk for edited transcripts of the talk.

33   Historic Scotland Statutory List of Buildings HBNUM 50272 for a description of the building.

34   Londei, 2007, p5

Section 3

1   Curl, 1999, p158

2   Curl, 1999, p162

3   Bath City Council, 1993, p29

4   Pearson, 2005, p477

5   Bath City Council, 1993, p26

6   Pearson, 2005, p 477

7   Curl, 1999, p490)

8   Curl, 1999, p500

REFERENCES AND SOURCES

Abel, Deryck (1960) *House of Sage: A Century of Achievement 1860-1960*, www.fredericksage.co.uk .

Adams, Ian, H. (1978) *The Making of Urban Scotland,* Croom Helm Ltd, London.

Adams, Steven (1987) *The Arts & Crafts Movement,* The Apple Press Ltd, Herts.

Adburgham, Alison (1989) *Shops and Shopping 1800-1914,* Barrie & Jenkins, London.

Allen, James Parnell (1893) *Practical Building Construction,* Crosby Lockwood & Son, London.

Anon. 1829 (13 August). 'Traditions of Perth: Sketches of Society'. *Perthshire Courier.* Dundee.

Anon. 1931 (9 December; 12 December). 'Perth Firm's Enterprise.' *Perthshire Advertiser.* Perth.

Ashurst, John and Ashurst, Nicola (1998) *Practical Building Conservation: English Heritage Technical Handbook,* Gower Technical Press, Aldershot.

Bailey, Rebecca M. (1996) *Scottish Architects Papers: A Sourcebook,* Rutland Press, Edinburgh.

Ballantine, Ian (1997) 'Cast Iron' in *Traditional Building Materials,* Historic Scotland, Edinburgh.

Bannister, Turpin (April 1950) 'The First Iron Framed Buildings' in *Architectural Review,* Vol 107, pp231-246.

Baren, Maurice (1996) *How it All Began up in the High Street,* Michael O'Mara Books Ltd, London.

Barker, T. C. (1977) *The Glassmakers: Pilkington the Rise of an International Company 1826-1976,* Weidenfeld & Nicolson, London.

Barnard, Julian (1972) *Victorian Ceramic Tiles,* Studio Vista, London.

Bartram, Alan (1978) *Fascia Lettering in the British Isles,* Lund Humphries, London.

Bath City Council (1993) *Bath Shopfronts: Guidelines for Design and Conservation,* Bath City Council, Bath.

Bayer, Patricia (2003) *Art Deco Architecture: Design, Decoration and Detail from the Twenties and Thirties,* Thames and Hudson, London.

Beatts 1873 *The Municipal History of the Royal Burgh of Dundee,* Beatts, Dundee.

Beeching, C. L. T. (Ed.) (Undated) *The Modern Grocer and Provision Dealer,* Caxton Publishing Company Ltd, London.

Benson, John and Ugolini, Laura (Eds.) (2003) *A Nation of Shopkeepers: Five Centuries of British Retailing,* I B Tauris & Co Ltd, London.

Birchall, Johnston (1994) *Co-op: The People's Business,* Manchester University Press, Manchester.

Blackman, Janet (1967) 'The Development of the Retail Grocery Trade in the Nineteenth Century' *Business History,* IX, 110-117.

Bonnar, Arnold (1961) *British Co-operation,* Co-operative Union, Manchester.

Burford, James (1922) 'The Design of the Shop Front from Ancient to Modern Times' *The Architects Journal,* January 4 1922, pp9-20, p33.

Burnett, John (1963) 'The Baking Industry in the Nineteenth Century' *Business History,* V, 98-108.

Burns, Wilfred (1959) *British Shopping Centres: New Trends in Layout and Distribution,* Leonard Hill (Books) Ltd, London.

Byrne, Katriona (2007) *A Material Modernity: A Study of Vitrolite and Vitrolite Shop Fronts,* University College Dublin Masters in Urban and Building Conservation.

Chapman, R. W. (1970) *Johnson's Journey Through the Western Isles of Scotland* and *Boswell's Journal of a Tour Through the Hebrides with Samuel Johnson,* Oxford University Press, London.

Civic Trust, (1962) *Shopfront,* Civic Trust, London.

Clark, David (2000) 'The Shop Within?: An Analysis of the Architectural Evidence for Medieval Shops' *Architectural History,* 43**,** pp58-87.

Colville, A. (1822) *Dundee Delineated,* A. M. Sanderson, Dundee.

Corporation of the City of Glasgow (1914) *Municipal Glasgow: its Evolution and its Enterprise,* Glasgow Corporation, Glasgow.

Curl, James Stephen (1990) *Victorian Architecture,* David & Charles, London.

Curl, James Stephen (1993) *Georgian Architecture,* David & Charles, London.

Curl, James Stephen (1999) *A Dictionary of Architecture,* Oxford University Press, Oxford.

Dan, Horace and Willmott, E. C. Morgan (1907) *English Shopfronts: Old and New,* BT Batsford, London.

Davey, Andy, Heath, Bob, Hodges, Desmond, Ketchin, Mandy and Milne, Roy (1995) *The Care and Conservation of Georgian Houses,* Butterworth Architecture, Oxford.

Davidson, Liz (2008) 'The Role of Design and Shop Frontages in Urban Regeneration', Conserving Scotland's Retail Buildings Seminar, Glasgow http://www.historic-scotland.gov.uk/design-and-shop-frontages.pdf .

Davis, Dorothy (1966) *A History of Shopping,* Routledge & Kegan Paul, London.

Dean, David (1970) *English Shopfronts from Contemporary Sourcebooks 1792-1840,* Alec Tiranti, London.

Defoe, Daniel (1726) *A Tour Thro that Part of Great Britain called Scotland* (Folio Society reprint, London, 1976).

di Folco, John, 2009 'Restoring the Past' *The Scots Magazine,* March 2009, pp245-247.

Dixon, Roger and Muthesius, Stefan (1978) *Victorian Architecture,* Thames & Hudson, London.

Draper-Stumm, Tara and Kendall, Derek (2000) *London's Shops: The World's Emporium,* English Heritage, London.

Duncan, Alastair (1988) *Art Deco,* Thames & Hudson, London.

Durbin, Lesley (2005) 'Nineteenth Century Tiles Industrial Mass Production and Construction Methods of Interior Tiles Schemes in the Nineteenth and Early 20th Centuries' in *Construction History Society 2nd International Congress,* Vol. I, Cambridge.

Dyson, Carol J. (1995) 'Structural Glass' in *Twentieth Century Building Materials* (Ed, Jester, T. C.) McGraw-Hill, New York.

Earl, John (1997) *Building Conservation Philosophy,* The College of Estate Management, Reading.

Eldridge, Mary (1958) 'The Plate Glass Shopfront' *Architectural Review,* 123**,** pp193-195.

Ellis, George (1906) *Modern Practical Joinery,* Stobart & Son Ltd, London (1987 republished version of original 1906 publication).

English Historic Towns Forum (1991) *Shopfront Advertisements in Historic Towns,* English Historic Towns Forum.

English Historic Towns Forum (1991) *Shopfronts Seminar Proceedings,* Halifax.

English Historic Towns Forum (1993) *Book of Details and Good Practice in Shopfront Design.*

Evans, Bill and Lawson, Andrew (1981) *A Nation of Shopkeepers,* Plexus, London.

193

Evans, Richard (1997) *Regenerating Town Centres,* Manchester University Press, Manchester.

Fawcett, R. 1992 'Medieval Structures as Historical Documents' in *Materials and Traditions in Scottish Building.* Riches, A. and Stell, G. (Eds). Edinburgh: Nic Allen.

Fellows, Richard (1995) *Edwardian Architecture: Style and Technology,* Lund Humphries, London.

Fletcher, Sir Bannister (1928) *A History of Architecture on the Comparative Method,* B T Batsford Ltd, London.

Frew, John M. (1991) 'St Andrews Shopfronts 1830-1930' in *Three Decades of Historical Notes* St Andrews Preservation Trust, St Andrews.

Frew, John (Ed.) (1984) *Building for a New Age: The Architects of Victorian and Edwardian St Andrews,* The Crawford Centre for the Arts, St Andrews.

Gardiner, Leslie (1983) *The Making of John Menzies,* Hunter & Foulis Ltd, Edinburgh.

Glendinning, Miles and MacKechnie, Aonghus (2004) *Scottish Architecture,* Thames & Hudson, London.

Gloag, John and Bridgewater, Derek (1948) *A History of Cast Iron in Architecture,* George Allen and Unwin Ltd, London.

Gomme and Walker (1987) *Architecture of Glasgow,* Lund Humphries, London.

Graham, Henry Grey (1906) *The Social Life of Scotland in the Eighteenth Century,* Adam & Charles Black, London.

Gray, Iain (1994) *A Guide to Dean of Guild Court Records,* University of Glasgow, Glasgow.

Gregory, Neil (2003) 'Monro and Partners: Shopping in Scotland with Marks & Spencer' *Architectural Heritage,* XIV, pp67–85.

Grigg, Jocelyn (1987) *Charles Rennie Mackintosh,* Richard Drew Publishing, Glasgow.

Grundy, Joan (1982) 'Inter-war Shop Fronts' *The Thirties Society Journal,* pp41–44.

Hall, Catherine (1993) 'The Butcher, the Baker, the Candlestickmaker: The Shop and Family in the Industrial Revolution' in *The Victorian City: A Reader in British Urban History 1820-1914* (Eds, Morris, R. J. and Rodger, R.) Longman, London, pp307–321.

Hand, Owen F. (2003) 'Structures Associated with the Retail Trade' in *Scotland's Buildings: A Compendium of Scottish Ethnology,* Vol. 3 (Eds, Stell, G., Shaw, J. and Starrier, S.) Tuckwell Press, East Linton.

Heal, Ambrose (1988) *Sign Boards of Old London Shops,* Portman Books, London.

Herbert, Tony and Huggins, Kathryn (2005) *The Decorative Tile in Architecture and Interiors,* Phaidon Press, London.

Herbert, Tony (1996) 'The Manufacture and Design of Victorian Tiles in Relation to their Conservation' in *Architectural Ceramics, their History, Manufacture and Conservation,* James and James (Science Publishers Ltd), London.

Hermann, Levy (1947) *The Shops of Britain: A Study of Retail Distribution,* Kegan Paul, Trench, Turner & Co Ltd, London.

Historic Scotland (1998) *A Guide to Conservation Areas in Scotland,* Historic Scotland, Edinburgh.

Historic Scotland (1998) *The Memorandum of Guidance on Listed Buildings and Conservation Areas,* Historic Scotland, Edinburgh.

Historic Scotland (2006) *A Guide to the Protection of Scotland's Listed Buildings: What Listing Means to Owners and Occupiers,* Historic Scotland, Edinburgh.

Historical Publishing Co (1888) *Glasgow of Today: Industries of Glasgow,* Glasgow.

Hoey, Peter, 'Shopfront Security: Roller Shutters and Insurance Companies' *Context,* 43, http://www.ihbc.org.uk/context_archive/43/PeterHoey_dir/PeterHoey_s.htm

Honeyman, Katrina (2000) 'Tailor-made: Mass Production, High Street Retailing, and the Leeds Menswear Multiples, 1918-1939' *Northern History,* 37, pp293-305.

Howard, Deborah (1995) *The Architectural History of Scotland: Scottish Architecture from the Reformation to the Restoration,* Edinburgh University Press, Edinburgh.

Hudd, Fiona G. (2009) *Saving Surfaces: The Conservation of a 1930's Building Material* Oxford Brookes University and University of Oxford Department of Continuing Education MSc, unpublished dissertation.

Hume, John R. (1992) 'Iron in Buildings in Scotland' in *Materials and Traditions in Scottish Building* (Eds, Riches, A. and Stell, G.), Scottish Vernacular Buildings Working Group, Edinburgh.

Jackson, Peter (1987) *George Scharf's London,* John Murray Publishers Ltd, London.

Jefferys, James B. (1954) *Retail Trading in Britain 1850-1950,* Cambridge University Press, Cambridge.

Jennings, Arthur Seymour (Undated) *The Modern Painter and Decorator: A Practical Work on House-painting and Decorating,* Caxton Publishing Ltd, London.

Jester, T. C. (Ed.) 1995 *Twentieth Century Building Materials,* McGraw-Hill, New York.

John Menzies & Co Ltd (1958) *The House of Menzies,* John Menzies & Co Ltd, Edinburgh.

John Menzies (Holdings) Ltd (1965) *The Menzies Group,* John Menzies (Holdings) Ltd, Edinburgh.

Johnson, Walker C. (1995) 'Terrazzo' in *Twentieth Century Building Materials* (Ed, Jester, T. C.), McGraw-Hill, New York.

Jones, Ronald (1979) 'Consumers Co-operation in Victorian Edinburgh: The Evolution of a Location Pattern' *Transactions of the Institute of British Geographers,* New Series 4, pp292-305.

Kenna, Rudolph (1985) *Glasgow Art Deco,* Richard Drew Publishing, Glasgow.

Kenna, Rudolph (1987) *Scotland in the Thirties,* Richard Drew Publishing, Glasgow.

Kenna, Rudolph (1996) *Old Glasgow Shops,* Glasgow City Archives, Glasgow.

King, Elspeth (1991) *People's Pictures: the Story of Tiles in Glasgow,* Glasgow Museums, Glasgow

Laing, Margaret (2005) *A Social History of Blairgowrie and Rattray* Blairgowrie, Rattray and District Local History Trust, Blairgowrie.

Lamont-Brown, Raymond and Adamson, Peter (1980) *Victorian and Edwardian Fife from Old Photographs,* The Ramsey Head Press, Edinburgh.

Lennie, Lindsay Ann (2006) *The Conservation of Historic Shopfronts in Perth and Perthshire,* Heriot-Watt University, unpublished PhD thesis.

Lennie, Lindsay Ann (2008) *The Historic Shopfronts of Perth: An Architectural History,* Perth and Kinross Heritage Trust, Perth.

Lennie, Lindsay (2009) 'Scotland's Bow-fronted Shops' *Architectural Heritage XX* pp75-92.

Lennie, Lindsay (2009) 'The Tiled Shops of James Duncan Ltd' *The Tile and Architectural Ceramics Society Journal,* 15, pp3-13.

Lion Foundry Company Ltd *Illustrated Catalogue of Cast Iron Manufactures,* Lion Foundry Company Ltd, Kirkintilloch.

Londei, John (2007) *Shutting up Shop,* Dewil Lewis Publishing, Stockport.

Lothian Regional Council, (1995) *Edinburgh Streetscape Manual,* Edinburgh.

MacFarlane, Walter & Co (1882) *Illustrated Catalogue of MacFarlane's Castings,* MacFarlane's, Glasgow.

MacGibbon, David and Ross, Thomas (1887) *The Castellated and Domestic Architecture of Scotland from the 12th to 18th Century,* David Douglas, Edinburgh.

MacKeith, Margaret (1985) 'The Changing High Street' *The Planner,* pp9-12

MacKeith, Margaret (1985) *Shopping Arcades: A Gazetteer of Extant British Arcades 1817-1939,* Mansell Publishing Ltd, London.

MacKeith, Margaret (1986) *The History and Conservation of Shopping Arcades,* Mansell Publishing Ltd, London.

MacKinnon, James (1921) *The Social and Industrial History of Scotland,* Longmans, Green & Co, London.

MacLaren, James and Thomson, James (Eds.) (1874) *The History of Dundee,* John Durham & Sons, Dundee.

MacMillan, Andrew (1992) *Six Scottish Burghs,* Canongate Press, Edinburgh.

Madsen, Stephen Tschudi (2002) *The Art Nouveau Style,* Dover, New York.

Mair, Craig (1988) *Mercat Cross and Tolbooth,* John Donald Publishers Ltd, Edinburgh.

Martin, G. H. (1968) 'The Town as a Palimpsest' in *The Study of Urban History* (Ed, Dyos, H. J.), Edward Arnold, London.

Mathias, Peter (1967) *Retailing Revolution,* Longman, London.

Mayall, Colin (2004) *Images of Scotland: Around Crieff and Strathearn,* Tempus Publishing Ltd, Stroud.

McBain, J M (1887) *Arbroath Past and Present,* Brodie and Salmond, Arbroath.

McFadzean, Ronald (1979) *The Life and Work of Alexander Thomson,* Routledge & Kegan Paul, London.

McGrath, Raymond and Frost, A C (1961) *Glass in Architecture and Decoration,* The Architectural Press, London.

McKean, Charles (1987) *The Scottish Thirties: An Architectural Introduction,* The Scottish Academic Press, Edinburgh.

McWilliam, Colin (1975) *Scottish Townscape,* Collins, London.

Mitchell, David (1866) *The History of Montrose,* George Walker, Montrose.

Moon, Karen (1993) *George Walton: Designer and Architect,* White Cockade Publishing, London.

Morrison, Kathryn (2004) *English Shops and Shopping,* Yale University Press, London.

Moss, Michael (1989) *100 Years of Provisioning Scotland,* The Scottish Provision Trade Association, Glasgow.

Moss, Michael and Turton, Alison (1989) *A Legend of Retailing: House of Fraser,* Weidenfeld & Nicolson, London.

Mullay, Sandy (1996) *The Edinburgh Encyclopaedia,* Mainstream Publishing, Edinburgh.

Murray, Andrew (1911) *Fifty Years of Slamannan Co-operative Society 1861-1911,* Slamannan Co-operative Society, Slamannan.

Naismith, Robert J. (1985) *Buildings of the Scottish Countryside,* Victor Gollanz Ltd, London.

Naismith, Robert J. (1989) *The Story of Scotland's Towns,* John Donald Publishers Ltd, Edinburgh.

Neumann, Dietrich (1995) 'Prismatic Glass' in *Twentieth Century Building Materials: History and Conservation* (Ed, Jester, T. C.), McGraw Hill, New York.

Newlands, J., (Ed.) 1990. *The Carpenters Assistant: The Complete Practical Course in Carpentry and Joinery,* London: Studio Editions.

Pearson, Elizabeth and Pearson, Tom (1998) *Old Newburgh,* Stenlake Publishing, Ochiltree, Ayrshire.

Pearson, Lynn (2005) *Tile Gazetteer: A Guide to British Tile and Architectural Ceramics Locations,* Tile and Architectural Ceramics Society and Richard Dennis Publications, Shepton Beauchamp.

Pennant, Thomas (2000) *A Tour in Scotland in 1769,* Birlinn, Edinburgh (facsimile reprint of edition).

Perry, Trevor (1933) *Modern Shopfront Construction,* The Technical Press Ltd, London.

Pevsner, Nikolaus (1968) 'George Walton' in *Studies in Art, Architecture and Design,* Vol. II (Ed. Pevsner, N.), Thames and Hudson, London.

Pevsner, Nikolaus (1976) *A History of Building Types,* Thames & Hudson, London.

Plant, Marjorie (1952) *The Domestic Life of Scotland in the Eighteenth Century,* Edinburgh University Press, Edinburgh.

Porter, J. H. (1971) 'The Development of a Provincial Department Store 1870-1939' *Business History,* XIII, pp64-71.

Powell, Christopher (1996) *The British Building Industry Since 1800: an Economic History,* E &F N Spon, London.

Powers, Alan (1989) *Shopfronts,* Chatto and Windus Ltd, London.

Pride, Glen L. (1996) *Dictionary of Scottish Building,* Rutland Press, Edinburgh.

RCAHMS (2004) *Creating a Future for the Past: The Scottish Architects Preservation Papers,* RCAHMS, Edinburgh.

Rees, Goronwy (1969) *St Michael: A History of Marks & Spencer,* Weidenfeld and Nicholson, London.

Renwick, Robert (Ed.) (1912) *Extracts from the Records of the Burgh of Glasgow with Charters & other Documents,* Glasgow Corporation, Glasgow.

Richardson, Harry and Aldcroft, Derek H. (1968) *Building in the British Economy Between the Wars,* George Allen & Unwin Ltd, London.

Rickards, Lynne C. and Urquhart, Gordon (Eds.) (1999) *The West End Conservation Manual: A Guide to the Maintenance, Repair and Conservation of Victorian and Edwardian Buildings in Glasgow's Historic West End,* Glasgow West Conservation Trust, Glasgow.

Riddell, Ian (2008) 'The Shop in the Lawnmarket and Other Edinburgh Shop Frontages' in Conserving Scotland's Retail Buildings Seminar, Glasgow http://www.historic-scotland.gov.uk/design-and-shop-frontages.pdf.

Robertson, Howard and Yerbury, F. R. (1928) *Examples of Modern French Architecture,* Ernst Benn Ltd, London.

Robertson, Uiga and Robertson, John (1999) *Kingussie: Caught in the Light,* Kingussie Arts Network, Kingussie.

Robertson, Uiga and Robertson, John (2002) *Kingussie: At the Head of the Pines,* Kingussie Arts Network, Kingussie.

Robertson, Uiga and Robertson, John (2006) *Kingussie: Lasting Impressions,* Kingussie Arts Network, Kingussie.

Robinson, Peter (1983) *Tenements: A Scottish Urban Tradition* unpublished paper.

Roche, Nessa (2001) *The Historical and Technical Development of the Sash and Case Window in Scotland,* Historic Scotland, Edinburgh.

Rodger, R. G. (1981) 'Sources and Methods of Urban Studies: The Contributions of Building Records' *Area,* 13, pp315-321.

Ross, Michael (1995) *Planning and the Heritage,* E & F Spon, London.

Sanderson, Elizabeth (1996) *Women and Work in 18th Century Edinburgh,* MacMillan Press Ltd, Basingstoke.

Schmiechen and Carls (1999) *The British Market Hall: A Social and Architectural History,* Yale University Press, London.

Scotsman, The, 19 October 1839 *Instructions, Rules, Regulations, Orders and By-Laws made by the General Commissioners of Police for the City of Edinburgh and Adjoining Districts,* p1

Scott, Frank T. (1986) 'J. P. Allison, Architect' *Hawick Architectural Society Transactions,* pp24-29.

Scott, N. Keith (1989) *Shopping Centre Design,* VNR International, London.

Scott, Peter (1994) 'Learning to Multiply: The Property Market and the Growth of Multiple Retailing in Britain, 1919-1939', *Business History,* 36, pp1-28.

Scottish Executive *Planning Advice Note 52: Planning and Small Towns,* Scottish Executive, Edinburgh.

Scottish Executive (1998) *NPPG8: Town Centres & Retailing,* Scottish Executive, Edinburgh.

Scottish Executive (1999) *Planning Advice Note 59: Improving Town Centres,* Scottish Executive, Edinburgh.

Scottish Executive (2006) *SPP8: Town Centres and Retailing,* Scottish Executive, Edinburgh.

Service, Alastair (Ed.) (1975) *Edwardian Architecture and its Origins,* The Architectural Press, London.

Seth, Andrew and Randall, Geoffrey (1999) *The Grocers: The Rise and Rise of the Supermarket Chains,* Kogan Page Ltd, London.

Shairp, J C (Ed.) (1981) *Dorothy Wordsworth 'A Tour in Scotland in 1803',* James Thin, Edinburgh.

Shaw, Gareth and Wild, M. T. (1979) 'Retail Patterns in the Victorian City' *Transactions of the Institute of British Geographers,* New Series 4, pp278-291.

Simms, Andrew, Kjell, Petra and Potts, Ruth (2005) *Clone Town Britain: Survey Results,* New Economics Foundation, London.

Sinclair, Sir John (Ed.) (1976) *The Statistical Accounts of Scotland 1791-1799 Volumes I-X,* E P Publishing Ltd, Wakefield.

Slavin, A and Checkford, S (1986) *Dictionary of Scottish Business Biography 1860-1960,* Aberdeen University Press, Aberdeen.

Smith, Andrew and Sparks, Leigh (1997) *Retailing and Small Shops,* The Stationery Office, Edinburgh.

Smith, Andrew and Sparks, Leigh (2000) 'The Independent Small Shop in Scotland: A Discussion of Roles and Problems' *Scottish Geographical Journal,* 116, pp41-58.

Smith, Gavin and Smith, Ruth (2000) *Scotland in Old Photographs: Perth,* Sutton Publishing Ltd, Stroud.

Smout, T C (1987) *A History of the Scottish People 1560-1830,* Fontana Press, London.

Stamp, G. (1982) 'Conversation with Erno Goldfinger.' *The Thirties Society Journal* (2): pp19-24.

Stratten & Stratten (1891) *Strattens Glasgow and its Environs: A Literary, Commercial and Social Review,* Stratten & Stratten, Glasgow.

Stratton, M. J. (1993) *The Terracotta Revival,* Gollancz, London.

Summerson, John (1996) *The Classical Language of Architecture,* Thames and Hudson, London.

Sunday Herald (2003) 'The Big and the Beautiful: Guide to Art Deco in Scotland'

Swailes, T. (2006) *Scottish Iron Structures,* Historic Scotland, Edinburgh.

Taylor, Jonathan (1994) 'Retail Detail' *Building Conservation Directory,* http://www.buildingconservation.com/articles/shop/retail.htm

Taylor, D.B. (Ed.) (1979) *The Third Statistical Account, Volume I-XXI,* Culross The Printers, Coupar Angus.

Taylor, Michael (March 2000) 'In Search of Vitrolite' *Context,* 65.

The Illustrated London News Supplement (15 March 1856) 'Iron and Glass Building in Glasgow' pp281-282

The US National Park Heritage Preservation Services (1984) *Brief 12: The Preservation of Historic Pigmented Structural Glass (Vitrolite and Carrara Glass),* Technical Preservation Services, Washington DC.

Topham (1776). *Letters from Edinburgh written in the years 1774 and 1775,* James Thin, Edinburgh, facsimile of 1776 edition.

van Lemmen, Hans (2000) *Victorian Tiles,* Shire Publications, Princes Risborough.

van Lemmen, Hans and Blanchett, Chris (1999) *20ᵗʰ Century Tiles,* Shire Publications, Princes Risborough.

Walsh, Claire (1995) 'Shop Design and the Display of Goods in Eighteenth Century London' *Journal of Design History,* 8, pp157-176.

Watkins, David (1982) *The Buildings of Britain: Regency,* Barrie and Jenkins, London.

Weaver, Martin E. (1993) *Conserving Buildings: Guide to Techniques and Materials,* John Wiley and Sons Inc, New York.

Westwood, P. J. & Son (1950) 'Analysis of Self-Service Shops', *Architects Journal,* pp50-56.

Williams, Bridget (1994) *The Best Butter in the World: A History of Sainsbury's,* Ebury Press, London.

Wood, Marguerite (Ed.) *Extracts from the Records of the Burgh of Edinburgh,* Oliver & Boyd, Edinburgh. Years: 1642-55 (pub 1938), 1655-65 (pub 1940), 1665-80 (pub 1950).

Wood, Marguerite and Armet, Helen (Eds.) (1954) *Extracts from the Records of the Burgh of Edinburgh 1681-89,* Oliver & Boyd, Edinburgh.

Woodforde, John (1985) *Georgian Houses for All,* Routledge & Kegan Paul, London.

Wordsall, F. (1979) *The Tenement: A Way of Life,* Chambers, Edinburgh.

Youngson, A. J. (1988) *The Making of Classical Edinburgh 1750-1840,* Edinburgh University Press, Edinburgh.

BIOGRAPHY

Dr Lindsay Lennie worked for many years as a Chartered Valuation Surveyor in the public sector. She completed the RICS Post-graduate Diploma in Building Conservation in 2001 and was awarded a PhD in Building Conservation in 2006 at Heriot-Watt University for her thesis 'The Conservation of Historic Shopfronts in Perth and Perthshire'. This led to a three year Research Fellowship with Technical Conservation Group, Historic Scotland researching traditional shops across Scotland. Lindsay has written a number of articles on this topic and since November 2009 she has been working freelance providing specialist advice on the conservation of historic shops.